The Early Politics
and Poetics of
William Carlos Williams

Studies in Modern Literature, No. 73

A. Walton Litz, General Series Editor

Professor of English
Princeton University

Consulting Editor:
Paul Mariani

Professor of English
University of Massachusetts/Amherst

Other Titles in This Series

The Early Politics and Poetics of William Carlos Williams

by
David Frail

U·M·I Research Press

Ann Arbor / London

Produced and distributed by
UMI Research Press
an imprint of
University Microfilms, Inc.
Ann Arbor, Michigan 48106

Library of Congress Cataloging in Publication Data

Frail, David, 1952-
The early politics and poetics of William Carlos
Williams.

(Studies in modern literature ; no. 73)
Bibliography: p.
Includes index.
1. Williams, William Carlos, 1883-1963—Political and
social views.   2. Poets, American—20th century—Political
and social views.   I. Title.   II. Series.
PS3545.I544   1987   811'.52   87-9202
ISBN 0-8357-1802-6 (alk. paper)

British Library CIP data is available

The sense of beauty is the mainspring of civilization.
                                                Noble Lives and Deeds

All artists are moved by real human relations and not artificial [ones], which all the rest of us need to respect. If the ordinary people have to be divided by social relations, the artist has to get away from that to real human truth.
                              William Carlos Williams to Walter Sutton

The problem with literary theory is that it can neither beat nor join the dominant ideologies of late industrial capitalism.
                                                        Terry Eagleton

Contents

Acknowledgments

I am grateful to a number of institutions. The Danforth Foundation and the Graduate School of the University of Massachusetts at Amherst provided fellowships; the Graduate Program in English at the University of Massachusetts gave me support and two degrees. The staff of the Rutherford Free Library, David Schoonmaker and the staff at the Beinecke Rare Book and Manuscript Library of Yale University, and Robert Bertholf and the staff of the Poetry Collection of the Lockwood Memorial Library, State University of New York at Buffalo all made research a pleasure.

More people than I can thank here helped in more ways than I can say, but I must name a few of them. This study would not have been written without Paul Mariani's faith in Williams's work and in mine. I owe him. David Porter and Sarah Lennox read the orignal version and did much to improve it. Jim Gauer taught me the problem of poetry's responsibility to the world. F.S. shared two cats, shop talk, and the hard times starting out. Kerry Buckley, Lynne Ambrosini, Nancy Elwell, Pamela Lowitt, Ron and Sue Perry, Bill Shullenberger and Bonny Alexander, Jack and Mary Grace Smith, John Surface, and Dan Warner helped me live and work. My mother and brothers took me in; this book is for Jim and for them.

Abbreviations

The abbreviations used in my text refer to the following books and texts by William Carlos Williams:

A	*Autobiography*
AG	*In the American Grain*
BU	*The Build-Up*
CP	*The Collected Poems, Vol. 1*
CLP	*The Collected Later Poems*
EK	*The Embodiment of Knowledge*
FD	*The Farmers' Daughters*
I	*Imaginations*
IM	*In the Money*
Int	*Interviews*
IWWP	*I Wanted to Write a Poem*
LRN	"The Little Red Notebook," ed. Dr. William Eric Williams, *William Carlos Williams Review* 9.1–2 (Fall 1983), 1–34
ML	*Many Loves*
P	*Paterson*
PB	*Pictures from Breughel*
RI	*A Recognizable Image*
Rome	*Rome*, ed. with an introduction by Steven Ross Loevy, *Iowa Review* 9.3 (Summer 1978), 1–65
SE	*Selected Essays*
SL	*Selected Letters*
VP	*A Voyage to Pagany*
WM	*White Mule*
YMW	*Yes, Mrs. Williams*

Full information on the texts appears in the Bibliography.

Introduction

This study is perhaps best read as a biography of William Carlos Williams's early politics, their relation to his poetics, and their expression in his poems. As such it is a narrative, dividing into three periods: from the decade before his birth to 1913 (chapters 1 through 3); from the Armory Show to America's entry into World War I (chapters 4 through 8); and from 1918 through 1925, with a few glances ahead to the end of the 1920s (chapters 9 through 11).

As an attempt to define what Williams meant when he called the poet a "revolutionist," however, this study's organization may not be so clear. Three major themes underlie my chronology and become clearest in the chapters on the early 1920s, the period when Williams himself became most articulate about them: the fate of the individual and the small community—and American individualism—in a modernizing, urbanizing society; the relations of the autonomous artist and socially concerned art to such a society; and the relation of a poetics of self-expression and immediacy, and the poems written out of it, to an indifferent and hostile social order.

There has been some difficulty seeing Williams as a political writer at any point in his career, much less early on. No one doubts that he "had politics"—he voted Democratic—but he was disinclined to participate in organized political action or thought. Moreover, although he occasionally went on "enthusiasms," as one of his sons puts it, such as for Al Smith in the late 1920s or Social Credit in the 1930s or consumer cooperatives in the late 1930s and 1940s, they were not activities we would call revolutionary (though in his Republican hometown they easily seemed "radical").[1] Nor was the little writing he did about them all that sophisticated; nor do they seem to have shaped his poetry. Compounding his apparent naïveté and lack of interest is his constant emphasis on the writer's concern with form and the necessity of his freedom from political "dogma."

Those who have taken his politics seriously vary in their characterization of them according to what part of Williams's life and work they consider, and, of course, their own politics. Bram Dijkstra, looking at Williams's writing on the visual arts, detects a "conservative cast" to Williams's thought; Mike Weaver, focusing mainly on the 1930s, has classified him as a middle-class "egoist" committed to owning property and himself, but also emotionally committed to the Constitution; poet George Oppen, recalling Williams in the early Depression, recently called him an anachronistic "populist"; Williams's biographer, Paul Mariani, presents an undoctrinaire "democrat" who was "at heart apolitical, a loner."[2]

As for whether Williams's politics are expressed in his poetry, the apparent absence of didactic or occasional poems expressing a specific ideology has left even his admirers unsure of how to explain their gut feelings that Willliams was indeed a political writer. Denise Levertov acknowledges that Williams wrote few such "classifiably" political poems, but insists that "all of his work is imbued with social concern." And as for whether his poetics—that is, his conception of poetry and his formal concerns—express his politics in more indirect ways, the assumption has been made that because he wrote about the commonplace and the overlooked, his poetics were therefore somehow "democratic"; as James Breslin defines them, "the poet fulfills himself in intimate relation to his locality."[3]

Given their points of view, all of these scholars, critics, and poets are correct, and I have learned much from all of them—particularly the fact that there are contradictions in our understanding of Williams's politics and poetics that need to be explained. How can a writer who so self-consciously conceived of himself as an "American" poet not express more about the politics of American democracy in his work? If Williams's work glows constantly with social concern, how can he not be a political writer? Why, if Dijkstra is correct about Williams's underlying conservatism, does Williams so often sound like a "Jacobin," as Mariani calls him—and about more than poetry?

By treating Williams's political views, and his view of politics in general, as specific responses to events and forces of American history, I think we can understand how his politics have come to seem so contradictory to us, if not resolve the contradictions. I have treated his early years accordingly—years which, except in Mariani's biography, are largely undiscussed—because it seems logical in Williams's case to think in terms of origins. I accept—with proper respect for context, I hope—the truism of Williams scholarship that most of the major elements of his later thought and writing are present *"ab ovo,"* as Rod Townley puts it, and find that this is true of his politics as well as his aesthetics. Thus by tracing Williams's early politics, his conception of the social function of the artist, and his early poetics and poetry, I aim to clarify the terms of discussion of his later work, especially *Paterson*.[4]

Granted, there is no ode to Bryan or the Bull Moose among Williams's early poems, nor does he make democratic politics as explicit a theme as Edgar Lee Masters did in the *Spoon River Anthology*. Nor is there much commentary on current political events or issues in Williams's nonpoetic writing. But in his 1909 *Poems* there is a "Hymn to the Spirit of Fraternal Love" that refers more to the brotherhood of man than to his brother Edgar; there are the early plays on themes from American history, the "townspeople" poems and numerous other brief lyrics, *The Comic Life of Elia Brobitza,* a fair amount of commentary on the civic affairs and mores of Rutherford, and more participation in those affairs than has been realized—not to mention the major works of the early 1920s. Yet even *In the American Grain* has been said to lack a civic sense.

But Williams's "civic sense" and its presence in his work become clearer when we place the young Williams in his local social contexts—suburban Rutherford and the artistic community of New York—and place these in the larger context of turn-of-the-century America. Listening to the political discourses spoken by Republicans, Progressives, socialists, anarchists, and the artists of the time enables us to overcome our resistance to calling Williams a political poet. For when we know of Rutherford's definition of "progress" and its pride in not mixing "politics" with "local elections," when we remember that prewar muckrakers and Progressives spoke more of moral reform than structural change, when we understand that the romantic rebels of Greenwich Village and Reds thought of revolution not as the victory of a party or an ideology but as a liberation of the individual—an imminent transformation of morality and culture—then poems such as "The Wanderer" or even "Tract" seem to be far less trivial or evasive political commentary.

In the context of his time, then, Williams appears to be a more engaged poet than we have allowed. But the more concretely we read the terms of his engagement, the more ambiguous and interesting they become: what does it mean to speak of right conduct or total honesty in a relatively small community in 1916, or of local government in 1923 when the New York skyline is visible from one's upstairs windows?

The answer is the major theme of my narrative: Williams's confrontation with "modernity"—the transformation of America from a small-community economy and culture to an urban, centralized, mass economy and culture—was the locus of his politics. By treating it as such, we can best explain both the politics he had and his apparent resistance to politics as a poet.

I refer throughout to aesthetic matters as "modernist," and use "modernization" and "modernity" to refer exclusively to the social changes occurring during Williams's youth and early maturity. Crucial among these, of course, was the fact that the industrialization of America was shifting into a new phase. By the turn of the century, the construction both of the base of heavy industry and the means of distribution over great distances (namely the railroads) upon which mass production depends was nearly complete; so, too, was the concentration into fewer hands and holding companies of the huge amounts of capital needed for such industry. Turn-of-the-century America was poised for a "takeoff" like that Britain experienced in the late eighteenth century, one that would solve the problem of using the country's now extraordinary productive capacity. When on January 5, 1914 Henry Ford announced that he would pay his workers five dollars a day as a minimum wage, he caused a riot of job applicants at his plant, enabled the few he hired to buy the Model Ts they made, and gave one of the first signs of America's transformation, fully underway by the early 1920s, from an economy of production and scarcity into one of consumption and "surplus."[5]

As mass production and consumption developed so did "urbanization," which, as Charles Tilly defines it, is not merely the growth of cities, but the centralization of financial, legal, and administrative systems in them, and the expansion of these systems to international scope. Beginning with Theodore Roosevelt's administrations, government authority started shifting from municipalities and state legislatures to the federal government, and within the federal government from Congress to the executive branch. By the end of Wilson's first administration, through the multiplication of agencies, commissions, bureaus, and administrations, the federal apparatus was poised to become what Robert H. Wiebe calls a "government of continuous involvement." Accompanying and fostering this new government was an emerging new power group, the middle-class "progressives" who viewed society not as a group of concrete individuals bound by personal loyalties but as an aggregate of anonymous, abstract forces or "interests" whose random "drift" and collision had to be controlled by the "mastery" of supposedly disinterested administrators. "The heart of progressivism," as Wiebe so cogently shows, "was the ambition of the new middle class to fulfill its destiny through bureaucratic means."[6]

Government and society, then, were making their presence felt in realms of life—the economic, familial, cultural, personal, even physical—to the extent that the boundaries between the private and the political or social began to vanish. The "confusion of politics and culture" by radical intellectuals of the Progressive movement and Greenwich Village, of which Christopher Lasch has disapproved, was in fact as much a response to modernity's fusion of the two as a flaw in their thinking. The meaning of "politics" was beginning to broaden beyond parties, legislation, and voting and refer to what we now call "the political": "the way we organize our social life together, and the power-relations which this involves," as Terry Eagleton defines it. Poets, too, were beginning to broaden the notion of "political poetry" so that it meant pretty much what Levertov calls Williams's "social concern." Her own definition of political poetry, in fact, is useful for understanding that of the 1910s: for her, politics are present in poems whenever they critically examine "our immediate social environment." These definitions may be considered so broad as to allow anything about a poem concerned with as few as two people to be called political, but such is the nature of our present social order, at whose birth the Progressives, the Villagers, and William Carlos Williams were present.[7]

On the one hand, then, we may justify seeing Williams as a political poet when he writes frankly about sex or hands out a "Tract" on funeral practices, because of the blurring of politics into social questions. More important, however, is the fact that Williams himself regarded his work as political because he wrote it for his own small community, Rutherford, in which conventional politics were as much a matter of mundane human concerns—schools and sewage—and concrete human relations—status, individual initiative, and ad hoc action—as of policy, legislation, and institutions. Ironically enough, it was modernity's particular fusion of the political and the social that most threatened the fusion forged by Rutherford and Williams, and produced the "political" poetry that we have had difficulty regarding as of more than "social concern."

Modernity's permeation of the small community and the self, then, created that "conservative cast" in Williams's thought. He was a true believer in American individualism as Alexis de Tocqueville defined it and I use it here: the assumption that one does "not belong to a group," be it a social class, a tradition-sharing solidarity, or an ancestry, and thus can "be considered absolutely alone." Even today the faith that one's self is constituted entirely apart from social structures remains the ground of American political discourse. Early in this century, Americans across the political spectrum, even those who benefited most from the centralizing state and mass society, replied to their emergence in the language of the old, smaller-scale social order; it is not surprising that most Progressive-era politics now seem either shortsighted or downright hypocritical.[8]

Williams's politics are no exception. Everything that contributed to their development emphasized the late-Victorian, middle-class conception of the individual as being constituted by his own inner "nature" and gifts, rather than by any social force from "outside" him. Although Williams was a willing agent of modernization when he felt that people would actually be helped or protected, especially from "special interests," the very basis of his politics was his need to defend his conception of individual autonomy from the abstract techniques of management and mass production and consumption that produced "prohibitions" and turned one's concrete experience of existence into mere "information."

I have termed Williams's politics "nostalgic" rather than using the conventional labels of left and right. He shared his nostalgia with figures as different in their apparent politics as Max Eastman and Ezra Pound. Although a few of the Greenwich Village rebels and radical intellectuals, particularly Walter Lippman, were willing to grant the state an active role, the words of Ralph Waldo Emerson and Walt Whitman, Orrick Johns recalls, rather than those of Karl Marx or Lippman himself "were the natural air we breathed, whether we had read them or not." As a group, notes Daniel Aaron, they were committed to the "extreme individualism" of their transcendentalist forebears. In their own social order of constantly shifting cliques, in their "paganism" and worship of nature and the "natural" self, in their attempt to preserve what Leslie Fishbein calls "the remnants of a craft tradition," the Village rebels inadvertently mirrored the world of the small towns and cities that so many of them came to New York to escape. Their politics, as Fishbein has shown, were full of unresolved contradictions between their desire for socialism and their uncritical quest for the liberation of the self. Williams never felt challenged by their radicalism, I suspect, because he shared their desires for immediate experience and individual autonomy, and differed only in the means by which he hoped to fulfill them.[9]

He and they, and virtually every artist of the time, also shared the assumption that the artist had a special kind of individual autonomy and that the artist's relation to society was a special sort of freedom. Whether they drew upon the nineteenth-century French tradition of the avant-garde, Friedrich Nietzsche's iconoclastic *Übermensch,* Oscar Wilde's exceptional Individual, Whitman's "simple, separate person," or Bliss Carman and Richard Hovey's Vagabond, and whether they held anarchist, socialist, progressive, or reactionary political views, for Village rebels and New York artists the artist was the figure of the free self, miraculously freed from the corruption of the cash nexus and the clichés of middle-class perception, emotion, vision, speech, and morality to experience and express life immediately and fully—not within society, however, but outside it. This figure of the artist was the most important influence on Williams's conception of the relation of his poetry and poetics to modern American society, and even on his politics.

The American avant-garde artist of the early 1910s was caught in a double bind. On the one hand, he defined himself as being in opposition to "conventions" of whatever kind; at his baldest, he thought he was a superior being or a Vagabond, completely free from society. Naturally, much ink was expended to defend the artist's right to express himself freely and fully, but the individualism of the artist led to more than the politics of censorship battles. An artist like Ezra Pound, or Williams, found that his liberty both as a citizen and as an individual artist was being threatened by modernity, and he made individual autonomy the center of his politics and poetics as well as his literary politics and social criticism.

On the other hand, the sight of the Woolworth Building or downtown Chicago stirred artists' sense of growing American power, and with a Shelleyan sense of the worth of their vocation they claimed a right to share in and contribute to it. Yet they found themselves completely disenfranchised as spokesmen for the truths they stood for by the "business mentality" erecting the skyscrapers that promised such power, and by the magazines and billboards of the new mass culture that promised them the means of reaching the broad "democratic" audience which American artists have felt a particular pressure to reach. As a result, they had to spend as much of their time defensively asserting their place in the culture or demonstrating that their presentation of experience in art was of more use than any specific advice as they did giving counsel on specific issues.

This bind, as Marshall Berman, Octavio Paz, T.W. Adorno, and Peter Bürger have argued within different conceptual frameworks—I use Bürger's here—has been inherent in the social situation of artists in bourgeois societies since the emergence of industrial capitalism and its quantitative, profit-motivated values. With the decline of religion and its integration of art in communal ritual, the quality of experience that we now call "the aesthetic" was divorced from everyday life and reserved as if in a game park in the autonomous institution—the mode of production, distribution, and reception—of "art."[10]

The paradox of art's autonomy is that it gives an artist the experience of freedom at the same time it aborts whatever attempts he might make to carry this freedom into life. As Bürger says, "Art in bourgeois society lives off the tension between the institutional framework [which releases] art from the demand that it fulfill a social function[,] and the possible political content . . . of individual works." Almost no artist in 1910s America conceived of the problem in these terms. What Martha Sonnenberg has observed of these most politically radical writers and illustrators—those of *The Masses*—applies to their more conservative contemporaries as well: none of them conceived of a rigorous "synthesis between art and politics, of art as a form of revolutionary activity, or of radical consciousness as a liberated aesthetics."[11]

Max Eastman, for instance, condemned "Futurism, Imagism, Vorticism, the 'Sceptric [*sic*] School,' and Polyrhythmic Poetry" as "Lazy Verse" in the *New Republic* in 1916, and, never seeing the potential challenge to consciousness inherent in new form, never considered how it could be used to reenvision the world in new political terms. To him, a poem was revolutionary only by virtue of what it said; as he said in his 1913 *Enjoyment of Poetry*, "the poetic" was simply an "added power" that could enhance the impact of a discursive statement. It did not occur to him that conventional poetic form in itself might bear the very values that a socialist wanted to overthrow. Conventional poetic form, in fact, was a "bourgeois" habit that in their own work Eastman and the *Masses* writers never broke.[12]

The contradictions in bohemian radicalism's ideas about art and its relation to social revolution—and the nostalgia underlying and trivializing them—explain why more conservative innovative artists felt no challenge to their own assumptions. The *Masses* crowd were saying little about the artist that was much different from anyone else, and when they did express their politics in poems, the poems seemed more conservative than those of an innovative reactionary such as Pound. Not until the dadaists and surrealists tried to make their artistic revolution spill over into life by attacking not only the forms of conventional art but also the institution of art which shaped the meaning and force of those forms did artists suggest a way to resolve the disjunction between revolutionary politics and autonomous art. And, as Bürger admits, even the surrealists failed to carry the values and experience of their work across the boundary into life, making at most a formal revolution within the still-sealed-off realm of aesthetics by overthrowing the concept of the "organic" work and supplanting it with the idea of the "new."

So did William Carlos Williams, though with quite different political intentions. Declaring to his brother in 1909 that "art is intrinsic[,] it is not a plaything," Williams came of age despising the idea that art was only for art's sake as strongly as he believed that the artist was an autonomous Individual. He set out to make art that not only would be made of commonplace life more than the art of anyone before him, but would become "common" among his townspeople in Rutherford and eventually among Americans. By the early 1920s he rose to meet Marcel Duchamp's challenge and tried "to free the world of fact from the impositions of 'art.'" But the assumption of autonomy underlying both his image of the artist and his politics of individual liberty led Williams not to formulate a more radical politics. Despairing about the possibility of changing the world, or even of saving the small-scale world of concrete experience in which he had grown up, he fell back on the concept of art as a refuge—or rather, a scatter of hard-shelled "seeds" from which someday a better world might flower. He never gave up the hope that art would break down the barrier separating it from ordinary life.

If one of Williams's "seeds" took root, what kind of society would grow from it? What were the politics and social vision encoded in his poetics? The content of many of the early poems is plain enough: Williams defended the liberty of individuals, though most often not in conventional political terms. Rather, he spoke as a member of a small community about ethics and morals, urging his fellows to speak honestly and "nakedly" to each other and damning them for their pretensions to being better than anyone else in the small town. This ethical discourse on concrete human relations remained the terms in which he spoke of politics for the rest of his life. The pattern of imagery in two of his early major poems, "The Wanderer" and the sequence of *Spring and All,* opposes wild nature and the city; it reveals how ambivalently he felt about the urban world that was changing the terms in which he spoke of experience, political or otherwise, and shows how his desire to carry art over into life was frustrated by the power of modernity to erase his language. Against his own wishes, he became the lone guerilla of Santiago Grove.

In short, Williams defined his politics in terms of individuals and concrete human relations, and his poetics as the expression of the self and its immediate experience—of the words of the poem themselves, of the sheer "presence" of human beings, of the world of which they spoke. Modernity, however, threatened not only the autonomy of the individual but the immediacy of his experience; it displaced the artist with scientists, philosophers, critics, and the new mass media, the priests and instruments of what Williams and Robert McAlmon called the vapid "information culture." But because of his individualist belief in the existence of words, things, and selves "in themselves," in a *logos* constituted prior to social existence, Williams's efforts to recover "contact" with the world did not succeed in offering a way to transform the social world, the "information culture," so that it recovered such immediacy.

Williams had grown up distrusting the "dogma" of religious creeds, and he came to use the term to refer to any kind of a priori or abstract thinking about concrete human beings, particularly that of science, philosophy, and politics. His desire for concreteness led him to view all experience in terms of one's aesthetics. Williams manifested his own aesthetics in his efforts to show that poetry could compete with science and philosophy and politics not only as a way of experiencing the world but as a set of principles according to which social life could be organized. Thus he pressed for a "local government" commensurate with his poetics of immediate experience. Although after the 1920s he did not speak much of local government, the urge to make social order out of poetry's order never really died out. Poetry, he wrote in 1950, "will actually eat out the heart of the political dogmata and build a world to supplant."[13]

Such efforts place Williams squarely in the tradition of the "revolutionaries of the word" from the German romantics through the surrealists, whose demands, Octavio Paz reminds us, were deeply incompatible with political thought, even the political thought of those revolutionaries with whom so many of them sympathized. Paz's explanation of this mutual attraction and hostility between political and artistic radicals describes well Williams's uneasy relations with the Village socialists and indeed with all political "dogmatists" and activists:

> The reason for rejection is the same as for attraction: both revolution and poetry attempt to destroy the present, the time of history which is that of inequality, and to restore the other time. But poetry's time is not that of revolution, the dated time of critical reason, the future of the Utopias; it is the time before time, the time of *la vie antérieure* which reappears in the child's timeless glance.[14]

Williams translated American history into a version of this myth of "the time before time" in *In the American Grain,* making an Adam out of Columbus, and the moment of poetry out of the historical moment of discovery of the *Nuevo Mundo.* In his own history, he lived out a Fall from small-community autonomy and concreteness into the modern fragmentation of the individual and the abstraction of experience. He knew full well, and often said, how constricting the small community can be for an exceptional individual, and he also knew that such myths as the *Nuevo Mundo* are to think with, not to live out. But, fearing that it was "too late to be Eric" the Red (I, 182), he gave in at times to the power of his deepest assumptions and imagined that one could escape time and live deep in the woods of a presocial self.

Despite my assertions that one must define Williams's politics broadly, I have neglected his attitudes toward several issues that we now take for granted as part of "the political." I discuss in passing some of his comments on immigration and ethnicity—an extremely powerful social force in the period I cover, and a crucial influence on his nationalism—but nowhere do I dwell on it. I also merely touch on his attitude toward race; I can only add here that his assertion in *In the*

American Grain that the black slaves "were just men of a certain mettle who came to America in ships, like the rest" (AG, 208) suggests to what extremes his resistance to acknowledging the power of social and economic forces reached in the early 1920s. The bright side of this individualism is the fact that he treated his black patients "like the rest," which was not always true of many other doctors in Rutherford at the time.

I have said even less about Williams's difficulties with what was both a powerful social force and an explicit issue in the 1910s, namely feminism. Mariani acknowledges the fact of Williams's sexism, so merely to detail its existence would be redundant. To go further with it would require a full-length study of Williams's views on sexuality and gender and their crucial relation to his poetics. The Williams who said early on, "It is the woman in us who makes us write," but who later defined the tradition-based writer as being trapped in a sterile "androgynetic mode" (as opposed to the innovative poet who generates new forms through his mating with the female present) deserves a book of his own.

I have presented a Williams who found it both imperative and deeply troubling to approach the American present. I have found Williams's early politics in his ambivalent responses to broad and deep social changes, the effects of which still shape our lives and our politics, and I have found these politics expressed constantly in his poems, not only in their subject matter but in their very origins. Our difficulties in seeing Williams as a political poet, then, are the result of Williams's difficulties in adapting his small-town political discourse, his conception of the individual, his image of the artist as an Individual, and his assumptions about the relation of language to the new world of consumer capitalism, big government, and what he called "mass movement like a sea" (I, 175).

If I seem to have dwelt on the forces that undercut Williams's best intentions, I do not discount those intentions. Ironically, the individualism that limited his social vision also made him a good man. De Tocqueville believed that the exercise of the "local liberties" granted by American political institutions fostered a sense of civic duty and voluntary participation that was the only thing preventing American individualism from degenerating into a mean egotism; he could have held Williams up as an example. As a skilled professional, as a young Unitarian, and as a poet, Williams was persistently exhorted to offer his services, and volunteer them he did.

We can wish that by being more willing to acknowledge the constituting power of forces "outside" the individual and art and perhaps arriving at more radical politics, Williams could be held up as a model for our America instead of de Tocqueville's. However, such a feat would have made him not an impure product of Rutherford, New Jersey in the early decades of this century, but an intellectual giant who solved the problematic relation between art and politics that post-Marxists and poststructuralists have only recently articulated. We must also keep in mind that most of the modern American poets who translated their nostalgia for an immediately given world into political ideology veered far to the right, into fascism, Christian royalism, Southern plantation aristocracy, or the specious Yankee agrarianism of Robert Frost. Williams, in contrast, wrote a campaign poem for Al Smith and treated each of his patients like the rest. If Williams was politically and socially conservative, he was so only in the sense that he wished to save the social framework in which his liberalism—let us take that as "generosity"—would make sense.

And if his poetics are nostalgic, his poems preserve seedlike the possibility of making an art "intrinsic" to life and a demand for a kind of freedom and experience that any social revolutionary must take into account. Williams valued the image of Washington "retreating across Jersey to win in the end''; I present the image of Williams retreating across modernity to win the respect I hope is expressed in my criticism.

1

The Hometown and the Civil Servant

In 1890, the year that Frederick Jackson Turner defined "The Significance of the Frontier in American History" as its creation of individualism and democracy, the small town was the form of community and government in which three-quarters of the American population lived. But over the next ten years, the small town reached a cusp. Since the end of the Civil War, the processes of "incorporation" and urbanization had been producing huge economic firms with nationwide markets, great and middle-sized cities, a federal government, and a national mass culture.[1] The small town would soon become either an object of derision or a repository of a kinder past.

Not a few small towns began growing as swiftly as cities in the 1890s, and, where local governments began to dicker with traction companies over trolley lines, replace backyard pumps with "city" water pipes, and collect taxes for "services" that older towns never dreamed were a collective responsibility, habitual ties of cooperation between families were unraveled and rewoven into more formal, institutional, urban modes of service—a looser social fabric. As clubs, lodges, fraternal organizations, ladies' improvement associations, and the like sprouted, the older values of familial self-reliance, "mutual aid and self-culture" began to be displaced by municipal service, "exclusiveness and getting ahead."[2]

Although William Carlos Williams would remember spending his boyhood in "a country town," Rutherford, New Jersey was never a model small town. From the moment it was conceived in the minds of a few real estate men as a nice proposition for a "New York business man of family," Rutherford was that new and ironic form of American community, the suburb.[3]

Like other suburbs, Rutherford was founded on a railroad line and the Faustian drive of Woodrow Wilson's "man on the make," on his eagerness to build and enjoy "a considerable share of urban conveniences," as pioneering suburban planner Frederick Law Olmsted forthrightly put it.[4] But it was also based on Wilsonian man's fear of the impersonal urban world that gave him his energy, a dread that fostered his nostalgia for small-community virtues such as self-sufficiency, independent and relatively participatory local government, familiar and secure social relations, and harmony with the magical nature he was marking out in lots.

One certainly can call the suburban ideal a "pseudo-pastoral," as Richard Lingeman does, but it is the attraction of the vision, not the truth of it, that is important. As a way of life and a form of community, the suburb, in Kenneth T. Jackson's elegant phrase, offered the individual "the promise of an environment visibly responsive to personal effort," be it the effort to trim the lawn of one's detached home or to persuade one's neighbors to build sewers.[5] The power of this promise shaped the Rutherford in which William Carlos Williams came of age, and it shaped his vision of society and the individual, of politics, and of the relation between the artist and his people. It also made Williams into an individualistic, iconoclastic moralist—and a curious kind of political artist, the artist as local civil servant.

Among the first nonfarmers to settle in the Rutherford area in the 1860s and 1870s were real estate agents. They formed companies called land associations, the most prominent of which was the Rutherford Heights Association. The area's first civic organization, the Rutherford Protective and Detective Association, was formed in 1878 to keep residents safe from the growing number of tramps jumping rides on the trains that delivered farm products, prospective land buyers, and commuters. The two associations were the seed of Rutherford's borough government, and their mutual interests in selling property and enabling middle-class people to live comfortably on it were the concern of borough politics and civic life well through 1912: how to continue to make the town's "advantages" such "that they bring to us the best class of people only," as the Rutherford *News* puffed in 1889. In a 1951 novel, set in Rutherford late in the first decade of the century, Williams called the period *The Build-Up,* punning on the town's growth and the self-satisfying hype that accompanied it.[6]

The byword was progress—the kind achieved through "improvements" of the borough's physical plant. The desire for such "advantages" divided area residents in the late 1870s, causing one of Rutherford's most memorable political disputes, that over the incorporation of the borough itself. At bottom, it was a struggle to control taxation: the newer, urbanized residents wanted to be able to spend the taxes they paid on their own town rather than have them distributed over the whole of Union Township. Older residents—mostly farmers and some wealthy families—could not have cared less about macadamizing the roads and laying sewers; they feared, and rightly so, that their tax bills would increase. (Some farmers, however, suffering through the agricultural depression of the late nineteenth century, welcomed a chance to sell off parcels to the real estate associations.)

The vote to incorporate was close, and would have been closer if the proborough faction had not drawn one of the proposed boundaries down the middle of one road so that a number of anti-incorporation voters who lived on the other side were cut out. Incorporation won, 90 to 71, and Rutherford's residents, fewer than a thousand of them, took their government into their own hands in 1881.[7]

Of course, some of the opponents of borough incorporation became opponents of borough taxation, notably Peter Kipp, a wealthy banker who still worked a farm he owned at the heart of the borough. In his autobiography, Williams vividly recalled how Kipp lived up to his reputation as the town crank by drop-kicking Williams over the fence dividing his farm from town for playing the local boys' sport of trampling his rye; he was a town character even after his death in 1920. Williams used him as one of the models for Johan Bach, the crusty Dutchman with fixed, "common" tastes, in his 1910 play *Sauerkraut to the Cultured*.[8]

In some older towns in the 1890s, older residents could block tax-raising improvements. They could not in Rutherford. Peter Kipp paid every rise in assessment rather than sell off a square inch, but as Williams suggested in his short story "Old Doc Rivers," others were neither as defiant nor as well cushioned. In the short story the conflict that founded the town is embodied in the figure of a "hot and eccentric" farmwoman, "peculiarly childish" from isolation, who reels off profanities at the young police surgeon (Williams in 1917) while he tries to test her for drunkenness after she has run her car through that symbol of town progress, the Park Avenue railroad crossing (FD, 99–100).

For years before the auto was introduced and for years after, Rutherford residents were killed at that crossing; it was one of the few situations in the borough that, because it required negotiations with the railroad, could not be "improved."[9] But otherwise, the "country town" of Williams's memory quickly made its kind of progress. By 1889, the *News* was announcing, "We are no longer a little country town"—Rutherford was already "a suburban village."

Between 1881 and 1900 Rutherford "developed" at a breakneck pace. In two decades the population quadrupled. Four bond issues were passed to macadamize roads, which were lit, curbed, guttered, and sidewalked as well. Sewer and gas lines were laid. Dozens of hydrants were installed, and two fire stations were built. Two new schools relieved overcrowding at the original school, and a fourth was already badly needed. A new freight house and a lavish new railroad station were built, and the first trolley began running in 1897.

The four denominations with churches became six. The leading women established the Reading Club, which in turn established a public library. The leading men founded and built the Union Club, modeled after the Republican political club of the same name in New York City. The merchants around Union Square stayed open Saturday nights so shoppers from all over the township could get in to buy in the region's new commercial center. In 1898, one long-time resident lamented that, what with the influx of newcomers, people did not know their neighbors anymore. His complaint would echo in the local newspapers through 1928.[10]

Throughout this period of growth—in fact, until the 1970s—Rutherford was, as its two major local newspapers proudly announced every November, "the banner Republican town of Bergen County." The voting totals bore out their boast. Conservative Democrat Grover Cleveland won the borough's presidential vote in 1892, but after him the Republican candidate carried Rutherford in every election through the 1920s but one, when former Republican Theodore Roosevelt ran in 1912 as a Progressive and defeated Woodrow Wilson in the borough by about 100 votes. Most of Rutherford went for "sound money," the protective tariff, international "expansion," and the regulation rather than the breakup of monopoly and the "money power."

The Democratic party's presence in early Rutherford was small but strong. The party's paper, the Bergen County *Herald,* began there before moving to Hackensack in 1897, leaving the *News,* which the *Herald* absorbed in 1900. The *Herald* was edited in the mid-1880s by Rutherford resident Nelson Young, a founder of the Typographical Unions in New York and undoubtedly acquainted with a fellow organizer, Williams's father-in-law Paul Herman. From 1895 to 1901, the *Herald* was owned and edited by Captain Addison Ely, one of the most powerful Democrats in the county and the party's nominee for Congress in 1896. He appears in *The Build-Up* as Captain Ellice, who lived in "semi-squirelike isolation" and "more or less defied the town"; one of his daughters is the playmate of Flossie Stecher (BU, 56–57).[11]

In state and local elections, the borough voted straight G.O.P. Only when progressive, "independent" Democrats coattailed along with Woodrow Wilson in the gubernatorial race of 1910 did Rutherford give any state office to a Democrat. Wilson himself told the borough he was a "Progressive" rather than a Democrat when he spoke there in that campaign, but he won Rutherford by only 50 votes out of 1,332. Besides losing Rutherford to Roosevelt in 1912, when Wilson ran for reelection to the presidency in 1916, he lost the borough two to one. As for county offices, the borough went straight Republican from 1892 to 1912. Only in 1912 did Republicans lose a borough election, and then to a slate of T.R.-inspired Progressives. A few Democratic mayors were elected—with Republican endorsements.

More than ambition and contempt for her neighbors, then, moves Gurlie Stecher to push her husband Joe into county politics in *The Build-Up.* A Rutherford Democrat did better to run for a county office and appeal over the heads of his townsmen to voters in the less affluent towns surrounding Rutherford—the immigrants in Carlstadt, Wallington, Lodi Township, and across the tracks in East Rutherford, where a Democratic Jeffersonian Club was founded around 1902. But after the "Hackensack Ring" of bosses were turned out in 1893 because of a scandal over a race track proposal, the Democrats' days of power in the county were numbered. By the turn of the century, Republicans ran the region as well.[12]

As for more radical political creeds, they had less hope of prevailing in Rutherford than the Democratic party. But they did have a few local adherents. There were always a few Prohibition party votes and some unorganized advocates of Henry George's single tax. Each presidential election from the 1890s through the 1910s yielded three or four socialist votes, either for Eugene Debs or Socialist Labor party candidate Daniel DeLeon. But even in this period of significant socialist success in municipal elections, no socialist candidate for county or local office is listed in the vote returns, and nothing of substance on radical politics (or Democratic politics, for that matter) appeared in either Republican newspaper until 1910, when the *Republican* reprinted an essay defining socialism from the *Appeal to Reason*. The shibboleth that socialism threatened not only private property, but all of a free man's "opportunities," marriage, and public morality apparently held complete sway in the borough.[13]

At the Union Club, his brother told interviewer Stanley Koehler, William Carlos Williams was "always the liberal."[14] In Republican Rutherford, he was assigned the role of the perennial dissenter who can never expect to acquire the power to change things. Such a person's participation in politics can become a mere rhetorical gesture demonstrating the moral superiority of his own principles to those of the prevailing party and allowing him to remain more idealistic than if he were given the power to translate ideals into impure practice. Williams's combination of political concern and practical passivity was caused by far more than Rutherford's domination by Republicans, but his membership in the town's liberal minority undoubtedly reinforced both his fervent idealism and his disinclination to participate in organized politics.

Judging politics in Rutherford by its parties, however, gives only a partial view. The *Republican* itself high-mindedly noted in 1914 that Rutherfordians had no politics at all, at least where town matters were concerned: "Rutherford people have never been very fond of mixing politics with their elections for local office." For politics pejoratively referred to the seeking of concrete personal gain—a job, a favor—through personal loyalty such as was practiced by city, county, and state "machines." The middle-class, Protestant businessmen who ran Rutherford saw themselves as loyal to principle, not to men with power, as the strength of Progressivism in the borough suggests.[15]

Aiding this antiparty devotion to the "best interests of the community as a whole" was the fact that in local elections, people could vote according to their judgment of men with whom they were familiar, and the man they elected was still able to be responsible primarily to townspeople he knew. Even in the 1890s, local governments had a degree of independence from county, state, or federal involvement that is hard to imagine today. The concentration of power in larger units of government was only just beginning (with the actions, ironically enough, of that strenuous individual Theodore Roosevelt), and for a long time one could believe in local self-determination—especially if, like the Populists and Progressives (and later Coolidge Republicans, the Ku Klux Klan, and William Carlos Williams) one felt it slipping away. Williams's call in his 1928 "Democratic Party Poem" for "the return of responsibility to the county, the town, the individual in matters which relate solely to the locality and the individual" derives more from his experience of such power in Rutherford than from his reading of Jefferson.[16]

Although Rutherford was not a conventional small community, as its attitude toward politics shows, the borough government was at least felt to be as much a network of concrete personal relationships as a set of abstract institutions, the kind of "direct" government that Progressives wished the federal government could be. Although from the start the borough government assumed functions such as sewer contracting that require impersonal processes, Rutherford's citizens could and did participate in the civic life of the town to a great degree.

Citizens' groups and determined individuals, in fact, helped define the functions of the borough government, as ad hoc movements for shade trees, parks, and even some welfare and child care were institutionalized as a Shade Tree Commission or Lincoln Park. Such citizens' groups, of course, were one of the few ways that disenfranchised women could have a voice in political affairs. It is Gurlie Stecher, not Joe, who becomes a political power in *The Build-Up* by joining the Riverdale Town Improvement Association (T.I.A.) and raising funds for borough parks and a hospital, pushing for school playgrounds, and making sure that the poor got some kind of relief—all of which Rutherford's T.I.A. performed between 1905 and 1910, and which Williams, who often helped the organization out, memorialized in his novel.

Perhaps the most telling scene about local politics in Williams's work occurs in *The Build-Up*, when the well-to-do Mrs. W. bribes the young fifth-grade teacher into recommending that the next year's two classes be divided by social status; the coin of her bribe is an invitation to one of her fashionable teas and a rare chance for the teacher to get ahead socially. If one defines politics as the relations of power between people on whatever scale, much of Rutherford's local politics, as one would expect in a relatively small, young, and therefore fluid community, concerned the power and status conferred by wealth, social standing, and taste. Graft, Williams argues, is paid in the politics of daily life as well as in government.

It is difficult to describe in detail just what the social structure in Rutherford was and what position the Williamses occupied in it; however, some generalizations can be made from a few revealing bits of evidence. To judge from young Williams's remarks and some of his later reminiscences, one gathers that the Williamses were an anamoly, being in the class of "the best sort of people" but not really part of it.

There was real wealth in Rutherford. As Paul Mariani notes, there was "comfortable old Yankee money" such as the Bectons and Dickinsons of medical supply fame had, and there were some very old Dutch families. Peter Kipp could trace his line back beyond the chief councilor to Peter Stuyvesant, and the Kipps had owned property in the area since the early eighteenth century.[17]

There was clearly some real poverty as well. Few immigrants seem to have moved into town even through 1915, when the *New Jersey Industrial Directory* noted in its Rutherford entry that "the immigrant population consists of ten Italians." But the author was disingenuous. So, perhaps, were the *Republican* and *American,* which gave little indication before the mid-1910s that either foreigners or poor people lived in town. But the poor family that Gurlie Stecher wants to help in *The Build-Up* (137–45) is Irish, and William Eric Williams notes that there was a "not inconsiderable population" of blacks, more of whom were probably descended from the 2,000 free Negroes and 600 slaves living in Bergen County in 1830 than had lately come North. In towns all around Rutherford, significant numbers of Germans, Italians, and Poles were settling. Any factory could have found a labor force.[18]

The majority of "the best sort of people" whom the Rutherford *News* was so proud to attract were in fact middle-class aspirants to the title. They were headed by businessmen like Paul Herman, owner of a small printing company, and they were generally quite well off, enough so to dwell on how others spent their money more than on how one was to earn one's own. Since they were new to town, they needed to establish themselves in the social scheme of things. Often they were second-generation Americans—the German Gunzes, the English Sheafs, the Norwegian Nanny Herman—and some of them, as Gurlie's speech on her Norwegian roots to a Southern friend's Grange meeting (BU, 225–27) suggests, were anxious to be accepted as real Americans by those W.A.S.P.'s of old family and breeding. And having the Ivison "castle"—"a positive medieval French chateau" (BU, 60)—in the middle of town, they meant to acquire some real "tone." Indeed, the borough acquired a reputation as thinking itself just a bit better than other places that has persisted to this day. Little wonder that Williams considered Thorstein Veblen's *Theory of the Leisure Class* fundamental reading.[19]

Just how one told true from false tone could only have been decided by cautious imitation. Gladys Eckart, the present director of the Rutherford Public Library, says of Rutherford social life that "the accent was on culture, with a capital C." She is referring to the town of the 1940s and 1950s, but it seems safe to say that earlier Rutherford, with its Women's Reading Club discussing Ibsen and hearing Bach recitals by young Charlotte Herman, had a "hunger," as Andrew Giarelli puts it, for an "idealized culture" of refinement and light.[20] Perhaps there was more emphasis on refinement than light, as Williams charged in *The Build-Up*: "'Ain't that something? We're getting stylish these days,'" says the town assessor when he sees the printed program for Lottie Stecher's piano recital (BU, 85–86).

Williams's father, William George Williams, was a salaried professional with a difference; as the advertising manager for Lanman and Kemp, he made long trips to countries in Central and South America to oversee the establishment of factories and distribution networks of the company's cologne. Said Williams,

"Pop never in his life made more than the barest possible income on which to support two families, his own and his mother's." But he managed to send his two sons to a school in Geneva while he was away for a year in Argentina and then put them through Horace Mann High School, the University of Pennsylvania and M.I.T. And, said Williams, "we did have an occasional case of Chateau Lafite in the cellar" (A, 50).[21]

If William George could afford such fine wine only rarely, he knew what to buy when he could; he was of sufficient cultivation and standing to be a charter member of the Union Club. But he was "slightly outside the accepted circle" (BU, 228) of town social life; after all, he was a British subject with sympathies for socialism, not an American Republican, a Unitarian rather than an Episcopalian or Presbyterian—and a lover of the arts as well as a businessman.

William George was highly active in local stage productions, which made him "slightly suspect on moral grounds" and perhaps even on grounds of sexual preference as well. Culture, after all, was part of "woman's sphere," although to *père* Williams it was simply part of a traditional English liberal education. Williams's mother passed on her hunger for the "real culture" of Paris to her son, but although she was a member of the Reading Club through the 1920s, she "felt ill at ease" in town society and took much less part than her husband.

The Williamses' relatively tight financial status and their long memories of European refinement and culture combined to make their son feel both slightly shabby-genteel and something of a snob about his hometown's cultural life. In 1909, when he was in Leipzig, Williams wrote a revealing comment to his brother about class in Germany—and his perception of it back home:

> The houses are well built but poorer than New York houses. In fact everything is cheaper looking in every way than in New York. This fact bothered me a lot at first. In New York the rich people own the place, that is, all the best things are for the rich, but here the middle class runs things. That is, suppose all the people of about our means in New York were to get together and say we are going to have theaters in which we can afford to buy orchestra seats twice a week, etc. The same with restaurants and, in fact, all public establishments—then you would have about the "speed" of Leipzig. It bothered me because I thought I was "getting in wrong," but this is not the case or it doesn't seem so as yet. (SL, 18)

The aspiring gentleman never got in wrong in Rutherford—he and his brother Edgar were part of a crowd that included the Becton and Dickinson scions—but he never quite got in right, either.[22] Circulating among people whose money he could never hope to match and whose taste fell so far short of his standards, he came to question their terms of inclusion in the social community and became an iconoclast of middle-class pretensions.

His sense of alienation also led him to idealize art in compensation for his sense of inferiority; significantly, in the early 1910s, when he was facing the condescension of the community toward a new doctor, he wrote a play (now lost) about "a tough guy"—undoubtedly the alter ego of the big-eared young gentleman now budding into a poet of common life and speech—"breaking up from under into local society" (A, 133). Williams may have doubted his community's values, but he still wanted to belong to it, and as an artist. Rutherford never got used to having its own poet; throughout his writing career Williams suffered a love-hate relationship with the townspeople who would not or could not accept the gifts he offered them.

But offer them he did, early on in the form of drama. Rod Townley suggested in 1975 that Williams wrote his early plays to do more than exorcise some private psychological conflicts: by putting them on with his friends, Williams "was able for an evening to view art as socially unifying, rather than alienating." This is truer than Townley suspected: Williams banded together not just friends in a cast, but the town of Rutherford in an audience of public performances. Indeed, the plays were his form of community service, performing the civic function of revealing and testing the values by which his townspeople lived.[23]

And he did so for tangible civic gain. *Betty Putnam* was performed as a benefit in July 1909, netting $18.60 for renovations to the public library; the performance of *Sauerkraut to the Cultured* in early November 1910 was part of a week's worth of fund-raising activities (including the Kirmess dances described in *The Build-Up*) by the T.I.A. for the Y.M.C.A. and a local hospital the association hoped to build.[24] It is this locally oriented civic-mindedness, rather than a concern with abstract principle or national issues, that defines the young Williams—and to a great extent the Williams of the 1910s and 1920s—as a political artist.

His first political comments in a work of art were thoroughly local. In May 1909, playing the Mikado in a production by Our Own, the town drama group, he sang revised lyrics mocking a current proposal to construct a new borough hall, the advocates of which included the "artless boss," "Who rants about taxes and modern improvements / And how we have fallen behind." But "most people" in town, he sang, "ne'er see real money at all"; anyone not content to renovate the old hall (which included the stage on which he was performing) should be made to sit by the Passaic River for ten years and "tell / If its odor grows richer with age."[25]

It isn't clear that Williams wrote these lyrics. In both *Betty Putnam* and *Sauerkraut to the Cultured,* however, Williams subordinated the obvious political dimensions of the subject matter to concerns of particular relevance to Rutherford. *Betty Putnam,* as David Fedo points out, ignores the political or social implications of the Salem witchcraft trials, and none of the major historical figures and events of that time figure in the play; in Fedo's words, the play is "a study, and finally a comedy, of greed."[26] Greed happens to have been a national political issue in 1909, and Williams attacked it as such in *A September Afternoon.* But in *Betty Putnam,* he focused on greed as it underlies social conformity in Rutherford and threatens the right of the individual to express herself, especially, in art.

Rutherford in 1909 was hardly in a state like that of 1692 Salem where, as

Betty's father says, "men who yesterday moved by a code of common sense today make law the toy of frenzy."[27] But the extreme circumstances of the Massachusetts town enabled Williams to criticize his New Jersey home bluntly. No one in the play believes in witches, but the characters subscribe to them under pressure to conform to the social code. The elder Noyes, the most powerful man in Salem, uses both his power and the pressure of the hysteria to try to acquire Betty's land from her. The villain of the play, then, is the hypocrite who masks greed with respectability.

Opposed to Noyes is Betty, who lives by "being true to one's own disposition," which is inquisitive, skeptical, risible, and entirely frank. Unlike her father, who asks her to keep his disbelief in witches secret, Betty speaks hers. And unlike everyone around her, she believes in culture and art. Having gone away from home to school (like Williams and his love of 1909, Charlotte Herman), Betty can find no worthy "diversions" in Salem such as the books to be found in Boston. Nor in Salem can she create her own "diversion"; she cannot laugh, sing, or rhyme without the danger of being accused of witchcraft: "I may not even think. And yet I do think!"

Williams would dissect the "puritanical" repression of art more subtly in the Cotton Mather chapter of *In the American Grain*. In his 1909 play, he did little more than protest Rutherford's genteel stuffiness and the sensibility that regarded artistic activities as trivial "entertainments." *Betty Putnam* itself was praised by the *Republican* as a "clever bit of comedy" written by "one of Rutherford's own bright young men," so it seems not to have had the impact upon the town which Williams intended.[28]

Sauerkraut to the Cultured is more obviously a local play than *Betty Putnam*. It takes place in the 1680s, just after the Dutch have surrendered New Amsterdam to the British and about 200 years before the Dutch-descended farmers of the Rutherford area lost their town to the foreign commuters. Like *Betty Putnam*, *Sauerkraut* concerns itself with the politics of expressing one's self honestly in spite of community disapproval. However, *Sauerkraut* focuses more explicitly than *Betty Putnam* on questions of culture and class. In fact, it recasts the fight over Rutherford's incorporation as a competition between two sets of aesthetic and social values.[29]

In *Sauerkraut*, two young men, one Dutch and one English, compete for the hand of Dutch-German Johan Bach's daughter by designing a lamppost for his house. The real competition, however, is between the style and values of "common" Old Bach and those of the gentlemanly Englishman, Fred Pickle. Pickle, one of New Amsterdam's "bright young men," sets out "To liberate Old Bach from his dull life" by "improving" every single item in it. "All old habits and worn out things must be done away with," announces Fred, for "to break the old is a symbol of progress." Fred answers Bach's criticism of his fancy design by proposing to improve the front of the house to match the post, the inside to match the front, and so on until Bach himself has been improved into a gentleman: "Habits, manners, all shall be raised to one level, that of my lantern."

The lamppost has been required by a new city ordinance intended to reduce the growing number of burglaries, and no doubt Williams's 1910 audience smiled at the memory of similar borough laws. Old Bach thinks the ordinance reasonable, even though it will, as suitor Karl Minnewit says, "cause you an expense." But it is the only change which Old Bach accepts. "They would have torn down my fence to widen the street," he says; as for the changes in taste and style that Englishmen such as Fred plan, he flatly opposes them. When Fred tells him he should "improve" the "advantages" he has, Bach replies:

> Why must I? You new ones in the city are so busy improving that you never have time to learn, but I live by profession evenly. All your misery comes from mixing levels. As long as men keep to their levels all is happiness but if a man live at the knee level and pretend to the chin level his end is fixed. I sir live little above the knees, I confess it, I am frankly common, yet my life is well ordered, I pretend to nothing. That is living by profession.

Old Bach's dread of change may make him laughable, but his clutching to his "rare common strong tastes" makes him poignant as well. "And when I have learned what you teach," he asks Fred after the gentleman has cracked his favorite chair, "will all my old things be broken?" Old Bach may be something of an inverted snob, but he, unlike some of Rutherford's leading citizens, is honest about who he is. "Well let no man call me a gentleman," he says, "I can still pretend to some honesty if they cannot." His daughter finally marries the dull Karl, and his lamppost is made plain with a lantern of solid tin. That suits Old Bach, who says: "I am no hypocrite."

So Old Bach lives by forthright "profession" of his common self, refusing to "mix levels" of class and status, and allowing Williams to mock the pretensions of his upwardly mobile neighbors. The aesthetics of "the common" which Williams developed over the next decade are by no means the same as Old Bach's, but the qualities Williams celebrates in the character—particularly his forthrightness and his concern for the quality of something rather than its power as status symbol—were permanent items on Williams's Rutherford agenda. "The cult of the gentleman," he declared to Walter Sutton in 1961, "will always lead him to double-cross a man" (Int, 49).

Thus in 1909 and 1910 Williams did his civic duty by teasing his progress-minded neighbors out of their pretensions, exhorting them to speak frankly and to pay attention to the paradigm of honest self-expression, the artist. Williams would continue to try writing his way into a place in the Rutherford community—addressing poems to his "townspeople," reading at the Polytopic Club he helped found, and assembling *Many Loves* for the local Little Theater group. He imagined the ideal relationship with his townspeople as that between George Washington and a group of soldiers he came upon swimming naked in a river, everyone laughing at the joke of revelation (CLP, 15). But in Rutherford there was more bewilderment or inattention than laughter, and Williams felt he was forced to keep silent and withold the benefits of self-knowledge that he wanted to confer.

In an unpublished poem dated March 16, 1939, now in the Williams collection at the Rutherford Free Public Library, Williams summed up his uneasy sense of his place in the community by imagining himself as the local post office clerk, the civil servant who knows who everyone in town really is—but who never says what he knows:

The Post Office Clerk and His Daily Duty

Some with faces
like a shrivelled quince
Some the manners
of a prince
Some hiding sins
their eyes disclosed
Or masking truth
in a gruff pose
I stand here looking
and serve you all
without distinction
big and small
the pale, the painted
gentle and crude
the timid, the ignorant
and the rude
By practice
grown familiar
I size you up
for what you are
But ask no questions
standing there
What I think
is my own affair.

Yet Williams did not withhold even this poem: the copy is signed, "William Carlos Williams / by request March 16, 1939."

And perhaps Rutherford did not shrug him off quite as indifferently as he often said, or so that little tag "by request" implies. In late 1938, Williams mentioned proudly to H.H. Lewis that the waiting list for his books at the public library was up to 200 names.[30] Of course, in his young manhood there were no books and no waiting list at all, and the gap between Rutherford's pretensions to culture and its shortcomings that fired his determination to make genuine art out of his local environment never closed to his satisfaction. He would always be out to prove something to his townspeople as well as to his later cosmopolitan artist friends.

Only a curmudgeon would note the irony, but when the chamber of commerce named Williams Rutherford's citizen of the year in 1954, it did so not so much for his writing as to give a beloved doctor and a decent man a "vote of confidence" in his "American-ness," which had been impugned by a few right-wing poets who wanted to deny him an appointment to the Library of Congress. At the award dinner, however, when Williams haltingly thanked the gathering of 400 of his townspeople, he left little doubt about how much he wanted them to recognize him for his writing:

> All that remains of communities and civilizations, all that remains of their worth and dignity exists in the art they leave. That is my excuse for existence. Your lives, your problems, are the things that make the artist go. The things you hide in your hearts and cannot tell about, even to yourselves, that makes art. I've come to know some of the things that make people great. You see, you see, you are here for a purpose, even if I am the recipient of that purpose. You are doing a warm thing in your hearts, and my heart is warmed. You are united, together, in . . . that is the greatest thing.[31]

But few Rutherfordians would hearken to his early plea, "Let us be conscious and talk of these things" (CP, 40). More than a few would always see him as the policeman questioned by an F.B.I. agent in 1942 did: he said the doctor was perfectly loyal, but, having seen Williams walking around town looking at the ground and talking to himself, he thought him a bit "odd." Had that cop realized that Williams was composing a poem, no doubt he still would have thought the Doc odd.[32]

One of the great ironies of Williams's career, then, is how many people think he lived in Paterson; it was Rutherford politics and culture that shaped his politics in several important ways. As a relatively small community on the verge of the bureaucratic era, Rutherford gave Williams the experience of something close to disinterested, direct participation in civic affairs by which he defined American democracy ever after. His life there also taught him that politics did not exclusively concern parties, factions, institutions, or ideologies, but consisted as well of the informal relations between people in daily life. The borough's economic prosperity and its sense of success reinforced Williams's own inclination not to make economic exploitation the center of his politics, turning his attention to the social and cultural and to the artistic shortcomings of his "suburban village."

The political discourse of Rutherford's leading citizens taught Williams the language in which to curse them. Social life there was about achieving a progress measured by material growth; Williams spent his life attacking such commercial values and the culture of pretension-to-culture they produced. Given his anamolous social position in a community aspiring to be upper-middle-class, it is not surprising that he was so concerned with challenging the values of merely material progress and exposing the hypocrisy and constriction of the self produced by the pressure to conform to Rutherford norms. Progress and improvement and the advantages that made people members of the best class: these were the terms of Rutherford politics. They molded William Carlos Williams's politics, which, local and national, were expressed largely as an exhortation to people like Rutherford's leading citizens to live up to the ideals latent in their real estate promotions. Answering such values made him, as Edgar said, "always the liberal" at the Union Club.

2

"So American!" Growing Up Liberal in the Progressive Era

The small-community style of politics and civic life in his well-to-do, suburban hometown left a lasting mark on William Carlos Williams, defining politics for him as concrete, unideological participation by individuals in the public life of their own place, and allowing him to feel that he could fulfill his civic responsibilities through his art and the improvement of his hometown's culture. Being an artist, however, made him something of an outsider in Rutherford society, and in many other important respects—ionality, religion, and politics—he was shut out of full membership in its upper crust. But even if the Williamses were not quite "right," they were by no means cut out; with the influx of middle-class, commuter families, the town's social structure was both too homogenous and too fluid, and the Williamses too long settled and too cultured, for them to be truly excluded.

William Carlos Williams, then, was an outsider inside his hometown—and as in social status, so in politics: if he was the liberal at the Union Club, he was nevertheless in the club. The very things that made him feel socially displaced—his multinational origins, his membership in the "small sect" (A, 22) of Unitarianism, and his father's unconventional politics—helped shape his politics into the liberalism that he expressed in some of his early work. So, too, did turn-of-the-century liberalism, the politics of Progressivism.

While Rutherford was busy building itself up and the town fathers were singing the virtues of Republican party and material progress, the nation as a whole was becoming aware that small-community values no longer served an industrializing nation. The memory of the Civil War never let people forget that the nation could be shattered, and several severe economic crises, including depression, labor-management war, and the widespread failure of family farms, along with the "invasion" of immigrants from southern and eastern Europe, set the agenda of American politics in Williams's youth and young adulthood as the struggle to "reform" industrial capitalism and save agrarian, Yankee, small-town democracy and individualism in the face of the financier and the corporation, the city machine and urban anonymity, and the wop, the Polack, and the Jew.[1]

This economic and social stress stirred up unusually intense anxiety about America's identity during the 1890s. American historians of this time, Michael Kammens notes, "de-revolutionized" the nation's origins in violence, presenting the past as an orderly evolution toward stability and prosperity. Among ordinary citizens, patriotism and "Americanness" became fevers. Those who could do so traced their lineages back to Colonial-era forebears, and local historians' profiles of leading citizens became recitations of impeccable genealogies. The Grand Army of the Republic (G.A.R.) and the recently founded Daughters of the American Revolution both mounted campaigns to teach public school students the numinosity of the symbols of the flag and the Constitution.[2]

In New Jersey, the G.A.R. strove to have some public object named after Lincoln in every town in the state. Rutherford had Lincoln Park and Lincoln Avenue by 1905, a bit late, considering that Charles Burrows, its postmaster in the early 1890s, was one of the leaders of the state G.A.R. Although Burrows did not boast about it, noted *Rutherford Illustrated,* his American "pedigree" as traced by county historians was "one such as would bring joy to the soul of the most ambitious member of the coteries of anglo-maniacs who ape the aristocracy of the old world."[3]

For William Carlos Williams, the son of recent immigrants from England and the Caribbean who spoke as much Spanish as English at home, the pressure to prove he "really belonged" in Rutherford and the United States was overwhelming. There is no small irony in the inscription he made on the first page of his address book on Christmas Day in 1906 ("Patriotism—Let every man love his native land!"), for in a nation protesting its Anglo-Saxon "purity" so loudly, only self-conscious acts of will and imagination like this could make Williams's birthplace his native land. As he told the Bergen *Herald-News* in 1949, he wanted so badly not to be considered a "foreigner" that he tried to excel in athletics in grammar school and at Horace Mann. Heart trouble blocked his athletic career, however, and he turned his desire to belong to Rutherford and America from sports to art, inscribing his own self-conscious nationalism into nearly everything he wrote.[4]

The urge to possess America, then, and create an American identity for himself possessed him very early on. But just when he began the reading in American history and politics that eventually issued in *In the American Grain* is hard to tell. In his autobiographical writings about his primary and secondary schooling, he says nothing about classes in American history; there is only a fragment about his course in English history at Horace Mann, which he did not much care for. "I more or less remembered the date of the Magna Carta," he said, "but that was all." In medical school at Penn he had little time for reading outside the curriculum, as his letters home suggest, but he did find some. In 1904, he wrote Ed to tell him that he was reading "Gen. Grant's personal memoirs" and laughing at Grant's talk about "it," which apparently was masturbation: "he hit it up pretty steadily for a long time. He did just like you and me. . . . "[5]

Although Williams recalled that his college friend Ezra Pound was "completely indifferent" to the American present—"he was absorbed, completely absorbed" in "the romantic times"—Pound had taken Principles of Government and American Colonial History the year before they met, and in the 1902–3 school year would take two more history courses. In fact, two months after they met, Pound published his first poem, a Riley-derived monologue by a farmer praising President Roosevelt for settling the coal miners' strike of that year. The two young men probably spent more of their "many, many sessions" talking about art and girls than trusts, but undoubtedly politics came up, if only in the playful tone of Pound's letter of 1907, when he told Williams not to let his brother know about Viola Baxter and "try to run the monopoly—I am opposed to trusts you know."[6]

Whatever history and politics he was learning, by 1907 Williams was acting on his desire to "belong" to America by helping the country's art and culture to flower as richly as its democracy seemed to be doing. Seeing Isadora Duncan dance in late August 1908 inspired a sonnet to her and a letter to Ed, both of which expressed his aims:

> It fairly made my hair stand on end Bo and best of all she is an American Bo, one of our own people and I tell you I felt doubly strengthened in my desire and my determination to accomplish my part in our wonderful future. You Bo and I must be what we crave to see in those around us and what this great girl has shown is possible of accomplishment now. Oh Bo I could see all our future before us in her dancing. . . .

Nor was present American culture quite so rude as Europeans made it out to be. Williams's nationalism was bolstered by a review of Nicholas Murray Butler's *The American as He Is* in *The Outlook* in March 1909, which sided with Butler's defensive contention that "The Real American" was creating fine works of art. "Be sure and read it," Williams told Ed.[7]

When that summer he himself became the American abroad whose usual boorishness Butler was trying to counter, Williams found virtues in his supposed cultural defects. The "New World spirit," he told Ed in a letter from Leipzig, was "young, ignorant but enterprising . . . with contempt for old forms and the unpractical in art" (SL, 16). The "enterprise" so highly valued in American business had only to be matched by the American artist's; when it was, America would be complete. Williams would soon find out, however, that his contempt for the "old forms" of art led to mutual contempt between him and America's businessmen: they continued to view all art as "unpractical," while Williams protested that it was more useful than the electric irons and washing machines produced by the American dynamo.

In 1909, Williams was aiming to usher in this future by making Americans aware of their own past. On his way home from Leipzig in May 1910, just after he made a pilgrimage to Palos de la Frontera, Columbus's point of embarkation for his first voyage, Williams wrote his fiancée that he wanted "to infuse Americans with the strength and purity of their own traditions which are lying all about us unused." Two reading lists he made between 1908 and 1911 list 13 works on American history, ranging from Francis Parkman's five volumes on French colonization to P.H. Bruce's *Institutional History of Virginia* to the autobiography of P.T. Barnum. One infers from the absence of anything concerned with American political theory that Williams was more concerned with finding subjects for art than with tracing the subtleties of states' rights or direct elections.[8]

He was writing plays set in the American past and completed at least seven between 1907 and 1911.[9] One of the reviews he received particularly pleased him; when he read *Betty Putnam* to Charlotte Herman and a friend, he wrote Ed, they praised everything about it, "and best of all they called it 'so American.'" His third surviving early play, *A September Afternoon*, is quite self-consciously about American tradition, American politics, and "Americanness," examining the motivations of those who fought the War of Independence and asserting the urgent relevance of those motivations to contemporary times.

In a time of anxiety about the national identity, Williams's own anxieties to be part of America probably led him not to question too sharply the principles upon which American political democracy was founded. Whatever his motives, Williams did wholeheartedly believe in what he called "the regular Fourth of July stuff" (Int, 83). While he never went into great detail about what he meant by the phrase, his writings make clear that at heart he meant Jefferson's agrarian-based vision of individual liberty and responsibility, or, later in his career, the Jacksonian revision in terms of the independent artisan and small entrepreneur—the basis of the American community and politics whose power as a mythology was being drained by industrialism throughout Williams's early life.

This is not to say he was uncritical of American politics. But even at his most exasperated, in the 1920s, when he questioned the worth of democracy itself—calling it "a thin, scientifically, philosophically perfect film . . . a magic lining between men everywhere and their desire" (EK, 27)—he decried the perversions of the system wrought by men rather than flaws in the system itself. To him, the country's political failures were caused by the "cheap self-interest" of the "ruling moneyed class" (SL, 158) whose champion, Alexander Hamilton, had undermined democracy almost from the start. But Williams never asked if capitalism made a Hamilton inevitable, or if the robber barons were only the double edge of the individualism he hoped to preserve. For Williams, the contradictions of capitalism had either psychological causes—Americans' fear of "contact" with the environment drove them to follow Puritan morality and the Franklinian virtues—or ethical causes—corruption was bred by greed.

Of course there was much more to young Williams's patriotism than any overcompensating anxieties he felt, and although he never became a Marxist, his idea of democracy was more literal, and thus further to the left, than that of most bourgeois Americans. The economic crises of the 1890s and the 1900s generated radical movements founded on economic issues; even the Democratic party was captured by William Jennings Bryan and the free silver crusade. Williams thus became aware of alternatives to American democracy early on, acquiring an understanding that democracy might extend even to the economic democracy of socialism. In fact, it is worth asking why, given his early political sympathies, Williams did not become more of a leftist in the 1910s. The answer, I think, is to be found in the nature of those sympathies themselves, in the kind of liberal politics he learned from his father, from Unitarianism, and from Progressivism.

In *The Build-Up,* Williams described his father (called "Bishop" in the novel) as one of three British residents who were the prime movers of local dramatic activity: "slightly outside the accepted circle of the local club world, perhaps from their own wishes as English, holding themselves apart, they were slightly suspect on moral grounds among their fellow townspeople" (BU, 228). Although his father was a charter member of the Union Club, heading the printing committee that ran off the program for their grand opening fair in 1892, and a founder of the Unitarian Church that year, William George Williams went largely unmentioned in the local papers; his obituary in 1918 spoke mostly of the quality of his drama productions.[10]

Williams's characterization of his father's social position applies neatly to his politics as well. As a lifelong British citizen, William George could not vote, but he was interested in politics, including one of the period's radical American movements: "Pop, he was a single taxer" (A, 15). In *Progress and Poverty* Henry George held that the source and the measure of all value were land and natural resources—which, he also argued, were fundamentally common property. A single tax, George argued, on the rise in value of land (and on those holding monopolies in land and resources) and distributed over the whole community would remedy all economic and social injustices.

George detailed his plan far more concretely than most other utopian schemes of the 1890s, and its appeal to Americans' uneasy sense that the frontiersman had been displaced by the real estate agent kept it alive from the 1890s even through 1920, when the Single Tax party nominated its last presidential candidate. Rutherfordians, who knew firsthand how land values could go up overnight without a shovelful of earth being turned, counted a number of "genial single tax men" in their midst, one of whom even proposed in 1893 that the borough set its own tax valuation rates according to George's principles.[11]

The borough council voted the measure down, and Williams apparently never went too far along with his father's interest in George. "Damned right not to read it [*Progress and Poverty*]," Ezra Pound wrote him in 1958; "have never known a cure for infection. Look at Upton [Sinclair]!!!" But whether or not Williams read George, he became disposed to distrust industrial capitalism's measurements of labor and value, and learned that there were other measures to make and take.[12]

Had Williams plowed through *Progress and Poverty,* he might have sympathized more positively. As Daniel Bell says, George's single-tax scheme was "perhaps the boldest attempt to restate an individualist America" yet made, and the alternative measures that Williams sometimes did take had the same bent. In the early 1920s, in fact, Williams had a momentary enthusiasm for *The Freeman,* though he enjoyed its acerbic anti-big-government attacks more than its single-tax solution. During the Depression he expressed sympathy for "radical" movements aiming to preserve individual freedom as defined by the middle-class man, and even joined a few of them, particularly the Social Credit movement to redistribute wealth through dividends given to consumers, and the Bergen County Consumer Cooperative that flourished during the Depression. We may safely imagine that young Williams, like young Pound, was opposed to monopolies on more than girlfriends.[13]

Williams also acquired something of his father's sympathy with contemporary socialism, though not very much. The elder Williams's library contained a number of works by late Victorian, British radicals and political economists, Williams told Walter Sutton in 1961, but, he said, "I didn't bother to read [them] very much" (Int, 51). They have disappeared, and one cannot know whether along with the work of, say, John Stuart Mill or the Webbs they included work of Ruskin and especially William Morris, which might have had some appeal to the budding artist. We do know, however, that for several years after he left home, William Carlos Williams was curious to know what a few socialist authors had to say about art. At any rate, we should recall the nature of turn-of-the-century socialism to understand why young Williams did not pursue his father's interest further.

British socialism of the 1880s and early 1890s was a heterogenous compound of foreign rigor and native radicalisms with strong evangelical and middle-class bents. For the British radicals, capitalist society would inevitably evolve into socialism—smoothly and gradually, not catastrophically, through an Armageddon of class war. In fact, an upper- or middle-class socialist could remain upper- or middle-class; his or her duty was to assist history by bringing workers into present political institutions (the Webbs especially hoped to create a benevolent bureaucracy) and raising their culture up to bourgeois standards, rather than enabling workers to destroy such institutions and replace them with their own. Bringing about such change, then, would be accomplished through exhortation to individual reform. As Fabian leader Sidney Webb once explained, "It would be easier to moralise the capitalist than to expropriate him."[14]

The Webbs' careful statistical studies undoubtedly would have bored young Williams, and their faith in government management would not have appealed to the young individualist. Nor did the American Socialist party, which reached the height of its popularity between 1900 and 1912, when it overcame its scruples against working for short-term legislative reform and its obsession with the purity of members' "working-class-ness" to make what leader Morris Hillquit called in 1910 "a new appeal to [the] small middle-classes." During this time, as Daniel Bell notes, the party gave many nonproletarians an outlet for their "moral indignation at poverty and the promise of a better world."[15] Williams, however, who then had plenty of indignation and apocalyptic hope, was not one of them. By 1910, his friendship with his future father-in-law Paul Herman may well have instilled in him a thorough distrust of socialism's ends.

Nor would Williams ever entertain the Marxist premise, however specified, qualified, or modified, even by Marx himself, that economic relations in some sense determined one's consciousness. The mind, in whose power Williams believed so strongly, was for him constituted free of the relations of production. He was not being hyperbolic when he told the *Partisan Review* in 1943, "In my world are no classes but the good guys and the bastards" (Int, 83).

On the other hand, the Williams who refused to believe in the material basis of history would have responded warmly to the evangelical rhetoric that some American socialist leaders used, especially about the world after the apocalypse. As John Spargo wrote in a work that Williams may have read in late 1910, the arrival of socialism in this country would mean "nothing less than the redemption of our national life from crass and soul-destroying materialism."[16] This sort of rhetoric was hardly the property of socialists, though, and Williams heard it from sources that had much more impact on his politics, shaping his sense that politics were more a question of individual conscience and ethics, of being a "good guy," than of economics and class. The greatest influence on his political thinking, in fact, was his religious training in the Unitarian faith.

Williams's Sunday School class was presided over by Rutherford lawyer E.J. Luce, who was characterized by *Rutherford Illustrated* as "an enthusiastic upholder of that liberalism which distinguishes that denomination from all others." Luce read from Plato and Immanuel Kant to his pupils. He calmly informed them, in accordance with the faith's historicism, that circumcision was "a formal rite of mutilation practiced by the Jews." And he instilled in them the "modern" theology expressed by William C. Gannet: always to value "character" over creed, to trust one's own reason and conscience rather than religious dogma, and to assist "the growing nobility of man" by leading a "self-forgetting, loyal life" of service to others. As the copy of "Our Faith," the placard ("suitable for framing") that hung on the wall behind Luce, put it, "The Fatherhood of God, the Brotherhood of Man, the leadership of Jesus, salvation by character, the progress of mankind onward and upward forever."[17]

Such theological liberalism made Unitarians social and political liberals as well. Luce held "several public positions" as a Democrat and doubtless helped

Williams to see the faith's tenets as political principles, as the church encouraged its members to do. "It appealed to me," Williams remembered, "that Christ was divine by the spirit that was in him and not by miraculous birth. This seemed democratic and to the point" (A, 22). The democracy of another point of doctrine was made clear by Rev. George H. Badger, the first pastor of the Rutherford congregation, in an 1893 sermon on the need to redefine the medieval idea of "a tyrannical, Emperor-like God":

> In our day the King who would deal with his subjects, the landlord who would deal with his tenants, the employer who would deal with his workmen according to the ethical principles by which the Almighty God was supposed by the Medievals to deal with his sin-smitten children, would be hooted from civilized society with deserved opprobrium.[18]

Hearing such sermons, Williams came to conceive of Jesus as a "socialistic figure, related to a generous feeling toward the poor" (IWWP, 76), and presented him thus in his 1948 poem, "Choral: The Pink Church." At the service opening the Rutherford church in 1892, 9-year-old Williams dedicated himself to "the service of humanity, that the humblest and poorest child of God may be helped to the way of better living, may have life and have it more abundantly."[19] In 1904, the 21-year-old Williams and some other members of the University of Pennsylvania fencing team gave a demonstration at a Philadelphia settlement house, and he wrote his mother how "bright and quick" some of the poor boys were, and concluded that "the only way to be truly happy is to make others happy" (SL, 5).

He would come to serve the poor through his medical practice and his writing. The service ethic, however, left wide room for interpretation, and Williams could feel that he was helping without necessarily having to change the social circumstances that contributed to poverty. Several elements of Unitarian liberalism reinforced Williams's disinclination for politics, allowing him to be socially concerned but not a social activist.

The first was the faith's combined generosity toward, and resistance to, dogmatic statements. "Unitarianism is not exclusive," declared one of the ministers at the Rutherford congregation's 1892 dedication service; three decades later the Unitarian Society restated the point for the Bergen County Historical Society's annual report: "It is important, not so much that a person shall profess any given beliefs, as that he shall, in fact, believe that which he may be willing to profess." Such tolerance was founded on Unitarianism's respect for the "religious sentiment" in itself and the denomination's belief in both the limits of human reason and the necessity of using it freely to arrive at truth.[20]

But in Williams's youth, the church's trust in individual reason and conscience over sectarian "dogma" became difficult to reconcile with its strong imperative to assist reform. As George Willis Cooke explained, Unitarians' "attitude toward reform . . . has been qualified by their love of individual freedom," which disposed them to resist "any attempt to coerce opinions or to establish a despotism over individual convictions." For instance, they were reluctant to join the temperance movement because they preferred to use "moral suasion" rather than "legislative power." Cooke feared, however, that in 1902 Unitarianism's individualism was becoming "excessive" and was "in opposition to the altruistic and associative spirit of the time." Nevertheless, the church would continue to appeal to conscience rather than organize action.[21]

Williams acquired just this ambivalence along with his faith's political liberalism. He valued character over dogma highly enough, it seems, to wade through a churchman's 1901 tome of comparative religion which condemned abuses committed by Christianity because of its dogmatism. Throughout his own writing Williams used "church" as a figure for repression of the individual. Moreover, he always gave priority to the concrete human presence over abstract ideas. When in the early 1920s he wrote *In the American Grain,* he rejected the concern of some historians with "events" and "generic patterns" to assert that history is "all humanity" and organized his history as a sequence of biographies. This echoed the structure of one of his Sunday School texts, *Noble Lives and Deeds,* which offered 40 biographies, each illustrating a virtue of character. George Washington, for example, exemplified "Self-Control," the very virtue for which Williams excoriated him in *In the American Grain.* Williams had a copy of *Noble Lives* all his life.[22]

Such respect for the individual presence also helped stir Williams's distrust of logic and dogma, be it the philosophy of John Dewey or the Leninism of Bolsheviks. In a 1906 letter, Williams cautioned his brother Ed against falling into "the magical circle of careless reasoning" and advised him: "Don't reason from feelings or rather don't reason at all. What's the use? For the only thing that's worth while is truth and that doesn't need any reasoning about. What it does need though Bo is faith. Yes Faith." Williams would always insist on the limits of logical thought, and yet felt he could arrive at truth by sloughing off a priori abstractions, whether from the past or the present, and thinking for himself. Williams placed his own faith in the ability of his senses to grasp truth in the here and now, as an immediate revelation of the present.

And so he went on in his letter to Ed to speak not of political problems and interests, but of "ignorance" that caused "wrong":

> Bo it takes patience and grit and it doesn't mean being too careful about rules that custom has made laws but just say "I know that's wrong and I'll be darned if I know why but it will come right in the end for it can't help it because I'm doing my best" and if you don't get everything about you that is wrong, an uneven roadway, a false woman, an ugly dress, everything. Then I ask you honestly are they not ignorance, misconceptions of the eternal truth. Now comes trusty old Faith with his cheerful smile and says "Sure I see 'em what do you expect but just you wait a while and you'll see everything come right!" And I tell you he's a fine old comrade to have along.[2]

The badly paved new roads in Rutherford, then, were for Williams the product of an intellectual failure (as were any ethical irregularities in the contracting procedures), not of the alienation caused by capitalism. All one had to do is see straight, and the solution would come clear and everything would come out right. Williams would recurrently speak of social problems as failures of intelligence or imagination rather than as questions of power or interest; while he sometimes acknowledged the inevitability of the political process of persuasion, negotiation, and compromise (and sometimes participated in it, as in the Rutherford high school fight in 1921), his own quickness more often than not made him impatient with politics as such.

As a result of his distrust of dogma as well as his faith in the individual and in the mind, Williams often resisted the "associative" spirit, especially if he felt that it would subordinate his freedom of thought to a party or an idea. He would always be at his best defending individual liberties, especially the right of self-expression, but he was loath to commit himself to putting particular expressions into action and rejected any position that did not recognize a great deal of freedom for the individual. At times he even went so far as to defend the process of arriving at truth rather than commit himself to putting into practice the product of such disinterested inquiry. In a proposal he made to himself in his 1924 *Rome* journal, for a magazine of intellectual "clarity," he said that its "political and literary policy" should be "to study and reveal what is—to oppose nothing advocate nothing but move with everything in motion,, [sic] condemning nothing, wishing to change nothing but muddle headedness—leaving everything behind" (*Rome,* 58).

While Unitarianism reinforced the concept of freedom fostered by the American ideology of democracy and individual liberty, to which Williams was always devoted, it hardly led him to ignore political and social problems and rationalize his neglect. On the contrary, its emphasis on "practical" religion and service helped make him the constantly concerned doctor and poet that he was. However, Williams's boyhood faith created in him the tensions between the individual and society, ethics and politics, and art and politics which constituted and often limited his social thought and practice, by contributing much to his curiously apolitical understanding of politics.

Williams came to define politics in terms of individuals and ethics rather than group or class interests and power, as a struggle between greed, ignorance, deceit, conformity, and corrupting practice on the one hand, and selfless service, intelligence, honesty, and disinterested ideals on the other. If he first learned to speak such a discourse in the Sunday School classroom of a small-town, Democratic lawyer, he became fluent in it when he entered the larger world of Penn, Philadelphia, New York, and the muckraking magazines and heard the political discourse of "reform" in the Progressive era.

By the early 1910s, anxious small-community Americans had found a way both to express their pain and to accommodate themselves to the new world of trusts and cities. Progressivism, as Richard Hofstadter defines it, was a middle-class "revolt against industrial discipline . . . the complaint of the unorganized against the consequences of organization." Older entrepreneurs and professional men like those men who ran Rutherford, and members of the "new" middle class of technicians, salaried workers, clerical workers, salespeople, and public service personnel sought both to preserve the ideology of economic and political individualism and, as Robert Wiebe points out, make a place for themselves within the new industrial social order.[24]

Against both plutocracy and socialism, they hoped to preserve their economic "opportunities" and their faith that success was a question solely of individual effort and character. They also tried to continue to believe that American politics could be conducted according to disinterested, ethical principle by responsible individuals, rather than by the methods of the "corrupt," big-city machines and bosses, who consolidated power in their immigrant constituencies (and won power for them that disinterested leaders from the Yankee-Protestant tradition withheld) by satisfying and claiming more immediate personal needs and loyalties.[25]

William Carlos Williams was 17 when Theodore Roosevelt assumed the presidency, and he came of age in the peak of the Progressives' "strenuous" efforts to reform politics and society through exhortation. Little wonder he felt, as Unitarianism had taught him to hope, that humanity was progressing in spirit and the United States was moving onward and upward. In *The Build-Up,* he recalled the political mood of 1909 as "early spring"—"the world was on its way to the greatest triumphs for peace and plenty it had ever known" (BU, 257).

An earnest new doctor could believe it: in two terms Roosevelt had "busted" both trusts and coal strikers, assuring the country that if the federal government was going to enlarge its power, it would do so fairly. Taft, ineffectual as he seemed, actually saw through into law many of the reforms Roosevelt had only talked about, and raised hopes for world peace by trying to widen the scope of arbitration treaties and give the Hague Tribunal some genuine force. In 1910, Woodrow Wilson capped five years of the reform movement's efforts to cleanse New Jersey of Standard Oil and the bosses by winning the governorship as a Progressive, one who, he told a crowd in Rutherford that October, "insists upon returning to the reasonable, pure processes of popular government."[26]

Williams probably heard Wilson speak in Rutherford that night, but even if he did not, his own idealism and patriotism had had him talking the language of democratic "restoration" for several years. In 1905, he had written excitedly to Ed about the victory of "the decent people" over the corrupt bosses' machine in the Philadelphia city elections. In 1909, he was reading "The Real Americans" in the March 20 issue of the "uplift" magazine *The Outlook* (in which new editor Roosevelt explained "Where We Cannot Work with Socialists").[27] In August 1909, from Leipzig, he expressed to Ed the essence of progressive politics:

> Give me my country where there is water to drink and freedom such as they only dream of here. You can say what you want about rotten politics but it's rotten because I want it rotten but when I want it clean it will be clean, but here [in Germany] only bloodshed can wipe out tyranny. There is all the difference between the two. (SL, 18–19)

Among the "traditions" that Williams hoped to "infuse" in the audiences of his "American" plays was the ideal of ethically pure, personal participation in the political process. While *Betty Putnam* and *Sauerkraut to the Cultured* dealt mainly with local concerns, Williams's third surviving early play, *A September Afternoon,* is about the pure motivations of those who fought the War of Independence—motivations which, if "infused" in the audience, would kill their apathy, moving them to "want it clean" and thus working up the civic fervor that would renovate "rotten" American politics. *A September Afternoon,* in fact, is Williams's first work of national scope, and one of his most explicitly political works.

As British soldiers and American volunteers prepare in the far background to do battle, 17-year-old Barney Lane and his older sister Marjorie argue about Barney's joining the fight. Hotblooded Barney is the idealist, seeing the war as his chance to contribute to "the fight for liberty and against injustice and tyranny." Marjy, who fears that both Barney and their father will be killed and leave her and her mother to face winter on the farm, sees Barney's idealism as mere male bluster and "talk" stirred up by the papers. To her, Washington is no hero, but only "leads boys to be killed." As for the idea of the nation itself, she sees it as a mere smokescreen for greed:

> Loyal are they! They're fighting each other like a pack of lean dogs: I've heard father say it. And if you say it's any different in Philadelphia where the Congress of all the states is—the head of it all—I'll tell you they're worse than the rest; lying and backbiting and grabbing for the most they can lay hand to and fearing each other worse than England or the Devil himself even. It's true and you know it and that's the country you're fighting for![28]

The reformers saw just such a moral conflict between greed and self-interest, honesty and devotion to the larger good as the central problem of American politics, and Barney's reply to Marjy's cynicism is the quintessential Progressive solution: "General Washington needs me the more then."

The sources of *A September Afternoon* are unknown, but it is clear that Williams supplemented whatever he read about the Continental Congress with news of present-day corruption, such as the muckrakers' exposures of city and state governments, which, after trusts, were their favorite targets:

> B[arney]. It's such men as me will be the great heroes in the cities in time to come.
> M[arjy]. In the cities do you say, you poor fool? Where every man is fighting for himself and never bothers his head for lct alone one patriot of past times—not to speak of the hundreds are dead with him.

Marjorie also calls Philadelphia, which Williams knew from his college days, "worse than the rest," echoing Lincoln Steffens's 1903 article that judged the City of Brotherly Love not only "corrupt" but "content" to be that way.[29]

A September Afternoon, then, is a jeremiad on contemporary American politics, presenting the idealism of a figure from the past to criticize the failure of his descendants to live up to him. And it is a specifically Progressive jeremiad, echoing the reformers' charge that the failure rested in the failed zeal of "decent" people rather than in flaws or changes in America's social and political structure. As Barney tells Marjorie, "Everybody will care. We are the ones they'll look back to in the days to come and wish they could be like us." She replies, of course, "They'll be just as big liars and stealers as they are now." But he retorts that politics ever after will be determined by his example of dedication and decision to act. There will not be so many liars and thieves, he tells Marjy, "when enough of us has been brave," and goes off to die heroically and answer her cynicism and lack of will to make "good government" a reality with the ultimate self-sacrifice. Even Marjy ends up cheering the Americans as they win, at least until Barney dies.

In 1936, Williams would publish a similar exhortation to Americans, his libretto, *The First President*. George Washington is the main figure of civic self-sacrifice; however, Barney reappears as the sentry who climaxes a ballet in the snow at Valley Forge with his leap onto the bayonets of advancing British soldiers, sacrificing himself for the protection of his commander-in-chief and the nation (ML, 340–43).

Had Williams finished *A September Afternoon* after the fall 1909 elections, when Progressive administrations, some of them almost ten years old, were turned out by voters across the country, he might have decided to allow Marjy to keep jeering. But apparently people felt they had done enough penance for their municipal shame. Lincoln Steffens himself found that actually managing reform, as he had been invited to do in Boston, was impossible without some less-than-decent manipulation of voters' interests. And soon an overly serious Harvard student he had taken under his wing, Walter Lippman, would challenge the very basis of the reform movement by redefining politics as the "mastery" of the "drift" of interest groups rather than as the purification of those interests. Soon the bureaucratic discourse of efficiency and management through technique began to compete with rhetoric of individual ethical reform and "good government."[30]

Williams's own political discourse would take on new accents and inflections in the 1910s, but neither from "scientific" socialism nor from the new Progressive frankness about government and social "control." Like the Progressives, Williams hoped to preserve the middle-class version of individual autonomy, an ideal that led him to view participation in politics as a moral obligation to be directly involved, and to judge the ethics of individuals in politics rather than the ethics of the process. But Williams would not modify "the regular Fourth of July stuff" as readily as the Progressives did to suit the facts of social life in modernity. Long past the early 1920s, when it became clear that America had developed into a mass economy, society, and culture, Williams continued to defend the individual in the terms of the autonomy and concreteness he acquired in his early experience of American small-community life and his Unitarianism. The politics that would free this individual remained for Williams a question of the moral choice to serve others, and to do so ethically, intelligently, and face-to-face.

3

Iconoclasm, Professionalism, "Intrinsic" Art: Checks and Balances

If Unitarianism and Progressivism made William Carlos Williams a political liberal, why wasn't he more active and more radical when he became a poetic revolutionary in the 1910s? In the years between his graduation from Penn in 1906 and the momentous events of 1913, Williams's alienation from the Rutherford status quo was only slightly mitigated by his new status as a young doctor and local playwright, and he was learning new and harsher questions to ask of conventional morality. But two important elements of these years—his medical training and his friendship with his father-in-law—led him not to translate iconoclasm into political action. Above all, whatever political impulses he may have had were sublimated in his true vocation, image-breaking and image-making art.

Williams's iconoclasm was both fostered and limited by his faith. Unitarians thought of themselves as "pioneering the way for the development of the modern spirit within the limits of Christianity," and Williams grew up hearing the word "modern" being used to refer to his faith's rejection of traditional beliefs, with their constriction of individual intelligence, their involuted schisms so remote from "practical" human concerns, and their irrelevance to the ever-developing spirit of humankind. It was this modern spirit in which Williams advised Ed in March 1906 not to worry about breaking "rules that custom has made laws," and by which he was well disposed to conceive of modern poetry after the Armory Show as a "revolutionary" destroyer and reinventor of vital forms drawn from present life.[1]

A youth spent observing hypocrisies in Rutherford made him doubt social codes other than those of religion, and as he came of age, Williams started to suspect dogma of all kinds. Be it moral, legal, or political, dogma was somehow at bottom an arbitrary, and restrictive, convention. Iconoclasm took hold of him in 1909, when he had Betty Putnam challenge Puritan Salem's strictures against singing, laughing, and generally exuding vitality, and he wrote his "Hymn to Fraternal Love."

Williams was hardly an extreme iconoclast. For instance, he seems not to have read Nietzsche, for whom a vogue began around 1908 and 1909, when H.L. Mencken published his summary of Nietzsche's philosophy and the first translation of his complete works appeared in America. But a year of postgraduate medical study in Germany from August 1909 to June 1910, gave Williams a new skepticism as well as a homesickness for his rude free nation that he expressed in his letters to Ed. From Leipzig he wrote Floss Herman in late November 1909 that he hated "religious creeds and all dead forms."[2] He even let his hair and mustache grow.

At Leipzig he saw Henrik Ibsen and Richard Wagner performed and took a course on modern British drama, the teacher of which dismissed the Gilbert and Sullivan in which Williams had performed for the morally challenging new "realism" sparked by Ibsen and Ibsenism; the teacher measured a dramatist's worth by his willingness to challenge public opinion and conventional technique. Williams took methodical notes on, among others, Ibsen, George Bernard Shaw ("We must have a society in which we are not forced to sell our affections and convictions"), William Butler Yeats (whose "hero at war with all worldly institutions" was a "scornful protest against the English regime"), and Oscar Wilde—whose sad end showed the vanity of the "attempt of an artistic nature to assert itself in a community where no one distinguishes between art and morality."[3]

Williams returned from Germany to a career, a long engagement, and local civic service, but he continued to despise the constraints of such institutions. In the pocket notebook he carried while inspecting classrooms as the school physician of Rutherford in the fall of 1910 and early 1911, he wrote:

> Rule. Taught to obey the rule + not to distinguish between cause + effect.
> To make us safe instil[l] the things what will make us secure—reformers are nothing—and nothing dangerous to ourselves yet with both they could learn the same
> Teach to learn to obey—but in truth we teach them not to think, that is it
> They know it who are their heroes carved names reverenced traditions
> We make false heroes who are never worshipped[4]

His first poem of social commentary had not been so scornful. In "Hymn to the Spirit of Fraternal Love," published in his 1909 *Poems* before he left Rutherford, his iconoclasm was more Unitarian than Ibsenesque. In the poem, fraternal love, represented by the love of humble shepherds for one another, contrasts with a splendidly dressed dead Egyptian pharaoh, who goes "unfed" with love. This contrast between the shepherds and the "regal dead" is implicitly social, but Williams develops the conflict in ethical terms, contrasting the "naked," sincere love of the shepherds with the pharaoh's cloak of "flattery."

The poem's attack of the condescension of Rutherford's "pharaohs" toward "shepherds"—including Williams, who felt like a rustic before them—adumbrates the social commentary of Williams's "townspeople" poems of the 1910s. In them he speaks to the "leading citizens" of Rutherford on behalf of (not as) the poorer, "vulgar" people, holding them up as a model of the "naked" expression that bourgeois proprieties stifle. "Hymn" also foreshadows Williams's characteristic criticism, focusing on the ethics of human relations on a small-community scale and damning all discourse that, whether from self-interest, greed, or fear, blocked or twisted the expression of truth or self.

Thus Williams the young critic of middle-class social and cultural values acted in the name of the Unitarian brotherhood of man rather than the will to power, the spirit of youth, or anarchist freedom. Williams was deeply enmeshed in the social life of Rutherford, and he would view larger social networks from its point of view. When he drew support in the coming decade from the more cosmopolitan iconoclasm of some artists and radicals, such as in *The Egoist* or the *Little Review,* he did so not to disdain his townspeople but to improve them.

He was well on his way, then, to becoming the cultural iconoclast and poetic radical who declared in 1919 that the artist was a "revolutionist" who sublimated his potential, political radicalism into ethical and cultural criticism. His experiences in training to become a doctor, the nature of the medical profession, and the kind of mentality that the profession fostered all strengthened this tendency. Becoming a doctor enabled Williams to fulfill the role required of him by his liberal idealism and thus obviated the problem of political commitment.

In his internship at two New York City hospitals from 1906 to 1909, Williams had his first close contact with the urban environment, especially with its poverty and crime. French Hospital and Nursery and Child's Hospital were both located in wretched neighborhoods, and Williams could read the brutality of his patients' lives in their flesh. Treating unwed mothers, whores, knife-fight losers, and construction-accident victims worked much of the prig out of the 23-year-old would-be gentleman, who started to speak with his patients' cynicism about the "mean trick" he played on their babies by delivering them.[5]

But it was a vicarious toughness that Williams acquired. Although birthing and bandaging gave him one sort of intimacy with poverty, it was not the kind his patients had. As a doctor, he merely observed poverty's effects on others from within the enclosed and protected spaces of the hospital and the aura of his profession. He was right in the neighborhood, the context of actual poor life, but he knew better than to go out alone at night. And he did not have to.

Nor did his idealism venture into Hell's Kitchen. In none of his letters to his brother or mother at the time did he speculate on the causes of the squalor and crime, whose damage he was slaving to mend. It seems that for all his moral earnestness, young Williams never suffered the guilt, described in a *New Republic* editorial of late 1914, that wracked some of his middle-class contemporaries:

> Then suddenly, for reasons too intimate for analysis, the idea of what poverty means begins to burn into them, they are tortured with the thought of it. The feeling goes deeper than their reason, draws upon desire within them that is stronger than theory, and makes the war on poverty the central passion of their lives.

After all, as Hilda Doolittle admiringly told him in early 1908, Williams was acting on his "interest and love for humanity" by working in an overcrowded, bug-infested hospital.[6] The job undoubtedly exhausted whatever guilt about being better off he may have felt. When a friend visited and was shocked at the condition of some of the babies, Williams retorted, "You ought to have seen this brat when we got him" (A, 96).

Williams refused to see the "brats" and their parents in terms of abstractions such as poverty or the proletariat; social circumstances did not shape individual character, they provided a test of it. Consider his judgment of the prostitutes he met in the hospitals: he came to admire them because they "led a tough life and still kept a gentleness and kindness about them" that no man, he felt, could match. As Paul Mariani observes, several women who drew on personal resources to survive adversity and defy the proprieties became his heroines—in particular, his grandmother Emily Dickinson Wellcome.[7]

The poetry Williams wrote during his internships was Keatsian, a space sealed off from the slums' sordidness; not until 1913 did the urban world enter his poems. The poor entered his work then, too, as a result of his contact with those of his suburb, whom he came to know by face, name, ailment, and speech rhythm. Still, poverty remained for him a test of individual, moral character rather than a social or political problem, and a test for the well-to-do to pass rather than one for poor people to rewrite. Williams, like many other middle-class members of his generation, tended to romanticize lower-class life by thinking it more "real" than his own. Nevertheless, his eye and ear for detail enabled him to do better by poor people in his poetry than most.

If his hospital time both exposed Williams to and sheltered him from poverty, his experience with the powers of the institutions affected his sense of politics and ethics in much the same paradoxical way. Just before his graduation from medical school, Williams told his mother that he did not like the idea of having "to fight my way up by pushing others down"; he only wanted "to do all I have to do well, and be left alone to look on people and help them without myself being known."[8] But the nitty-gritty of business administration at Child's Hospital trapped Williams in politics. Even so, rather than cause him to reconsider his habit of judging politics according to ethical standards, his trial by fire confirmed him in it.

In March 1909, Williams resigned his internship (and gave up an offer of a place in a Manhattan practice) because he refused to go along with some hospital administrators' graft scheme, through which they gouged funds from the state by falsifying the number of patients treated each month. Williams had to verify the number with his signature; when he refused to sign without checking the figures himself, he was suspended for insubordination. His medical superiors, he recalled, pleaded with him to sign: "But look, we doctors cannot go against the business of an institution like this. Our business is to cure patients, not to ask where the money comes from" (A, 103). He resigned instead.

He almost went to the newspapers; he heard from a nurse, too late to withdraw his resignation, that an administrator was having an affair with the head of the hospital's board of governors, "one of the most distinguished figures in Wall Street banking circles" (A, 102). But his father advised him not to, and he himself felt that without support from his fellow doctors he had no chance. "Not a single doctor of the attending staff had stood by me. To hell with them all, I thought" (A, 105).

The event confirmed Williams's distaste for politicking. But in turn-of-the-century medicine, politics, especially because of the modernization of the profession and middle-class professionals' drive to power, were inescapable.

Burton Bledstein describes in *The Culture of Professionalism* how "idealism and monopolistic self-interest often played an indistinguishable role in the new images professionals cultivated about their expertise" as part of their effort throughout the nineteenth and early twentieth centuries to acquire authority, social status, and power. The model of authority for all aspiring, middle-class professionals was the scientist, with his objective methods and knowledge and his mastery of the forces of nature; naturally, doctors patterned themselves on the scientist.

Even so, the doctors' rise to status was quite slow until the early 1910s. The American Medical Association (A.M.A.) was founded in 1847, aiming to publicize doctors' claims to arcane knowledge and insist on the layman's dependence upon them for all things medical, formalize their own standards of conduct, and limit their number by setting admission standards and curricula in medical schools.[9] The 1890s saw the proliferation of local doctors' organizations, which pressed hard for the scientific standards they had learned from Louis Pasteur and Robert Koch, and the A.M.A. harnessed their energies and became a national, activist organization; its membership jumped ninefold to over 70,000 between 1900 and 1910. The Pure Food and Drug Act passed in 1906 with heavy pressure from the A.M.A., which loathed the patent medicines that the bill controlled. The bill institutionalized public health in unprecedented fashion and signaled the arrival of the medical "profession."

Thus in 1905, Sir William Osler could note with pride in a Penn commencement address (which Williams most likely heard) that "Everywhere now the medical student is welcomed as a member of the guild [of scientists]." Osler did worry about the narrowed vision of the specialists flourishing in "the larger cities," and in fact the advances of the profession in both knowledge and status were leading to the demeaning, if not the demise, of Osler's model of humanism, the general practitioner.[10]

Throughout his career Williams played both the old and new roles of doctor and medical professional. In the Child's Hospital imbroglio he lost a chance to become an elite, city specialist, but because of appointments to public health positions such as school medical inspector, he was more modern than many of his colleagues. At the same time he remained a general practitioner of the kind Osler eulogized. Williams believed more purely and simply than most in the ethical standards his profession often used to mask its drive for power. His seniors' failure to live up to them cut deeply, and all his life he castigated less-than-Hippocratic doctors. "Blatant ignoramuses. What a life! To them cash for cures," says his alter ego, Dr. Dev Evans, of his colleagues in *Voyage to Pagany* (148). Indeed, Evans is listed at the back of the A.M.A. directory with the nonmembers (189)—as was Williams.[11]

Williams also believed fervently in the science that gave doctors the right to call themselves professionals. He pointedly stripped away medicine's pretensions to rationality and expertise in his 1929 short story, "Old Doc Rivers," but more to expose hypocrisy than to discredit the ideal of science. Neither Unitarianism's "modern" questioning of tradition and dogma nor other iconoclastic currents led Williams to challenge the notion that truth was transcendental, constituted somewhere above history and human concerns, and his subscription to the truth of science undoubtedly turned him away from it.

One of Williams's fellow interns at French Hospital was staff pathologist Charles Krumweide, whom Williams remembered as "typically the German thinker, a man devoted to the literal truth, the born scientist." Krumweide's rigor (he was nicknamed "The Wrath of God") taught Williams "the value of a scientific awareness, a pre-Whitehead belief, shall we say, in science as the only possible faith of an intelligent man": such a man "keeps his senses open and detests only the obscurity which would occlude his detailed perceptions" (A, 88–89).

In his letters to Ed, Williams emphasized that his faith was practical, and that an artist's work was "truth in stone, wood, or iron." But Williams was no materialist; he felt that imminent truth was also "divine" and larger than man. Osler had emphasized that knowledge became wisdom only through its testing in one's actual medical practice, but he also acknowledged that the result could only be humility: "no human being is constituted to know the truth . . . even the best of men must be content with fragments, with partial glimpses, never the full fruition."[12]

Williams would seek these glimpses in poetic as well as medical practice, and he transposed the terms of the latter quest into those of the former. For him, truth manifested itself as a "radiant gist" emanating from the ordinary, but it nevertheless transcended the quotidian. The imagination glimpsing the gists was an untranscendent, "actual force"—it was simply the full use of one's senses. It was a scientific, "disinterested" attention with a mind clear of a priori dogma, as neutral as Krumweide's. As Williams told Harriet Monroe in 1915, "The minds of men in any profession"—he was speaking of poetry—"meet at a certain plane above which the greatest have not advanced. Here knowledge knows neither time nor place nor nationality."[13]

The transcendent nature of the truth Williams sought in both of his "professions" led him to believe in "disinterested" inquiry into matters about which there is no escaping interest. As Bledstein notes, scientific method appealed to professionals because it "transcended politics, the corruption of personality, and the exclusiveness of partisanship" and enabled them to present themselves as being above "business" and "politics."

Such an image also fostered a particular kind of extreme individualism. The professional, says Bledstein, "incarnated the radical idea of the independent democrat," who saw himself as

> a liberated person seeking to free the power of nature within every worldly sphere, a self-governing individual exercising his trained judgment in an open society. The Mid-Victorian as professional [and his descendant in the early 1900s] strove to achieve a level of autonomous individualism, a position of unchallenged authority heretofore unknown in American life.[14]

Doctors, in fact, were able to act out this belief far more easily than other professionals. As Paul Starr shows, the uniquely personal relationship between producer and consumer in medical care contributed both to doctors' individualism and the culture's willingness to allow doctors to preserve their autonomy. As a result, American doctors successfully resisted subordination to any bureaucratic structure—the corporation, the fraternal lodge, the hospital, or even a cooperative practice—that modernity sought to impose on them. Doctors remained self-governing in an increasingly closed bureaucracy.[15]

The individualism of the professional man, however, did not necessarily make him a political democrat. Autonomous professionals were tempted to regard others as similarly autonomous selves, whose "nature" was constituted solely by inborn talent and character. A doctor, moreover, worked with what he could believe was the very foundation of "human nature," the body that members of all races and classes share. But treating people as if they are the *same* is not democratic—treating people *equally* is, and to do so one has to acknowledge differences.[16]

Thus an American professional could acquire ambiguously democratic politics, as the courses of both Progressivism and William Carlos Williams, M.D., demonstrate. Williams's conceptions of poverty, democracy, and the individual were limited by his medical training, which also helped him believe in truth as transcendent and politics as a free individual's ethical choice to serve humanity. Williams made such a choice with extraordinary good faith; when he used the Hippocratic oath to mask self-interest, it was to practice what he called in 1919 "my illicit trade of smelling, seeing, hearing, touching, tasting, weighing" his patients as material for poetry. His own best intentions, however, may have blinded him to other political possibilities.[17]

The individualistic, apolitical ethics fostered by medicine were reinforced by another teacher. By late February 1908, Williams was spending his time off from French Hospital playing duets for violin and piano in Rutherford with Charlotte

Herman, whose sister Floss he eventually married. Through his difficult courtships of the sisters he became close friends with their father, Paul Herman. Williams surely was comforted by Herman's faith in the Democratic party, a rare thing in Rutherford; more important, however, Herman's experience with the labor movement and government contracting undoubtedly sowed the distrust of both unions and "business" in Williams.

As a leader of the New York local of the International Typographers Union (I.T.U.) in the 1880s, Paul Herman helped Samuel Gompers create the American Federation of Labor. He and Gompers, who led the Cigar Makers Union in New York, helped coordinate support for a crucial cigar makers strike in 1886, the success of which gave the union-federation movement, and Gompers's leadership of it, a big boost. In his memoirs, Gompers recalled how during the strike he and Herman put out a militant newspaper called *The Picket,* for which Herman designed a typeface in which "each vertical line culminated in a spearhead with a hostile flourish."[18]

Although Williams called his father-in-law "a sentimental socialist," Herman's union, the I.T.U., was notably conservative, sticking closely to "pure and simple" trade unionism. In fact, the I.T.U. was purer and simpler than Gompers, refusing in the American Federation of Labor's first year to yield member unions' autonomy to the central organization. Even so, Herman quit the labor movement early in the 1890s, disillusioned (according to Joe Stecher's comments) by strike tactics he considered unethical, the corruption of some union leaders, and the socialists' attempts to politicize the unions (WM, 98; IM, 90–91). He became the shop manager of the printing firm Wynkoop-Hallenbeck-Crawford and gave up his union membership.[19]

In 1903, Herman started his own business by underbidding his former employers for a federal post office contract that they had held for years, the bid on which he had always figured for them. His bid made national headlines that summer, for it led to the indictment of two of his former employers for graft, the firing of a government official and the resignation of the postmaster. President Roosevelt was quoted as saying, "I don't like this man Herman's way of doing business," and he summoned Herman to the White House for inspection, which he passed.[20]

Herman's experience is the basis of much of Williams's novels *White Mule* and *In the Money.* Although it is hard to say if protagonist Joe Stecher's politics are Paul Herman's, the novels are virtually our only source of information about Herman and his politics. But a man who knew Gompers and faced down Theodore Roosevelt was a rare figure in Williams's life, and we should draw what inferences we can.[21]

White Mule and *In the Money* are Williams's most eloquent defense of the ethics of the artisan and entrepreneur against the corruption of some who climbed to the top of the capitalist system and the federal government—and, to some extent, against the system and government themselves. The values of quality, honesty, personal loyalty, and economic "value for value"[22] that the novels defend probably were Paul Herman's; the "pure and simple" trade unionism for which he fought defended skilled workers like Joe Stecher and himself against a new industrial order.

By the turn of the century, master printers like Herman and Joe Stecher faced obsolescence. Their industry was entering the age of high-speed mass production, and in printing, as in the 1902 coal strike that Roosevelt settled, relations between a worker and his boss were becoming negotiations between "labor" and "capital" with the federal government intervening as arbitrator. A skilled tradesman was caught between his boss and the new labor unions, as Joe is in *White Mule* when he lies on his back picking a saboteur's screwdriver out of a press while a gofer calls him to the boss's office (WM, 48). As owner of a small business Joe is caught again, between "big business which won't tolerate you when it gets ready any more than a mosquito and . . . the upward drive from labor pinching you from below," as his fellow owner Mr. Lemon warns him (IM, 294).

The dynamics of modernization will force Joe either to expand to lower costs, risking the wrath of the corporations, or give in to the "iron law" and cut wages—and fight the union (IM, 285). But Joe bases prices and wages on his sense of justice rather than "business" values, which he defines as greed for profit. When Roosevelt tells Joe that he has a new policy requiring the government do as much of its own work as possible to cut down on the inefficiency and corruption of outside contractors, Joe tells him that a government cannot do what an honest man with "the knowledge" of the work can (IM, 177). On the train home, Joe thinks in disgust that, with policy, "You stop paying attention to the truth of the detail." "The only thing that works," he concludes, "is one man that pays attention to what he is doing and knows what to do about it" (IM, 180).

With Roosevelt, Joe makes a last stand before the very man who accommodated his small businessman's ideology to the forces of modernization. Joe's frustration is that of the self-made man whose moral universe, not to mention his livelihood, is being unmade by forces larger than the men he can see to condemn. He can play none of the roles offered him in a modernizing economy—friend of labor (though his shop is closed), grafter, Taylorite, or member of Lemon's club (he still votes Democratic)—and he defends himself only through a stubborn, passive resistance. Lemon tells him at one point, "Do you know, in a sense, and a very real sense, you're anti-social" (IM, 290). And he is correct:

> Very deep inside [Joe] moved another man—under water, under earth—among the worms and fishes, among the plant roots—an impalpable atmosphere through which he strode freely without necessity for food or drink, without breathing and with unthrobbing heart. How could a man exist there otherwise? (WM, 45)

Ironically enough, work—the task immediately at hand—is Joe's realm of freedom from necessity. But as Lemon warns him, work is "the worst drug in the world" (IM, 295). For the world of work is the business world, the world of social relations and therefore of politics; it always demands more than sheer craftsmanship.

Paul Herman may have warned Williams of this dangerous illusion, and Williams certainly was aware of it by the time he wrote *In the Money*. More important, the problems that Joe Stecher has reconciling his good faith in American ideals with American practices, especially with the changing economic structure, were implicit in Paul Herman's economic status. Herman could only have steeled Williams to live with the tensions between ethics and politics, and individualism and modernity, that were inherent in his own early politics.

To Williams, Paul Herman was "somewhat of the artist" (A, 129), and, as Floss recalled, he once told Williams "never to let anyone persuade him to write for money."[23] The master printer made an important contribution to Williams's understanding of the politics implicit in being an artist. They shared values about the nature of work—particularly the desire to measure it by its quality and the pleasure in the "job itself"—that the artist, more than any other laborer, tried to practice. When Joe Stecher concludes his indictment of Roosevelt, policy, and modernity on his train ride home, he speaks not only for Williams and Herman but for the generation of Progressive-era artists from John Reed to Ezra Pound:

> What good would it do for an artist to lie to a piano or a violin? No good at all. But they want to play the violin by telling it that "my policy" is to play the violin standing on my head or sitting in the bathtub, or—while I'm eating. Or use a shovel instead of a bow. (IM, 182)

The politics and social vision that Williams grew into—the white-collar, individualist, ethics-based, democratic-with-a-small-d liberalism he acquired from his father, his church, his profession, and Paul Herman—were catalyzed by his desire to be an artist and shaped by that desire into the politics of an artist.

Of course, his anxiety to belong in Rutherford and America made him a self-consciously nationalistic artist, and his optimism about the imminent fulfillment of America's promise enabled him to feel that he would participate in the nation's "wonderful future." As America came of age industrially, purifying its democracy and flexing its young muscles as an international arbiter and new colonialist, its artists would complement and complete the nation when their work flowered and demonstrated its sensibility and refinement. In this sense Williams's art was his patriotic politics.

But there was more to Williams's politics as an artist than his intention to write about America or somehow be American. His conception of the relations between society and the individual—that autonomous middle-class American whose soul was constituted separately from society—both reinforced and was reinforced by bourgeois culture's beliefs about the autonomous nature of art and the adversary relation between the artist and society.

Williams first learned that art was an autonomous realm of experience from his mother, who was cruelly disappointed in the late 1870s by the abrupt termination of her student days painting in Paris. "There life ended" (I, 188), she told him, and she lived more in nostalgia and pain than in mundane Rutherford. She taught him, he said, to think of the world of the imagination as a world both divorced from and more rarified than this one. Williams encountered this attitude all around him, negatively in the insensitivity of his neighbors, and positively in the presence of Charlotte Herman, who longed for the purity of Bach and despised Liszt, in no small part because Rutherfordians at her recitals always requested his songs (BU, 88–92). And so, as Bram Dijkstra says, art became for Williams "a privileged realm of transcendent experience" (RI, 11); several of the poems in his 1909 *Poems,* especially "The Uses of Poetry," say that art was a refuge for the harried intern from the overwhelming tide of daily events.

But as Cecelia Tichi notes, in Osler's 1905 valedictory he counseled young doctors to keep a notebook and cultivate "the power to recognize in your humdrum routine . . . the poetry of the commonplace, of the ordinary man, of the plain, toil-worn woman, with their loves and their joys, their sorrows and their griefs." If Williams heard Osler, he didn't take Osler's advice for several years; by 1908, though, he was asserting to Ed, "Beauty is nothing but truth in all it's [*sic*] magnificent detail." As Unitarianism taught him, although truth might be as transcendent as art, it was to be reached through the everyday and put into practice. So, too, was art.[24]

Even the precious *Poems* contained one look at a "A Street Market, N.Y., 1908" and the admission that Williams had been blind to a "patent wide reality." The month before his volume came out in 1909, he wrote Ed to say: "Art is intrinsic it is not a plaything, it is an everyday affair and does not need a museum for its exposition it should breathe in the common places and inspire us at the moments of decision in our work and play."[25]

The modesty of the "intrinsic" art that the Williams brothers had in mind may be inferred from a letter that Ed, studying architecture in Rome, wrote to the *Republican* in August 1910. In the letter he praised the borough's decision to buy a plot of land on Park Avenue for use as a public park, saying how its importance as "a beauty spot" had grown on him. He added that "only because of their prematureness have I not said anything before about the many plans evoked by my brother and me for that corner."[26]

Williams's plans for making art intrinsic would grow more ambitious when he learned how to make poems out of commonplace people and speech patterns and encountered the daring aesthetics of some of the New York painters, especially Marcel Duchamp. In the early Twenties, Williams would even call for the destruction of "Art" with a capital A. But accepting the definition of art as an autonomous realm of experience leaves the artist only with the power of exhortation, for the society he addresses grants him little more than that. This oxymoronic freedom and impotence, as Peter Bürger argues in *Theory of the Avant-Garde,* has been the relation of the European and American artist to his society since the Industrial Revolution and the Romantic era, and has plagued socially concerned artists who seek to erase the boundary between art and life; not even the dadaists and surrealists, who struck squarely at art's autonomous status by questioning both Art and the social order which imprisoned it within its institution, got much further than admitting new forms and objects into the rarified realm.

For all his zeal to make art an everyday affair and to serve Rutherford and America with it, Williams wound up leaving the boundary in place and fighting an interminable guerilla war. The guerilla could not risk destroying his base of operations outside ordinary life. Because he was so deeply committed to preserving the autonomy of the individual, as American society became a mass culture Williams sometimes found as much consolation as chagrin in art's autonomous realm; it was one of the few places where a man could feel whole and find "relief" from anonymity, conformity, and silence. For the artist was not only a free individual but superior in his Individuality, as Oscar Wilde, one of the few writers on art and politics Williams read early on, so wittily proclaimed.

In July 1908 Williams wrote enthusiastically to Ed about Wilde's *The Soul of Man,* saying, "It's as near an antidote to our weaker qualities as I know. . . ." Just which weaker qualities Williams meant is hard to say, but Wilde's sparkling assurance about the supreme importance of the artist and his absolute distinction from the ordinary run of humankind must have bolstered the budding poet. As for Wilde's politics, they probably comforted the artist and iconoclast in Williams and appealed to the extreme libertarian who lurks always in the middle-class American individualist.[27]

Wilde's vision of the social order was that of a libertarian anarchist, and not just any sort of anarchist, but an anarchist artist. "The form of government most suitable to the artist," wrote Wilde, "is no government at all." He denied the legitimacy of any authority outside the individual, dismissing kings, popes, the democratic populace, and public opinion in turn. Nor were "industrial tyrannies" of socialist worker-states any more acceptable to him. The socialist state would liberate man from the tyranny exercised by private property over his body and his spirit, but only if that state were no state at all, constituted only by voluntary association and mutual cooperation. For Wilde, "Socialism itself will be of value simply because it will lead to Individualism."[28]

Wilde's Individualism was the freedom "to realize some form of beautiful and intellectual life" in art: "Art," he said, "is the most intense mode of Individualism that the world has known. I am inclined to say that it is the only real mode of Individualism that the world has known." Although not everyone would become an artist when Individualism arrived, the populace would at least yield a public of

Individuals capable of regarding his work as "the unique result of a unique temperament" and thus of properly judging it.[29]

The present public, however, made the artist suffer. People "degrade the classics into authorities," demanding not "novelty" from the artist but conformity to what they already know—which for Wilde was not art at all. Wilde traced this boorishness to its root in the public's "barbarous conception of authority," which it applied not only to government but to drama criticism. Until Wildean socialism created an audience of Individuals, the artist would by nature be in revolt against society: "Art is Individualism, and Individualism is a disturbing, a disintegrating force. Therein lies its immense value. For what it seeks to disturb is monotony of type, slavery of custom, tyranny of habit, and the reduction of man to the level of a machine."[30]

No other single work contains as many of the terms Williams used in the 1910s and early 1920s to speak of the artist's revolutionary function as *The Soul of Man*. His own aesthetics of "the new" derived as much from another iconoclast, Marcel Duchamp, as from Wilde, but Williams defined the social dimension of his aesthetics in virtually the same generalized, classless, psychological terms of fear, habit, and the herd instinct.

Wilde's extreme definition of the artist as Individual, however, was probably the most potent ingredient of the "antidote" Williams found in the book. Just a few months before recommending Wilde to Ed, Williams had counseled his brother on the need to resist the "domination of a teacher," saying that "if there's anything can approach individuality in value I don't know it;" indeed, it was "the very motive of genius."[31] Art would always be for Williams the expression of "genius" or "personality." This complicated his notion of the relation between art and politics, for there is a self-centeredness at the heart of Wilde's social vision. Wilde is claiming status for the déclassé artist, a man without a place in the bourgeois social structure commensurate with art's crucial value to the world. Yet he is also demanding that the freedom this isolation gives him be a condition of his integration.

In the coming two decades, Williams sometimes defended the autonomy of both art and the artist in terms nearly as extreme as Wilde's. In fact, in the early 1940s Williams said that Herbert Read's anarchist testament, *The Politics of the Unpolitical*, expressed "the very core of all that I have ever wanted to believe or believed." In Read's vision, a society free of the profit motive would enable individuals to choose freely to cooperate mutually and be a society in which "every man is a special kind of artist." Politics would simply disappear. Until then, Read warned that "Poets should not go outside their own ranks for a policy" because "poetry is its own politics."[32]

The anarchist artist's vision inevitably appealed to Williams. The threat of modernity to American notions of individuality, the rise of mass culture, and the blindness of the guardians of Art to the avant-garde forced him to be as concerned with preserving his autonomy as with constructing a vision of society in which art and the artist truly breathed freely "in the common places."

But despite his alienation as an artist, Williams never went so far as to imagine an alternative society. His defense of the individual never became anarchist like Wilde's nor elitist like Ezra Pound's. His opportunity to be a free and whole individual in an energetically growing town and nation was too possible, and his faith in the kind of freedom promised by the ideology of American democracy too strong, for William Carlos Williams ever to feel so disillusioned as to desire more than America's renovation.

The most important influences on his politics—his father's socialism, his Unitarianism, his medical training, Paul Herman's disillusionment—all brought him to choose politics of liberal, democratic service bounded by the ideology of middle-class, American individualism and democracy. And just as in his politics there was a deep split between the free individual who chose to serve society, so in his art he grew up with the notion that the rarified, autonomous world that the artist had to will into being "should be intrinsic." This inherent contradiction between his need for autonomy and his zeal to serve American democracy was only intensifed by the ambiguous new relations between art and politics, and the uneasy relation between Wildean Individuals and one-dimensional American society, in the New York intellectual scene just beginning to flourish across the Hudson River.

4

Tinctures of Disestablishment: Williams and the New York Scene in 1913

"The dominant note of the present epoch is revolutionary," exulted *Camera Work* critic Maurice Aisen, "not only in the plastic arts and in music, but in everything that exists." To Aisen and most of the unconventional artists, thinkers, and social and political activists in New York City, life there in the spring of 1913 was one, long, unsealing scroll:

> [Revolution] is in ethics, in politics, in the community and in the individual. Life itself today is in revolution. It is perhaps the first time in history that all functions of intelligent life have reflected one another, each interpreting the others simultaneously. The wise student of today must be a specialist in universality.[1]

That study of today also had to be versed in the ways of loose analogy. Did cubism and ragtime, Bergson, Freud, and vers libre "reflect" or "interpret" anarcho-syndicalism, free love, or even Woodrow Wilson's "New Freedom" in any way more precise than a sense of significant coincidence? Few of the "wise students" of Aisen's day took the time to define clearly the relations, or lack of them, among their new mores, new politics, and new art; they were too busy practicing to reflect. Perhaps if they had, they might have realized that the very energies charging them with a sense of such possibilities would thwart their fulfillment.

The "great forces at work" in the city, which John Marin sensed and captured in his explosive 1912 watercolor of the new Woolworth Building, did produce a new social order, but one hostile to all that they, especially the artists, hoped to live out.[2] But in 1913, one could still read all the signs as portents of some vague, greater spring. A 29-year-old doctor in Rutherford, New Jersey could see the Woolworth Building receive its finishing touches as he made his daily rounds that year, and read them in the distance.

Two events that took place early in 1913 reverberated with overtones of revolution and stirred the sight of reflections between politics and art. On February

17, the International Exhibition of Modern Art opened at the Sixty-Ninth Regiment Armory and introduced avant-garde French and American painting and sculpture of the past quarter-century to the American public. The near-daily coverage of the Armory Show in the press and art journals was laced with analogies like Aisen's between artistic innovation and political radicalism. Besides calling the artists incompetent, immoral, and insane, conservative critics accused them of being anarchists, socialists, socially irresponsible individualists, and un-Americanists. Wendell Phillips believed that they threatened "to overthrow the established standards taught in the schools and respected in the homes."[3] The radical press responded more sympathetically, though it spoke more to the conservative critics than about the art itself.

The organizers and supporters of the show, of course, drew their own political analogies, the most powerful of which was expressed by the organization of the exhibition itself. Painter Arthur B. Davies had selected the European paintings forming the background section of the show so as to define art's history as a sequence of formal innovations made in defiance of the previous ones, which had stiffened into convention. The strange new works on the walls, then, were but the latest manifestation of the artistic spirit, which was by nature a revolutionary spirit. Adding rhetorical force to Davies's arrangement was the show's symbol, which countered nationalist bias against the "foreign" art by appropriating America's own tradition of revolution: it was the pine tree from the flag of Colonial Massachusetts. Branches of pine, along with banners with its image, were displayed high up on the walls of the Armory.[4]

The second signal event was more political than artistic in nature, but it suggested that radical art and politics could literally unite. On February 25, a week after the Armory Show opened, leaders of the International Workers of the World (I.W.W.) arrived in Paterson, New Jersey and led about 25,000 silk-mill workers off the job, turning a small, spontaneous walkout protesting a speedup order the month before into a full-blown city-wide strike for a minimum wage and an eight-hour day. These demands of the "Wobblies" were far more modest than their reputation for being ready to dynamite America into a worker-owned state would have led one to expect. The I.W.W. was in fact being pragmatic; it had just won its first foothold in the East in Lawrence, Massachusetts and was now hoping to dig in among the immigrants in Paterson. But its ultimate ends, and some of its means, were indeed revolutionary. One of the strike leaders, William ("Big Bill") Haywood, had been expelled in January from the executive committee of the Socialist party he had helped to found for allegedly advocating industrial sabotage—"direct action"—over the "slow-shalism" of the party's legislative and political means.[5]

While the strike was on, Haywood stayed with a young schoolteacher who lived in New York, and at her apartment in April he met a group of young intellectuals, journalists, and artists who wanted to help the Wobblies in Paterson as other city dwellers had in the Lawrence strike by taking in some of the workers' children. That meeting resulted in a march on June 8 of over 1,200 of the Paterson strikers from the Hoboken ferry landing through Manhattan's streets into Madison Square Garden, where they filled a huge stage with a pageant recreating the crucial moments in the still-ongoing strike. The planning and performance also resulted in Haywood's steady circulation among some writers' and artists' circles in New York. He began including in his speeches a vision of a workers' art collection better than the Metropolitan Museum's and was even discovered sitting on a bench in Washington Square Park one day writing poetry.[6]

To know of the members of the pageant's executive committee is to understand why Aisen saw revolution everywhere he looked. The committee met at the uptown apartment of Margaret Sanger, who had had her first run-in with censorship the week before the Armory Show opened, when her column in the New York *Call* telling "What Every Girl Should Know" about her reproductive organs was suppressed. Joining Sanger were Socialist party member F. Summer Boyd; Ernest Poole, muckraking novelist and worker in a lower West Side settlement house; anarchist Alexander Berkman, the would-be assassin of Henry Clay Frick; feminist Jessie Ashley; John Sloan, a Socialist party candidate in two municipal elections, two of whose "Ash Can School" oils hung at the Armory, and before whose sets the Paterson workers would act; Mabel Dodge Luhan, hostess of the four-month-old salon which many of the members regularly attended; and for the pack's joker, bohemian Harry Kemp, who was soon to cause a minor international incident by stowing away on a steamer to England and then claiming to some unamused immigration officials the right as a poet to visit the home of his "gods," Shelley and Keats, without passport or the price of passage.[7]

The committee's prime mover was 25-year-old journalist John Reed, who wrote the script for the pageant. Reed had made a name for himself in February by giving his neighborhood, Greenwich Village, a name for itself in a pamphlet poem, "The Day in Bohemia." The Village had been home for a number of writers, artists, and unconventional citizens for about a decade—one could go back farther to Edgar Allan Poe or even Tom Paine—but in late 1912 and 1913, most participants' accounts agree, some critical mass was reached that made it a "self-conscious" community aware of its own distinctive values and style, as Robert Rosenstone defines it. One Villager who had lived there for ten years left in July of 1913; when Alfred Kreymborg came back in September to find a publisher for an anthology of exotic "Imagiste" poems that the best-known of the new American poets, Ezra Pound, had sent him from London, his friends sent him straight to the Boni brothers' new bookstore in his old neighborhood and asked him, "Where have you been?"[8]

Reed had discovered several other forms of community when, inspired by Haywood, he went to do some reporting in Paterson and got arrested and jailed. He taught his cellmates, few of whom knew English, to sing radical lyrics he set to the tunes of his alma mater, Harvard. The experience turned him into the director of the pageant, and he turned out an exuberant piece of partisan journalism about the "War in Paterson" that appeared in the June issue of *The Masses,* which expressed the Village community's new self-conscious sense of rebel self even more fully than Reed's Bohemia poem. Previously a dull advocate of the cooperative commonwealth, the magazine was reborn in January 1913 as an irreverent monthly, fighting all at once, said editor Floyd Dell, for "Fun, Truth, Beauty, Realism, Peace, Feminism, and Revolution." Five of its illustrators, including John Sloan, exhibited at the Armory in February.[9]

Strangely enough, given Reed and Sloan's presence on the magazine's editorial board, come June and July there was not even a mention of the Paterson pageant in *The Masses.* (In fact, besides Reed's "War in Paterson" in the June issue, the only items on Paterson in *The Masses* in all of 1913 were an interview with a mill worker, a poem, and two brief items on court decisions.) The unpleasant fact was that the pageant failed politically, losing about $2,000 and hurting the workers the committee had hoped to help. But although it boded ill for an alliance of bohemians and proletarians, it confirmed to some of the New York crowd that artistic innovation and political revolution would be allied. Hutchins Hapgood, a confidant of Mabel Dodge Luhan's, wrote in his New York *Globe* column that the pageant foretold the coming of "a real democracy, where self-expression in industry and art among the masses may become a rich reality." Recent Columbia graduate Randolph Bourne, who was about to publish a call for generational revolt entitled *Youth and Life,* took the "crude and rather terrifying" spectacle for a sign that "a new social art was in the American world, something genuinely and excitingly new."[10]

Across the Hudson River that February, William Carlos Williams was hearing rumors of this new world while discovering one of his own. He was then two months married after a three-year-long engagement, and his growing medical practice now included a hospital appointment and weekly inspections of Rutherford's four public schools. He undoubtedly read about the Armory Show in the New York newspapers and heard talk about the Paterson strike around Rutherford—at least one resident had financial interests in Paterson—but his one "futurist" gesture was to speed on his rounds in one of Rutherford's first cars, his five-month-old Model T.[11]

But the compound of Unitarianism, Ibsenesque iconoclasm, cultural nationalism, and many-motived alienation from the culture of his hometown that had made the young Williams a local liberal was hardly simmering down. Nor was he settling comfortably into the role of town doctor—in fact, as he told his mother several years later, he had already "given up medicine for poetry."[12] He was well prepared to hear apocalyptic strains in the news from New York in 1913, even its political inflections. And news from beyond New York fed whatever urges that events in the city stimulated to make his poetry part of the impending new order. In the March issue of the four-month-old, Chicago magazine *Poetry* that his college friend Ezra Pound had been telling him about, Pound published the tenets of "Imagisme" under F.S. Flint's name and, under his own, "A Few Don'ts by an Imagiste."

Imagism's principles, Pound insisted, did not make the imagists revolutionary, but placed them "in accordance with the best tradition." However, the absolute economy and concreteness of language and the "free" rhythms tuned according to the laws of music and the accents of one's expression that Pound prescribed placed the imagists in opposition to nearly all current conventional verse. Pound's tradition was much like Davies's tradition of innovation in painting.

An image, moreover, aimed to create "that sense of sudden liberation . . . of freedom from time limits and space limits . . . of sudden growth, which we experience in the presence of the greatest works of art." Although he would have denied it, Pound's claim for art's power to cause this revolution of individual consciousness was in the best tradition of early British romanticism, and as one may judge from the younger and older William Wordsworth, the claim could cut either way politically. In 1913, such individual liberation had a powerful appeal; Williams and the Village poets would use both edges of the knife, sometimes both at once, to define art's relation to society.[13]

Williams received another text of liberation on March 1, when his wife Floss gave him a new copy of Walt Whitman's *Leaves of Grass*. The "poet of Democracy," dead only two decades, was revered by nearly every member of the New York scene, from Reed to Robert Henri to Alfred Stieglitz to Kreymborg to Emma Goldman. Even Pound made a "Pact" with the father, whose swelling rhythms Pound considered a disease. When Whitman's disciple Horace Traubel visited from Philadelphia, he paid visits to the office of *The Masses*, and he wrote for Goldman's *Mother Earth*. At Penn, Williams had read Whitman with the adolescent joy of hearing someone express his own passions (Int, 42), but in March, with the Armory Show in the papers, the grapevine from Paterson humming, and Pound's manifesto fresh from the mail, he seems to have reread *Leaves of Grass* for its celebration of the "simple, separate person" who, as its first poem said, uttered the words "Democratic" and "En-Masse."[14]

On March 5, the day after Woodrow Wilson's stirring Progressive inaugural address, Williams wrote to Harriet Monroe, editor of *Poetry,* to take issue with some revisions she had suggested in some poems, the first she had accepted from him. On behalf of his poems, he declared:

> Now life is above all things else at any moment subversive of life as it was the moment before—always new, irregular. Verse to be alive must have infused into it something of the same order, some tincture of disestablishment, something in the nature of an impalpable revolution, an ethereal reversal, let me say. I am speaking of modern verse. (SL, 23–24)

Through the rest of the spring, on through the year into the winter of 1913–14, the "functions of intelligent life" continued to signify with tinctures of disestablishment. While Wilson set about checking the power of the "money trust" by expanding the power of the federal government, the pageant strikers lined up at the Hoboken ferry, and Huertistas, Zapatistas, and Carranzistas turned Mexico's 1911 revolution into a civil war. The *Lyric Year* anthology for 1912 appeared and gave first prize to a "social" poem, Orrick Johns's "Second Avenue." The Paterson workers slouched back to the mills, the strike broken by August, when Ford Madox Hueffer explained in *Poetry* that the aim of his "Post-Impressionism" was "to register my own times in terms of my own time." While Liberal members of Parliament hedged on Irish home rule and a general strike in Dublin lit another slow fuse, feminist Henrietta Rodman and her supporters quit the genteel Liberal Club, rented space next door to the Boni brothers' bookstore, and began producing one-act plays.[15] Henry Ford's workers tried out some ideas he had had watching the conveyor belt used by meat packers and began assembling a thousand Model Ts a day. Eleven thousand Colorado coal miners struck, some of them moving out of Rockefeller company-owned towns into tents near Ludlow; during the bitter winter the tent colony was machine-gunned by the National Guard.

Off in London, Pound tried to exert a lunar force on the tide. He arranged for imagist Richard Aldington to edit the literary pages of a feminist-libertarian bimonthly, called on the American ambassador with Hueffer to try to secure Harry Kemp his "rights" as a poet, told Kreymborg to go meet Williams and Williams to go meet Kreymborg, continued to attack the conspiracy against "art of the best tradition" he saw operating between American monopolies and the press, and altered by omission some lines from John Reed's "Sangar" to make them head a poem of his own mocking the present "generation of the thoroughly smug." Reed, just before heading to Mexico late in the year to ride with the lately victorious (and newsworthy) rebel leader Pancho Villa, protested Pound's distortion in a letter to *Poetry* and twitted Pound for being so slow about making his "Pact." Accompanying Reed on the train south—after holding one of her "Evenings" of discussion on Mexico—Mabel Dodge Luhan decided, said Reed, that "the rebels are part of the great world-movement, whatever that may be."[16]

Whatever indeed it was, in 1913 artistic revolt was taken for one of its signs. Throughout the year, Williams—his wife pregnant, he and she moving in the fall to their own home at 9 Ridge Road in Rutherford—kept New York within the field of his peripheral vision and wrote the first of his own manifestoes. In the summer, in a prose draft, he argued that poetry should be governed by "Speech Rhythm."[17] And that winter, in a poem governed by the intentions of Whitman and "the great world-movement," he ventured out as "The Wanderer" into the streets of Manhattan and Paterson and asked himself: "How shall I be a mirror to this modernity?"

An asymptote is a line to which one loop of a hyperbolic curve draws infinitely closer but never quite touches. Such was the relationship Williams Carlos Williams had with the New York avant-garde scene, not only in 1913 but through the decade as well.

It is most likely that Williams attended neither the Armory Show nor the Paterson pageant; nor did he frequent Mabel Dodge Luhan's salon or any of the other circles, clubs, restaurants, and bars of the new Village scene in 1913. So one infers from the lack of references to specific people or events in his writing; although Williams dated from 1912 his weekly visits to New York to attend pediatrics clinics, the details he recalled date from 1915 on. Nor do any members of the scene recall him.[18]

Riding a train to Jersey City and a ferry across to lower Manhattan did not take much over an hour, but as William Marling points out, Williams was "a man of limited time," and even if he did get to the city, he was too pressed to stay very long. Nor did he know anyone in 1913 who could introduce him to kindred spirits among the poets and painters or bohemians and radicals. Of course, he might have walked on his own into 291 or, later in the year, into the newly opened Daniel Gallery, where Alanson Hartpence, best friend of Alfred Kreymborg (who was Williams's friend of a few years hence), was working. If Williams did so, though, he seems not to have introduced himself; even when he was in the same room with someone he really wanted to meet, as he was with Eugene O'Neill at the Provincetown Playhouse in late 1916, he might not get up the nerve to approach him.[19]

Thus it seems that Williams fought the artists' revolution in isolation at home, through newspapers and the mail. However, one must acknowledge the lack of positive proof against any city activity. There are a few suggestions that Williams drew at least a tangent with New York artists' circles even earlier than 1913, though without further evidence they remain only suggestions. Nevertheless, it is worth noting here both Williams's possible presences and his likely absences from the New York scene to get a sense of just how close (and yet how far) he was from its remarkable intermingling of politics and art, and to prepare us to see the nature of what he was missing but always facing throughout his development as an idiosyncratic, political poet.

In the little red leather notebook that Williams carried with him from September 1910 through March 1911, he jotted down the names of two art galleries and their current exhibits: "Knoedler Gallery (Rodin)" and "Scott & Fowles (Sorolla)." Perpendicular to these he wrote, "270—4th Ave.," Ezra Pound's address for part of his stay in Manhattan from the fall of 1910 until late February 1911.[20]

Around the corner from Pound's lodgings was a bookshop owned by Lawrence Gomme, which was frequented by some of the city's leading young writers:

there Pound met Joyce Kilmer, Harry Kemp, and Orrick Johns. Pound, who had told Williams two years before that Williams was "out of touch" with the latest in poetry, apparently wanted to take him to see the latest in painting and sculpture, and, perhaps, to meet his acquaintances at Gomme's. That Williams did get in to see Pound and be so edified is possible. Pound visited Williams in Rutherford on Thanksgiving Day of 1910 and again on February 13, 1911 and perhaps told him of the galleries then; on February 17, Williams entered into his notebook's financial accounts an expense for "n.y.c.f.," the New York City ferry. However, I have been unable to find out the dates of the art exhibitions and either confirm or deny this possibility.[21]

Nothing in Pound's letters to Williams in the next few years after his visit shows that they had met in New York. But in a 1920 letter, when Pound lamented to Williams the vanishing of the America he had known during the 1910 visit, he mentioned in the same nostalgic litany both Williams's father's *goldwasser,* which Pound drank on his Thanksgiving visit to Rutherford, and Mouquin's, the French restaurant under the Sixth Avenue El frequented at that time by Alfred Stieglitz and his 291 circle, Sloan, George Bellows, and other members of "The Eight." In December of 1911, members of both groups and others who ate at Mouquin's formed the American Association of Painters and Sculptors, which would produce the Armory Show. Pound named Mouquin's as if it were a shared reference, but Williams never mentioned the restaurant in his own letters or reminiscences, and Pound was more than capable of assuming that his world was Williams's.[22]

Williams did meet one New York poet, or at least had his West 36th Street address in his book—Robert G. Welsh. In "Patria Mia" Pound made Welsh an example of how American magazine editors' lack of critical standards stifled American poets; one editor, said Pound, had advised Welsh to hobble his natural gift for rhythm so that his poems conformed to conventional meter, and Welsh, not knowing any better, had complied. Welsh, Pound noted, was over 30 when Pound met him in 1910, and had "never had time to get 'educated.'" Judging from the conventionally measured poems that appeared in *Poetry* in 1918 and the *Literary Digest* in 1924, Welsh remained "uneducated," and, given the conservatism of the magazines in which he published, he and Williams had little in common after 1913. When Welsh drowned in July 1924 he was the drama critic for the New York *Telegram and Evening Mail.*[23]

Williams's artist friend from his days at Penn, Charles Demuth, could have made those introductions that Pound's dear "Carlos" found so difficult. As William Marling notes, Demuth was a friend of most of the artists that Williams met in the 1910s and may well have been Williams's "calling card."[24] But Williams did not present that card to anyone until 1915. Marling's claim that "the world that Williams decided to enter was this world that Demuth had assembled" may overstate a mere possibility.

Demuth was rarely in Manhattan until the spring of 1914; after three years in Philadelphia at the Pennsylvania Academy of Fine Arts, he spent 1911 and 1912 at his mother's home in Lancaster, Pennsylvania, and then left for a two-year stay in Paris. Even when Demuth returned to a studio on Washington Square South in the Village, he was often not there. He summered in Provincetown in 1914, 1915, and 1916; moreover, because of his diabetes, he spent parts of the next two years in the care of his mother.[25]

However, Demuth did get to know people in Manhattan fairly quickly. In Europe he had become friends with painter Marsden Hartley, who introduced him to Alfred Stieglitz in the spring of 1914; Hartley and Demuth's friendship soon cooled, however, because of Hartley's loyalty to Stieglitz, whose overprotectiveness of "his" watercolorist, John Marin, led to Demuth's never having a show at 291. But while Demuth was going to 291 in 1914, he met Alfred Kreymborg, who had published Demuth's one-act farce, *The Azure Adder*. Kreymborg had gotten art critic John Cournos, whom he knew from Mouquin's, to solicit material from his Philadelphia friends, including Demuth. Not until 1913, though, did Kreymborg have a magazine, *The Glebe*, in which to publish it.[26]

Thus Demuth certainly could have taken Williams in 1914 to meet Stieglitz and Kreymborg, who were then the two main movers and shakers in New York painting and poetry. In fact, Pound asked Williams in a December 1913 letter if he had talked to Demuth about *The Glebe*. On the other hand, Pound also urged Williams to "take my introduction" to Kreymborg at 96 Fifth Avenue and get him to "do" Williams's London-published book, *The Tempers*, in America. It is as likely that either Williams or Kreymborg finally took Pound's advice and contacted the other as that Demuth introduced them. In whatever way Williams met Kreymborg, the first certain time for him to have done so is not until the spring of 1915. Most likely the place was the apartment of Allan Norton, publisher of *Rogue*, whose dinners both Demuth and Kreymborg were then attending, along with wealthy art patron and poet Walter Arensberg and his college friend Wallace Stevens. However, Williams himself recalled, if doubtfully, that Arensberg wrote him to invite him to work on *Others*. At any rate, Williams published a poem in *Rogue* in mid-June 1915, and out of the *Rogue* circle came the conversation between Kreymborg and Arensberg that resulted in the founding of *Others* in the late spring of 1915 and Williams's first full membership in a New York avant-garde circle.[27]

In 1913, then, Williams most probably had few direct personal relations with New York artists. Even after he joined the *Others* crowd and the Arensberg salon, he kept his distance, if not always his detachment, from the political commitments and experiments in lifestyles being made below Fourteenth Street. He surely was aware of them, however. When Pound wrote Williams in late 1912 to announce the impending arrival of *Poetry*, he told him to "tell [Robert] Welsh & buoni [*sic*]" about it, which suggests that Williams at least knew of the Boni brothers' bookstore late in 1912. Had he ignored Pound's recurrent urgings to subscribe to *The New Freewoman* later in 1913 and chosen to buy it off the stands, the Bonis' was where he would have shopped.[28]

If Williams did browse there in 1913, he apparently did not venture through the passageway that connected the bookshop with the Liberal Club. Nor did he go downstairs to Polly's Village Restaurant in the basement to be served by the anarchist waiter Hyppolite Havel with dinner and the insult, "Bourgeois pig!" None of the radicals who ate at the restaurant, belonged to the Club, put out *The Masses*, and had begun meeting at Mabel Dodge Luhan's "evenings" mention Williams's presence at any of their gatherings. They include Floyd Dell, Hutchins Hapgood, Louis Untermeyer, Lincoln Steffens, Big Bill Haywood, Emma Goldman, Margaret Sanger, John Sloan, Art Young, John Reed, and Dodge herself. Only Max Eastman names Williams explicitly, and that is to say that he never met Williams even through the decade. Williams got to know a few visitors to Mabel Dodge Luhan's and contributors to *The Masses*, but only later in the decade and after: Orrick Johns and Robert Carleton Brown in 1915, Marsden Hartley in late 1915 or 1916, Stuart Davis in 1921, and John Marin in 1922.[29]

It is a pity, and also a strong indication that Williams remained an outsider in New York, that he did not yet know Alfred Kreymborg. As they discovered later on, they had a good deal in common, at least artistically. Kreymborg shared Williams's current interest in breaking out of old poetic forms and mirroring "modernity"; he was trying to figure out how to bring over into poetry the contemporary American material he had been using in naturalist prose, such as in his novel, *Edna, A Girl of the Streets,* and with the help of the imagist poems Pound had sent him he was looking for a new rhythm. He also had Williams's anticolonial fervor: the title of *The Glebe* referred to the sacred grounds of America and art.[30]

Kreymborg certainly could have made Williams feel more at home in the Village, for he had lived there since 1904. "Vortex" connotes too much energy to apply to a man like Kreymborg—full of dry charm, retiring irony, and small poems—but by 1913 he knew practically everybody that Williams had almost met or would meet: Hartley, who ate breakfast at the same bakery as he (as did one of Hartley's heroes, the "Ancient Mariner" of American painting, Albert Ryder); Stieglitz and the 291 crowd, including Cournos with his Philadelphia connections; Joyce Kilmer, Orrick Johns, and the poets from Lawrence Gomme's bookstore.[31]

Kreymborg missed some of the explosions in the Village by spending the summer of 1913 in a shack in Grantwood, New Jersey. Hoping to fulfill his recurring dream of starting a new arts magazine, he and his shackmates, painters Samuel Halpert and Man Ray, managed to print the first issue of *The Glebe,* a one-man show of poems by the anarchist sculptor and ex-husband of Ray's lover, Adolf Wolff. When Kreymborg came back to the Village in the fall, he quickly joined the new community, arranging for the Bonis to publish *The Glebe* and

Pound's *Imagist Anthology,* meeting Horace Traubel, Big Bill Haywood, Reed, Eastman, Margaret Sanger, and other new Villagers at the bookstore in the fall of 1913, and joining in the drama productions at the Liberal Club. By 1914, he was sufficiently established downtown to be caricatured by Herb Roth; seated in a group at the Liberal Club which included Floyd Dell and Orrick Johns, Kreymborg holds forth to Becky Edelson, who had made a stir by going on a hunger strike after being jailed for picketing in Paterson.[32]

Kreymborg, then, could have introduced Williams all around the radical crowd. However, like Williams, although his politics were hardly conservative, his priorities lay with artistic innovation and freedom, and even if Williams had sat with him at the Liberal Club while Roth was sketching, most likely he and Kreymborg would have remained absorbed in each other's conversation. It is appropriate that Kreymborg was responsible, in 1916, for bringing Williams into the closest contact he would have with the most prominent members of the Dodge Luhan–*Masses*–Liberal Club crowd, and that it was not for politics but for their most successful artistic venture, the Provincetown Players.

Several days before the opening of the Playhouse in early November 1916, Williams wrote to Orrick Johns that "The 'Provincetown Players' are the rage in Greenwich Village. . . . This is a group—not the 'Others' group—but a crowd that got together last summer out on Cape Cod. . . . " Ironically enough, Johns knew almost every member of that crowd—Eastman, Reed, O'Neill, Dell, Ida Rauh, Louise Bryant—none of whom Williams had met. Williams went on to describe the renovations of their space at 139 MacDougal Street in enough detail to suggest that he had actually seen it, or was excited enough to pass on every bit of what he heard secondhand. Kreymborg and Williams and the *Others* crowd had talked about expanding their activity beyond poetry and the magazine—in fact, Williams had just published their ambitions in a "New York Letter" to *The Egoist* (SL, 30–33)—and the Provincetown Players gave them a ready-made chance to do so. Kreymborg had submitted his play *Lima Beans* to them for production.[33]

It is not known whether Williams attended the Players' première bill the next week, for which Reed acted in his lover Louise Bryant's *The Game*. (Also on the bill were Dell's *King Arthur's Socks* and O'Neill's first publicly performed work, *Bound East for Cardiff*.) But Williams was soon on the MacDougal Street stage himself, rehearsing and performing in *Lima Beans* in mid-November and early December. The play was approved, though not without dissension among the Players, who favored realist drama like O'Neill's (and perhaps were wary of welcoming members of another New York clique to their turf). Fortunately, Reed had threatened to resign from the Players unless they took a chance and accepted Kreymborg's fantasy for "mannequins," and they were swayed.[34]

And so Williams's curve drew as close to the asymptote of the Village radicals as it would come; he even almost kissed Louise Bryant, though her part was given to Mina Loy before rehearsals began.[35] Even while Williams was in their presence at the Playhouse, he held back from the Players; he watched O'Neill walk around with his father, but he neither spoke with the playwright nor had any memorable conversation with Dell or Rauh or the friends who came by. Nor did he see Reed to thank him, for Reed was then in Baltimore recovering from the removal of a kidney.

Williams finally did meet Reed, but not until late in the decade at a party given by a Village rebel of long standing, Lola Ridge. By then the aura of revolution that surrounded both art and politics in 1913 shone as from separate sources, but perhaps the men talked about the prewar moment. Williams implied in his autobiography that they discussed the Paterson strike (A, 391), though no unique details appear in Williams's long poem. One may imagine that Williams asked about Pancho Villa, whom he would soon include in *The Great American Novel,* but the account Williams used of a raid by a group of Villistas is not from Reed's *Insurgent Mexico,* and there is no sign that Williams read it.[36]

Although Reed had no personal influence on Williams's life in the 1910s, he was then the embodiment of the Village faith in the inevitablity of the relation between art and politics, a belief in universal revolution which exerted as much force on American poets in the 1910s as imagism. As Williams did with the communism that Reed symbolized in the 1930s, he acknowledged its power at the same time he resisted its specific manifestations. In 1913, Williams's art, like every new artist's, was part of the "great world-movement."

But even in 1913 there was tension along the united front. In Williams's 1934 short story, "Life along the Passaic River," Williams vented his resentment at being told what to do by giving voice to the Paterson workers' sense of betrayal at the hands of the 1913 artists and radicals, who, after the pageant failed to give any concrete financial or political help, withdrew their interest (Reed himself, exhausted, sailed away to Italy to rest with Mabel Dodge Luhan):

> When they had the big strike at the textile mills, and that bright boy from Boston [Reed, Harvard '10] came down and went shooting his mouth around in the street here telling us what to do: Who paid for having their kids and women beat up by the police? Did that guy take a room down on Monroe St. and offer his services for the next ten years at fifty cents a throw to help straighten out the messes he helped get us into? He did not. The Polacks paid for it all. Sure. And raised up sons to be cops too. I don't blame them. Somebody's got to take the jobs. Why get excited? But they ain't moved away none; that's what I'm saying. They're still here. Still as dumb as ever. But it's more than that guy ever give up or could think to do to help them. (FD, 114)

Williams's anger in 1934 was directed not so much at Reed as it was at the manufacturers and consumers of Reed's legend—particularly Mike Gold of *The New Masses,* who was calling for writers to stop being "bourgeois intellectual observers" and somehow become proletarian "insiders."[37] But Williams clearly was also reliving his chagrin of the 1910s, when Reed's and his compatriots' notions of revolution and art had overshadowed Williams's less glamorous politics and poetics. Williams may have been a bourgeois doctor in the early depression, but he was rendering service to the Polacks and Irish and Italians and blacks, often at less than 50 cents a throw. In the more promising year 1913, Williams the bourgeois poet was captivated by the same sense of possibility as Reed, the pageant, and the Armory Show, and he was no less eager than the fair-haired boys of Bohemia to serve mill workers and bosses alike with poetry as forceful as a citywide strike.

5

Reflecting "Revolution": Art and Politics, Pound and *Others*

Although Williams confined his revolutionary activity to subverting poetic form and kept his distance from Village radicals, he shared with them a loose understanding of art's relation to politics like that presumed by Maurice Aisen in his celebration of the "reflections" of disparate intellectual and moral "revolutions" in each other. He also shared with them the uneasy sense of the situation of the artist in modernizing American society, which rendered ideas about the relation between art and politics in the 1910s so ambivalent and contradictory. In the most important relations Williams had in the early 1910s with other poets—with Ezra Pound, Alfred Kreymborg, and the *Others* group—he encountered nearly all of the contemporary notions about the relations between the artist and society and art and politics, and he made the best of a limited set of choices.

When artists and their supporters in the 1910s thought about those two relations, they did so in terms of some familiar disjunctions. Nearly all of the radical intellectuals, cultural revolutionaries, and artists in New York in the 1910s believed, often against their professed intentions, in politics based on individualism, which tended to undercut their avowed intentions to change society. If the rebels of *The Masses* were helping socialism to triumph, it was to liberate their middle-class selves more than to empower the proletariat. In fact, many of those who cheered the arrival of a new order of politics, morals, and aesthetics in 1913 were also nostalgic about the passing of premodern America, in which the individual had a concrete place in a community, even if it was a stifling one.[1]

Rebels and artists alike had also inherited from the romantic tradition an image of the artist as an individual who was autonomous but nevertheless, because of the insight his freedom conferred on him, deserved some social power. But if the emergence of modernity in America charged artists with the tremendous energies of construction—Randolph Bourne even announced that "We live in a new age of surplus value, economic and spiritual," and had only to figure out how best to express this new psychological abundance—modernity itself, with its dynamic of the profit motive, only seemed to threaten the self that the artist believed was his nature to express.[2] The immediate problem was to defend one's self, by withdrawing from the corrupt world into a purer realm of freedom and experience; art naturally became such a refuge for many artists and radicals.

Many of them also felt a moral duty to act as Bard, one who spoke to and for the society from which, paradoxically, he was detached. Everyone from socialist Max Eastman to Ezra Pound sought a way to regard the artist, who, Pound insisted, was "free from the beginning," as being also engaged with American society and therefore deserving of a position of power. Modernizing America, however, which was rapidly transforming aesthetic experience into mass culture and advertising, only intensified the "free," unconventional artist's sense of his isolation and impotence. Avant-garde and bohemian artists of 1910s New York, then, felt they had to defend the artist's freedom from social relations and claim a place of importance within them. They did not try to reconceive the autonomy of both the self and art and find a more accurate and perhaps more efficacious relation between modernist art and modernity.[3]

Pound, then, was not being all that much more extreme than his leftist contemporaries when he argued, as he did in 1918, that "respect for the peripheries of the individual may be . . . a discovery of our generation; I doubt [in fact that] it [is], but it seems to have been at low ebb in some districts (not rural) for some time." Those districts causing the individual such concern were, of course, the cities and the processes of urbanization; despite the vision of New York he had on his 1912 visit, Pound soon detested the modern metropolis for its erasure of personality.[4]

It is his deep anxiety before modernity and the nostalgia with which he responded to the artist's loss of his place that make Pound the dark double of the New York radical contemporaries at whom he usually scoffed. In a narrow sense, his views of the relation between the artist and society, and art and politics, make him the representative figure of the 1910s—that is, if one remembers that the representation is a caricature. For unlike *The Masses'* socialists and bohemians, Pound did not temper his individualism with an ethical sense of duty to society, and the artist's will to what he believed was his former power is expressed more bluntly in Pound's work than in the work of any other American artist.

Pound's vision of society throughout the 1910s was radically antimodern: "Humanity is a collection of individuals, not a whole divided into segments or units," he asserted in 1917. He had been more generous in "Patria Mia," in which he praised American society for presuming that "those things are right which give . . . the greatest opportunity for individual development." But even in that 1912 essay he had opposed forms of government—state socialism or syndicalism or democracy—that he felt leveled the important differences between individuals, and he grew more vehement as the decade went on. The great city he believed essential to a great civilization was not the centralizing Paris, London, or New

York of modernity, but the small Italian city-state of the Renaissance, in which, he declared, "any body of a few thousands of men who really wish independence, [and] liberty with responsibility, can achieve it under any system—under any feudalism—whether of arms or of money." The artist resisted such urbanizing forces, fighting "a new form of tyranny," namely "slavery to a 'State' or a 'democracy,' or some such corporation." By presenting "human variety" in his work, the artist stood for "the rights of personality."[5]

But for Pound there was variety and variety. In "Patria Mia," he speculated that only old countries or "old stock" could produce the kind of " 'Individuals' " that mattered to him. Excluded from this class were industrial workers, Jews, and the entire British and American middle classes, as comments in "Patria Mia" and *Blast* make clear. The individual liberty that Pound defended was finally only the right to power of an elite composed of the intelligent. As William M. Chace explains, "Emphasizing repeatedly the importance of those philosophies permitting the ultimate degree of personal freedom within the social order, [Pound] envisioned a cultural elite that would manage to lead and influence, but would not be subject to any of the deleterious consequences of political power." All of Pound's writing on politics until the 1920s can be summed up in this "parochial message": "society must maintain order so that the arts may be sustained."[6]

Pound's political judgments were "aestheticocentric"; that is, they were determined almost exclusively by his interests as one of the complete Individuals who kept true intelligence alive for the good of society. Neither British nor American society, however, acknowledged the artist's importance and gave him an appropriate position of influence, despite the fact that "the aristocracy of the arts," as Pound announced in 1914, "is ready again for its service." Such noblesse oblige failing him, Pound tried throughout his early essays to reclaim a place for the artist by defining him in terms of the roles that intellectuals were playing in the new urban-industrial order, while seeking to conserve or adapt the "aristocratic" and individualistic values of older social orders.[7]

When Pound visited New York in late 1910 and early 1911, the new skyscrapers evoked from him a prophecy of a "Risorgimento," which implied, he said, "a whole volley of liberations . . . from ideas, from stupidities, from conditions and from tyrannies of wealth or of arms." It also implied new patronage and power for the arts, which "respond to an intellectual movement more swiftly and more apparently than do institutions." But he did not see just yet which new "institutions" were coming to control progressive, professional America. Back in England in 1912, he quoted Wilson's campaign slogan, "The first duty of a nation is to conserve its human resources," and announced, "I believe that this sentence contains the future greatness of America."[8]

But was an Individual such as Pound conceived the artist to be a "human resource" in the new world of drift and mastery? Pound tried to situate him in several places. Thinking of his frustration in a program geared for philologically oriented scholars at Penn, he proposed to "drive the actual artist upon the seminary" and revamp schools so they produced artists. One wonders what he would think of giving poets the professional credential of M.F.A. Thinking that the new national press and periodicals could perform the function of the art-generating central city that America lacked, he urged that they serve as "clear channels for the transmission of intelligence" from artists.[9]

In "The Serious Artist," Pound made his strongest claim to a modern place for the poet, attempting to appropriate the status and claims to disinterested truth held by the scientist. Just as the scientist provided the data of physical behavior, so the artist determined the data of individual desire and thus provided "data for ethics." Pound drew out his analogy at length, arguing for the poet's "precision" in bearing witness and implicitly claiming that the poet was as disinterested as a scientist. But he undercut his claims by failing to note the difference between the objects of their respective research: men and societies are not natural objects, nor are human laws physical laws. The gap forced him to shift his terms from the epistemological to the ethical, moving from the scientist to the practicing doctor such as Williams: the artist who "falsifies his report as to the nature of man" commits an offense "of the same nature as the physician's."[10]

These roles—professor, mass communicator of intelligence, scientist—are not incompatible, and they were sometimes claimed by even a Vagabond poet, but there was a particular willingness to meet his enemy's terms in Pound's proposals between 1911 and 1913, and a particular impatience, a restless trying of the doorknobs into the modern world. His tone changed in 1914, when he vented that impatience as rage against the "aristocracy of commerce" in *Blast* and a notable review of "The New Sculpture" of Wyndham Lewis, Jacob Epstein, and Henri Gaudier-Brzeska. Disgusted with British middle-class culture, he gave up all attempts to accommodate the artist to modernity and reverted to the language of magic:

> The artist has been at peace with his oppressors long enough. He has dabbled with democracy and he is now done with that folly.
>
> We turn back, we artists, to the power of the air, to the djinns who were our allies aforetime, to the spirits of our ancestors. It is by them that we have ruled and shall rule, and by their connivance that we shall mount again. . . .
>
> Modern civilization has bred a race with brains like those of rabbits and who are the heirs of the witch-doctor and the voodoo, we artists who have been so long despised are about to take over control.
>
> And the public will do well to resent these "new" kinds of art.[11]

It was bombast, perhaps, but it was real rage at the exclusion from the new world of a man who set on art the highest value—too high a value.

As for claiming the role of political arbiter for the poet, Pound's Individualism led him to feel that art—the "data for ethics"—was fundamentally divorced from "civics." Nevertheless, he could not help asserting that the artist had civic effects. Pound's desire for power and disdain for political responsibility shaped his writing about not only the place of the artist in society, but also the relationship between poetics and politics. On the one hand, he persistently argued that an artist's concern was with form and the accurate observation of concrete things and individuals ("Go in fear of abstractions," in fact, applies to Pound's politics as well as to imagism). On the other hand, he just as persistently asserted that "a work of art need not contain any statement of a political or of a social or of a philosophical conviction, but it nearly always implies one." Although in 1918 he argued that Henry James's work was "wholly exempt" from "political connotations," he meant the bald political denotations and didactic rhetoric of current "social" poetry; the connotations of James's work, he said, were a defense of "freedom from tyrannies."[12]

But "fundamentally," he wrote in 1917, "I do not care 'politically,' I care only for civilization and I do not care who collects the taxes, or who polices the thoroughfares. . . . The only things that matter are the things that make individual life more interesting." The war would change his lack of concern with politics and economics, but largely because such minor matters had nearly destroyed the "civilization" for which he cared so much. Thus Pound came to make the ethical choice to connect poetry with politics; ironically, he did so with no more insight into their relation than the socialist poets of *The Masses* had, and he made the *Cantos* the most didactic poem of the century. Williams might sometimes echo the arrogance in Pound's defense of the artist's freedom and superiority, and there was a touch of noblesse oblige in his choice to serve his townspeople, but if Williams resented having to fulfill commitments to the mundane he nevertheless fulfilled them. Pound, the Vagabond of Provence demanding tenure in the modern university, forgot that myths are to think with, not to live out. In 1917, when Pound wrote that he did not care who collected the taxes, William Carlos Williams was the borough police surgeon.[13]

It is instructive to compare Pound's politics as an artist—and his style of delivering them—with those of Alfred Kreymborg, if only to remind ourselves that the more modest bohemian had as important an influence on Williams's poetry as their transatlantic matchmaker. Kreymborg's influence may well also have extended to Williams's notions of politics and art. During their close association from 1915 to 1918, Kreymborg showed Williams some of the possibilities in "the skillful use of small words," as Williams put it in his 1916 "New York Letter" to *The Egoist* (SL, 33). Moreover, their concern with formal innovations did not exclude social concerns, about which they slanted distinctly toward Village cultural and political radicalism. Their magazine, *Others,* and the writers and artists associated with it was a microcosm of 1910s attitudes about politics, the relation of politics to art, and the artist's relation to society.

Kreymborg was by no means a political activist, but he was not out of place at the table with the Village radicals in Herb Roth's cartoon. A precocious musician, writer, and art lover, he had seen his father's business making fine hand-rolled cigars wiped out by a United Cigars chain store that appeared across the street. Ever after he felt that the same forces that ruined his father's craft and all it stood for had corrupted "spiritual America and contaminated nearly everyone concerned with creative expression." Like Pound, he tried to earn his living through the arts: he sold player pianos in a fancy music store to "clients" such as Mark Twain, Arnold Dolmetsch, and Richard Strauss, which experience softened him toward neither the rich nor machine civilization. He free-lanced articles for the *Morning Telegraph,* led a mandolute "orchestra" in a restaurant, and gave chess lessons, all the while getting rejections from editors and dreaming of his own magazine.[14]

Not surprisingly, Kreymborg thought and spoke like a déclassé artist about the stifling of self-expression and individuality by the cash nexus (although, like even the socialist artists, he spoke not in political but in moral and aesthetic terms). Around 1908 he became friends with arch-individualist Marsden Hartley and got to know members of the 291 circle, who were soon proclaiming in *Camera Work* the artist's complete freedom from what Benjamin de Casseres called "the deadly dullness of group-standards and group technique." They urged the artist to defy such "social coercions," which, said John Wieschel, "from time immemorial [have] inhibited pure self-expression." However, unlike Pound or Stieglitz's iconoclasts, Kreymborg never consoled himself with the pose of the aristocrat—his piano customers, who disabused him of any notions about wealth and breeding, and his immigrant background turned his longing for identification the other way. Finding that he "could attach his affection to no other class in town," in the 1900s he developed "an incurable mania for writing about the poor."[15]

Then in 1913 he found a "class" of people just like himself in the Village, and though he regarded the goings-on there with as much bemusement as commitment, he became a full member of the bohemian community. The "mushrooms" that he wrote and published between 1913 and 1916 are a lexicon of the discourse of Village cultural radicalism, celebrating the deadness of the past and of social convention, the urge for "life," the falsehood of material progress, the nobility of idealists who live for "life" and the "spirit," and the poet's social role as a "pirate." But Kreymborg also wrote poems on political themes still neglected by even *The Masses'* poets, particularly racial prejudice and the insanity of war. He never published in *The Masses,* however, and played no part in political activity.[16]

In 1916, oddly enough, he did write the keynote speech of the Democratic party's presidential convention. He was then secretary to Alexander Konta, a Hungarian immigrant powerful on Wall Street and in the party, who insisted, over Kreymborg's protests that he had never even voted, that he ghostwrite the speech for him. Scanning the newspapers, Kreymborg could find no difference between what the two parties said, but he managed anyway. On the day the keynote speech was delivered in St. Louis, Kreymborg delivered his own speech in Chicago to an audience of 16 about the poetry magazine he had at long last managed to start, *Others*.[17]

This image of two speeches simultaneously delivered in two distant cities aptly embodies Kreymborg's sense of the relation between politics and art: the two were as far apart as St. Louis and Chicago, and he much preferred the Windy City. Yet his poetry expressed his liberal concern with issues beyond the artist's plight or the Village rebel's moral freedom. Such was also the relation between poetry and politics expressed by the poets and artists of the *Others* crowd and their work.

Others began when Kreymborg met poet and patron Walter Arensberg in the spring of 1915 at the home of Allan Norton, publisher of *Rogue*. After a conversation that lasted until dawn in Arensberg's apartment, Arensberg agreed to fund a magazine and Kreymborg, eagerly, to edit it. That summer Kreymborg moved back out to Grantwood, New Jersey, and it was north from Rutherford that Kreymborg's "new friend" Williams drove on the weekends in his Model T to join the community of sympathetic artists he craved and to work on the magazine that "saved my life as a writer" (A, 135).[18]

Grantwood was a neighborhood in Ridgefield of small shacks and houses set on a steep western slope of the Palisades; there one turned one's back on Manhattan toward a panoramic view of the Jersey countryside. For the artists and leftists who came there over the next two decades, it was a haven of sorts from modernity, a radicals' suburbia. When Man Ray moved there in 1913, he felt like Henry David Thoreau, "breaking free of all ties and duties to society." Ray considered making Grantwood into a Brook Farm for the arts, and Adolf Wolff, who taught sculpture at the radical Ferrer Center, talked of founding a "liberal colony," but the neighborhood never became quite so organized. By 1915, said Orrick Johns, who moved there that spring, it was "a country refuge from the fads and wartime hysteria that were taking possession of people in Greenwich Village." Members of the Provincetown Players and some Village radicals started moving out around 1917; Floyd Dell and Becky Edelson came in the 1920s, and Emma Goldman in the 1930s. A persistent legend has it that when he was in exile in New York in early 1917, Leon Trotsky spent the night on Rembrandt Terrace.[19]

If Trotsky did stay, he seems not to have visited what was then the social center of Grantwood, the imitation villa of "the plutocrat of the colony," as Williams called him, Robert Carlton Brown (A, 137). Bob Brown was a facile free-lance writer who not only believed in radical causes but also happened to make a lot of money. He published two best-sellers in 1913, took his royalties to Wall Street, and by 1915 could afford to give up writing (though by 1916, he later told H.L. Mencken, he had lost so much in the market that he had to start again). Brown loved a good time, and his parties in Grantwood were freewheeling affairs at which artists and radicals mingled, drank, danced, and argued about the worth of the floor-to-ceiling murals done by Manuel Komroff.[20]

Brown's politics were full of the man's high spirits and Village contradictions. He published a short story in *The Masses* in early 1914, and his wife Rose took food to John Reed when he was in jail in Paterson. But Brown, perhaps in the flush of his market success, also published in *Rogue* what is perhaps the baldest Vagabondia poem ever written, "Difference":

> You shall work to make my living,
> While I only sing you songs.
> And that is as it should be,
> Because I must sing to live,
> While you must work.[21]

Such was *Rogue*'s flippancy, mocking both the Protestant ethic and Village hedonism. Kreymborg said that "Paradox was the usual mode of discourse" at the evenings of its publisher, Allan Norton, who can be said to have set the tone of fey disdain which later drove socialist Louis Untermeyer to accuse the *Others* group of decadence. A mid-1915 *Rogue* antiwar editorial, "A Bas Patriotism, or To Hell with Arithmetic," surely infuriated socialists and Village radicals, some of whom would be jailed for believing what *Rogue* tossed off:

> War is silly! All wars are silly; but the silliest of all wars is a commercial war; that is what they call the present combat. Well! One man war, a war of genius, I can understand—he may get it. But a war for money? Who gets the money? Everybody losing money because everybody wants money, and everybody wants more than everybody wants money, to keep everybody else from getting money.
> Arithmetic is at the bottom of all the troubles of nations. . . .[22]

The Sunday afternoon gatherings of the *Others* group in the summer of 1915 were considerably tamer than Bob Brown's parties (Williams went to one of those, but not being a drinker he did not go back for another), but the *Rogue* spirit was present whenever Arensberg brought along some of his French artists, including Albert Gleizes, Jean Crotti, Henri-Pierre Roche, and Marcel Duchamp (who always asked why they could not meet in a civilized place like Manhattan). Whether they met at Kreymborg's shack or Arensberg's 67th Street apartment, their discourse was proto-dada, but nowhere near as charged with political content as the dada of Zurich, Berlin, or Paris. In the Arensberg circle, writes William I. Homer, politics was a subject for "tranquil avoidance."[23]

The *Others* group is often associated with Arensberg's cerebral salon, and the cosmopolitan disdain for politics and the interest in formal experimentation of its patron and his painters has colored the general view of the magazine. Williams remembered getting the invaluable chance to learn about modernist painting at Grantwood—"we'd have arguments over cubism which would fill up the afternoon" (A, 136)—and he mimicked their tone when he made an unfortunate reference to the war as "Europe's cruder affairs" in his "New York Letter" (SL, 33). The *Others* group was committed to quality and new forms of expression above all else. As Williams said, "One could actually get a poem published without having to think of anything except it be good artistically" (A, 136).

But they were open to poets who spoke explicitly of social and political issues—and the tendency of those who did, and of the magazine throughout its four-year existence, was to the wide-open left of the 1910s. Adolf Wolff was a thorough-going anarchist who condemned the "liberty" that denied him the right to express his "true self" and celebrated the New York garment workers' strike of early 1913 in Kreymborg's first issue of *The Glebe;* Orrick Johns felt himself to be "something of a socialist"; Robert Sanborn worked at a Y.M.C.A. in Boston; Mary Carolyn Davies was a settlement worker on the lower West Side of New York; Helen Hoyt, an occasional visitor to Grantwood, published poems about factory workers and women in *Poetry*; William Saphier, Emanuel Carnevali, Evelyn Scott, and especially Lola Ridge, all of whom worked on the magazine in its last two years, were political liberals or radicals.[24]

In *Others* itself, for every Arensberg poem on a part of speech there was a Carl Sandburg poem on political corruption. Many of these critical poems were on the usual Village countercultural themes of the debasement of art by the commercial mind or the rigidity of social convention. Marianne Moore's "To Statecraft Embalmed," however, made the political subtext of such work explicit, and her remarkable "Radical" managed to make a farmer's tending of a carrot a metaphor for a dialectic of both economic growth and poetic innovation. Adolf Wolff wrote a number of stark, free-verse poems while he was in prison, and he, along with Lelia Miller Pearce, Carl Sandburg, Helen Hoyt, John Gould Fletcher, William Saphier, and Lola Ridge published poems on various discontents of industrial work and life; Wolff and Sandburg also lamented the waste of life in the European war. The September 1916 issue was a "Woman's Number," whose editor, Helen Hoyt, argued that "at present most of what we know, or think we know, of women has been found out by men. We have yet to hear what a woman will tell of herself. . . ."[25]

Even this brief survey of the poetry in *Others* makes it clear that Williams associated with a group whose concern for form hardly made them indifferent to content, and whose poems were on the whole not much less leftist than the poems of *The Masses*. More important to them, though, was their conception of formal revolution as a political gesture in itself. Unfortunately, they were no more articulate about the political dimension they claimed for their aesthetics than anyone else in 1910s New York, but in the context of loose analogies between fauvism and anarchy created by the Armory Show, their stylistic experiments acquired more than a tincture of disestablishment. Given what Christopher Lasch calls the radical intellectuals' "confusion" of politics and culture, in which they found "political salvation . . . not in any particular program but in the state of mind with which one approached the solution of social problems," the act of creating a poetic form that would express one's "true self" and jolt a reader's inevitably resonated with political implications.[26] And Williams and Kreymborg did regard such form as a "democratic means of expression" (SL, 33). Perhaps they were finally making only a limited gesture of cultural nationalism, but their notion of what "democratic" meant was in practice wider and more liberal than that, for instance, of *Poetry*'s editor Harriet Monroe.

Others's conception of radical politics and its relation to radical poetry was best summed up by neither Kreymborg nor Williams, but by J.B. Kerfoot, a critic for *Life*. The two editors violated their policy of printing nothing but poems and quoted him on the last page of the November 1915 issue:

> Perhaps you are unfamiliar with this "new poetry" that is called "revolutionary." Perhaps you've heard that it is queer and have let it go at that. Perhaps if you tried it you'd find that a side of you that has been sleeping would come awake again. It is worth the price of a Wednesday matinee to find out. By the way, the new poetry *is* revolutionary. It is the expression of a democracy of feeling rebelling against the aristocracy of form.

Kerfoot's neatly turned figure became a habitual one of William Carlos Williams's. He paraphrased it in his "New York Letter" about *Others* the next fall, and by late 1917 had made it a part of his own vocabulary. In his first major essay, "America, Whitman, and the Art of Poetry," Williams identified traditional verse forms with aristocracies and argued that American poets had to carry Whitman's achievement further: "But back of these aristocratic forms lies the democratic groundwork of all forms, basic elements that can be comprehended and used with new force." When he went on to redefine free verse, a term he was trying to reject, he articulated for the first time a specifically political dimension of his own poetics:

> And yet American verse of today must have a certain quality of freedom, must be "free verse" in a sense. It must be new verse, in a new conscious form. But even more than that it must be free in that it is free to include all temperaments, all phases of our environment, physical as well as spiritual, mental and moral. It must be truly democratic, truly free for all—and yet it must be governed.[27]

For the rest of his life, whenever he related his poetics to politics Williams would use these terms: his formal revolution was in the service of a democratic inclusiveness. The "certain quality" of the poem's freedom, of course, was a classless and absolute individual freedom that was reinforced wherever Williams turned, whether to his hometown, his church, his profession, Greenwich Village, his fellow artists, or their magazines; the limitations of that freedom were obscured by the wilderness of mirrors in which revolution in art and revolution in politics reflected each other. However, Williams chose to defend his autonomy as an artist on different ground than most other 1910s artists. "The rhythms of everyday speech drive me mad," he told Edmund Brown in 1916. "Not with an artistic dementia due to horror at bourgeois ignorance but with a feeling of the perfections that mock me from ignorant mouths." Rather than escape bourgeois ignorance, Williams stayed in Rutherford and set out to enlighten it. The ambiguities of doing so form one of the subtexts of "The Wanderer."[28]

6

Santiago Grove:
The Politics of ''The Wanderer''

In October 1911, Williams told his New York friend Viola Baxter that he had "ceased approaching earthly semblances" and begun to woo "heavenly realities of soul + not of face for this reason":

> Not that I am tired not that the faces I see displease but that there shall be of my own creating a face beyond all others beautiful because of the soul which lives purely behind it.
> I am not a virtuoso. I am not a good-fellow. I am never happy in possession. I only wish to see myself creating those around me + within me into a beautiful reality.[1]

Two weeks before, he had written her to explain that he would have to "confine my resources of passion" for her earthly semblance because he had become officially engaged to Floss. The budding iconoclast of 1910, who had begun to "hate religious creeds and all dead forms," was evidently uncomfortable with the fact that his desires escaped the confines of social institutions, and he sought refuge in one of those "dead forms": his Unitarian-bred discourse of purity, soul, and heavenly ideals. He hated speaking in those terms, and punned on "virtue-oso" to kick some life into them and put some distance between them and him; on the other hand, he admitted to Baxter, it would take some time to get used to the presence of "gargoyles on my greek temple."[2]

Williams's uneasiness with the self-image of saint and the fact of Pan, however, was not matched by any doubt about his self-image as a poet. The high-toned old Christian terms he uses in his letter to Baxter refer to the function of his writing as well as to his sticky personal situation, and he seems perfectly comfortable with the genteel goals he sets for himself: he will invent an ideal individual, and an ideal world, a "beautiful reality." Of course, he aimed to make this ideal world not only true, but actual. He had insisted to his brother Ed in 1909 that "art should be intrinsic" to everyday life, and found in the "patent wide reality" of a New York street market plenty of vitality, along with genteel beauty. But the faces around him, as his hint of defensiveness implies, were not yielding to his transformative powers, nor had "beauty" lost its rarification and remoteness from the world just yet.[3]

Not long after, Williams faced the urban world and found that its truth was often not beautiful. Just seeing modernity, much less making art intrinsic to it, was not going to be easy. How would he respond to this problem in his poetry? Flight or fight? In his letter to Baxter, he uses the language of genteel idealism to shield himself from the quotidian, yet he suggests that such language is the way to engage it. His last line above opens the question: will he remake the world "into a beautiful reality" by taking it into another realm altogether—a self-deceptive realm—or by actually transforming it?

Two years later, after his marriage and the establishment of his medical practice, even after the Armory Show and his own declaration of artistic revolt, Williams kept that question open. In his first long poem, "The Wanderer," he set his gargoyle-dotted temple (no longer referred to as Greek) on the banks of the "filthy Passaic" River in his actual hometown and, crossing to Manhattan, announced his intention to be a "mirror" to "modernity." He acknowledged his need to look again at the urban, industrial landscape and culture and find a worth to which his poetics had blinded him.

If he required a transformation of his poetics, he also demanded that the "brutality" he saw be changed. But he was unclear about the extent, and the means, of such a transformation: does one learn to see the present world and social structure differently without acting on them, or, fired by a new vision, does one remake the actual world? Williams does not say. A further ambivalence in "The Wanderer" is more troubling, for it undercuts Williams's professed intentions to waken people with his poetry. The pattern of his wanderings implies that he hedged his bets: although he made his poetry mirror America in 1913, he also preserved the possibility that poetry could remain a haven from the actual and the social. This impulse to retreat would recur throughout his writing career, even as he came to develop poetics that included more of America's mundanities more charitably than those of any other modern poet.

Of all the ambivalences in the politics and poetics of Williams's 1910s poems—the split between his poetic radicalism and his political nostalgia, his viewing urban modernity from a small-town perspective, his preaching iconoclasm while being a devoted doctor, husband, and father—this one, between his desire to serve his "townspeople" as their poet and his conception of poetry as a space of transcendent private freedom, is the deepest. When thinking of Williams's politics, one must keep in mind the geography of his life: Manhattan visible in the distance, buildings and new houses going up all over Rutherford, and, at the heart of the growing suburb, Old Man Kipp's farm and woods.

How was poetry to express the era of the Woolworth Building and recover what Harriet Monroe called its "ancient prophetic function"? Some of the poets that Williams was reading at the time confirmed his feeling that if poetry were to play any role in this *Nuevo Mundo*, it would have to talk about and sound like that world. This was not a universal judgment, however; many poets felt that their work still had power and saw no need to change its voice. As Arthur Davison Ficke wrote in the lead-off poem of the first issue of *Poetry*, art was still "a refuge from the stormy days / Breathing the peace of a remoter world / Where beauty" lived. Of course, Ficke added, such poetry could also "with high passion shatter the bonds of sleep." For Williams, however, if poetry was to waken the world, it would have to speak in at least some of the world's terms, and it could not do so in a language like Ficke's.[4]

By the time Williams wrote "The Wanderer," in late 1913 or early 1914, he had received plenty of advice to this effect. One piece was that to be a truly modern writer, one's subject matter would have to be social issues. The naturalist novel and muckraking journalism and fiction had some influence on poets, if only to show that contemporary social problems could be written about in conventional forms. Williams never mentions fiction such as Theodore Dreiser's or David Graham Phillips's, which influenced Kreymborg, but he found a similar example closer to home, both in art and life. Ferdinand Earle, editor of *The Lyric Year* and current suitor of Williams's lost love Charlotte Herman, explained in the 1912 annual (published in the spring of 1913) that he had selected "poems fired with the time spirit."[5]

By this Earle meant a Whitmanic "robust optimism" such as he found in *The Lyric Year*'s prize poem of that year, Orrick Johns's "Second Avenue," which in octosyllabic ABAB quatrains prophesied the triumph in America of "song" over "gold," nature and pagan values over the city and commercial values, and "brotherhood" over greed-generated racism and anti-Semitism. However, Johns presented almost no details of Second Avenue or the Eastern European Jews who packed its tenements. Only about a dozen other poems in the volume were on social or occasional themes, and only James Oppenheim's "Pittsburgh" and Louis Untermeyer's "Caliban in the Coal Mines" expressed radical sympathies; the rest were in the keys either of Teddy Roosevelt's strenuous nationalism or Greenwich Village's protest against the neglect of art. (Johns, who later called his poem "the cry of the *plebs urbana* of my youth, the expression of the 'little' middle class of the previous century," thought he won *The Lyric Year*'s prize because of the insistence of one judge disposed to poetry with "a social content." The prize, John said, started "a literary dog-fight.")[6]

Williams had met Earle at the Hermans' summer house in July of 1912; Earle had offered to get one of Williams's poems published in the volume, but for some reason did not. When Williams saw what Earle had accepted, he smarted for personal reasons and for aesthetic ones as well. He had already worked Johns's poetic territory, writing about "A Street Market, N.Y., 1908" and seeing in it a promise of international peace (in a Unitarian version of Keats's "Ode on a Grecian Urn"):

> There die the wars which grew
> When first was quarrelling
> And gaily sing
> Slavs, Teutons, Greeks, sweet songs
> Forever new.

Since he published this poem in *Poems* (1909), he had been trying to modernize his work; in "On First Opening *The Lyric Year,*" a poem he published in a letter to *Poetry* in June of 1913, he equated the conventional forms of the poems in *The Lyric Year* with graves, in which lay the bodies of "socially well-ordered" conformists (CP, 27). Already Williams was locating the value of a poem not in its meaning, but in its form; to him, there was no "tincture of disestablishment" to be found in a poem like Johns's, no matter what its content. Nevertheless, Williams seems to have taken Earle's implicit advice to work with actual contemporary subject matter when he turned to "The Wanderer."[7]

Williams was not the only writer, of course, who felt that modernity, whether of subject or sensibility, required formal innovation. Throughout 1913 he got a good deal of support and specific advice from *Poetry*, the one magazine of the time we are certain he read. Editor Harriet Monroe complained in April 1913 that poets writing about social and political issues seemed "as unaware of the twentieth century as if they had spent these recent years in an Elizabethan manorhouse or a vine-clad Victorian cottage." However, she offered no practical advice on expressing "The New Beauty."[8]

Ford Madox Hueffer (Ford) was more detailed in a two-part essay, "Impressionism—Some Speculations," which greatly impressed Williams. Hueffer said his aim as a writer was "to register my own times in terms of my own time":

> I would rather read a picture in verse of the emotions and environment of a Googe Street anarchist than recapture what songs the sirens sang. That after all was what Francis Villon was doing for the life of his day, and I should feel that our day was doing its duty for posterity much more surely if it were doing something of the sort.

What were the contemporary terms that Hueffer would use? First, poets should leave country lanes and plunge into "the Crowd" (a prescription that may have sent Williams to Broadway in "The Wanderer"). Hueffer knew from writing fiction that the things of the day—"the comfrey under the hedge," "The ash-bucket"—could be charged with symbolic connotations. One needed no allegorical abstraction such as Johns's "alien Disarray" or "Bright lotos" to render immigrants or money into poetry. Most important for Hueffer, the language of poetry should be the language one spoke in life. The English, he regretted to say, had "a literary jargon" in which they had to write, unlike the French or Germans, who wrote much more as they spoke.[9]

Williams wrote to Harriet Monroe on August 30 to say that Hueffer's first half was "splendid." He also submitted to her an essay he referred to as "English Speech Rhythm" (he did not yet speak of the "American language"). In it he tried to show that *"vers libre"* was a "contradiction in terms," and that the new verse was governed by time and not accent. Williams said nothing in the essay that indicates a specific debt to Hueffer's piece, but he was at the least encouraged by it to articulate some formal concerns of his that would add further detail to the impressionist's practical advice. When Hueffer published his own experiment in speech rhythm in the June 1914 *Poetry,* the wonderful poem "On Heaven," Williams read it immediately and urged Viola Baxter Jordan to do so ("it's good"). A quarter-century later, he paid homage "To Ford Madox Ford in Heaven" (CLP, 60) in the long lines of Hueffer's 1914 poem.[10]

Williams already had heard Hueffer's advice on the power of contemporary subject matter and speech through Hueffer's pupil, Ezra Pound, one of whose imagist dicta was that "the natural object is always the adequate symbol." Pound's advice on rhythm, however, implied a difference between him and Hueffer—and between him and Williams—that Williams eventually made into his chief criticism of Pound's poetry and politics. Urging the poet to expand his means of expression beyond iambic pentameter, Pound recommended learning "the finest cadences, preferably in a foreign language." Williams would soon be filling a notebook with the cadences of speakers of American English, trying to establish the rhythmic terms of his own time and place. In his 1946 "Letter to an Australian Editor," Williams would argue that Pound's reliance on Greek, Latin, Provençal, Italian, and Chinese rhythms were part and parcel of his reactionary world view.[11]

For now he made no such claim, but listened to the friend who since 1909 had been telling him how to get in touch with modern poetry. Pound himself was on the lookout for new means of rendering the modern world, which to him for at least a time included an awakening working class. In "Patria Mia," he had said that a social revolution was certain (though he doubted that workers had sufficient backbone to take on such responsibility). In Henri-Martin Barzun's *Hymnes de forces,* however, he detected signs that the "proletariat would seem to be getting something like a coherent speech. . . . I am not sure that [Barzun] has not hit upon the true medium for democratic expression, the fitting method of synthesis." Barzun's work never became a cause for him, however; nor would Williams' quest for a similar, democratic medium.[12]

As the antennae for the poetic race, Pound registered in his reviews for *Poetry* and other magazines any evidence that a writer had discovered ways to express contemporary content. John Gould Fletcher, he thought, had made a synthesis less successful than Barzun's, but had at least escaped a dead diction and symbolism: "He is trying to use the speech of his time, which renders him inelegant. . . . Yet he talks about a factory as if it were a factory and not a mythological beast"—precisely the sin committed by Witter Bynner, who had suavely imagined office and factory workers he passed in the street as "fauns and nymphs" in a poem in *Poetry*'s February issue.[13]

In his letters to Williams, Pound gave similar criticism. In December of 1913, he told Williams that while the vocabulary of his poem "La Flor" was "right, . . . your syntax still strays from the simple order of natural speech."[14] Williams would consistently fault the poet who retained such "inversions" of spoken word order; some time between March of 1914, when he published, "The Wanderer," and its 1917 reprinting in *Al Que Quiere!*, he applied his rule to his own work and revised half a dozen or so offensive constructions in the poem.

Such was the way that the political implications of formal innovation were discussed by the contemporaries who stirred Williams to write "The Wanderer." Like the writers he read in *Poetry*, he concerned himself mainly with changing the form of poetry so that it would fittingly express contemporary life and sensibility, believing that this was the way to "win through," as Harriet Monroe put it, to an unspecified "freedom." "Go," Pound told a group of his own poems, "be against all forms of oppression."[15]

Few of these contemporaries said anything directly about the political or social views that a modern poet might hold or that formal innovations might in themselves imply. Instead they spoke the current language of the iconoclastic artist who opposed middle-class morals and the tastes of a "commercial" culture. While the poets identified themselves with "the new" or, as Williams did in a letter to Monroe, saw life itself as "subversive of life as it was the moment before," no one specified too clearly what "the new" was or how it translated into political values or actions (or what action besides ending Comstock laws and lifting import duties on foreign books would create conditions in which "the new" could be made and enjoyed). If they spoke of social issues in their poems, they did so in broad humanitarian terms such as Johns's, or proclaimed their own liberation from and superiority to conventional mores: as Pound boasted, "I mate with my free kind upon the crags."[16]

Williams gave "The Wanderer" the subtitle "A Rococo Study" because, he told Edith Heal in 1956, "I don't know except it was one of my mother's favorite words" (IWWP, 25). Probably he felt embarrassed that he had not fully achieved the language of modernity that the poem announces, and tried to imply that he intended its Keatsian anachronisms as self-parody. As his later revisions indicate, he was rightly dissatisfied with the poem's language; however, he did manage to write about some of the particularities of the time more discretely and vividly than almost any contemporary poet, especially in his portrait of workers in Paterson. Surely he pleased Hueffer.

The poem stands out from contemporary work because of the antifigurative, flat language of some of its passages, and it is distinguished from Williams's own work of the decade by its outspokenness about social and political concerns. He was evidently inspired by "the time-spirit" of poems such as Johns's and events such as the Armory Show and the pageant to follow once again the evangelical bent of his early letters to Ed. His rereading of Whitman early in 1913 no doubt gave him a precedent for the sort of witness to American modernity, and critic of it, that he becomes in "The Wanderer."

But what sort of Whitmanic witness to American democracy is Williams? The meaning of democracy was being remolded by the forces shaping the landscape of modernity that Williams wanders, but his response to urban anonymity and a mass society is based on values bred in smaller, more intimate communities such as Rutherford. As for the questions about the concentration of economic power discussed so widely and for so long, Williams overrides them, challenging their primacy with a call for moral and aesthetic renovation based on his older values. As is suggested by the disdain implicit in his saying that some people in a bread line are merely being "carried"—some of them were on strike—Williams retorts with the old-time religion of individualism. Furthermore, not only the content of "The Wanderer" but also its structure expresses both Williams's misgivings about the new American world and his concern for the artist's function—a concern that, ironically, nearly prevents him from fulfilling it.

Williams's wanderings divide into two journeys. The first takes place through the cities of Manhattan and Paterson, the second in still-rural New Jersey and a wild section of Rutherford. They cover the whole range of communities of America in 1913: New York, with towers of corporate commerce and anonymous Broadway crowds; industrial Paterson, its mills owned by many different self-made entrepreneurs and worked by immigrant proletarians; family-owned farms, set by themselves in the northern Jersey foothills; Williams's suburban home town, fast-growing, and an as yet still natural part of it on the Passaic River. The pattern of his journey, from the city to nature and poetry, implies a challenge to modernity and politics.

The poem opens with Williams at the prow of a Hudson River ferry, looking at the Manhattan skyline and asking how he can "be a mirror to this modernity." He glimpses his muse on the river as a woman, and then as a gull, and then becomes a gull himself, viewing the city as if it were the first day of creation. It is his vision as a poet, granted by his muse: "For me," he says, echoing his letter to Viola Baxter, "one face"—that of his muse—"is all the world!" This "old queen" is cast out of the modern world, however, "walking imperious in beggary," a wanderer. Seeking her, Williams vows (with an inversion he later revised), "In her I will take my peace henceforth!"

That Williams is parodying his own naïveté, if not his wonder at his new vision of the world, is made clear when, right after his vow, his muse strikes him and gives him a vision of Broadway. The urban world revolts him, especially the ghostlike quality of people in crowds:

> —men as visions
> With expressionless, animate faces;
> Empty men with shell-thin bodies
> Jostling close above the gutter,
> Hasting nowhere!

Williams does not see that such a face is not empty but is the characteristic urban walker's self-defense against the sensory overstimulation of encountering so many other faces. Compared to the townspeople he encounters in Rutherford streets, people whose presences are for him rich with his own knowledge of their lives, these strangers seem empty. Compared to the walks of Rutherfordians, the origins and destinations of which Williams would know, the New Yorkers may well seem to be in Brownian motion. But Williams's muse chastises his aesthetics and his moral vision by giving them a shock. Williams always represented the energy of the city as erotic, and here he recounts how he learned to do so. She appears to him as a gaudy overripe whore, "her might strapped in with a corset." The sight of her appearing as lewd as the Broadway environment sickens him, but she insists that he look beyond conventional morality: "Well, do their eyes shine, their clothes fit? / These *live* I tell you."

But Williams is not ready to acknowledge this. Instead he begs her for the power to present the Adamic vision of the city he had earlier, and so persuade the urbanites to seek such freshness:

> If I could only catch something of this day's
> Air and sun into your service,
> Those toilers after peace and after pleasure
> That toil and pleasure drive, broken at all hours—
> Would turn again worshippers at all hours!

She only sniffs "warily" at his prayer, implying that Williams's compassion is misplaced and that his chivalric tone is all wrong. When he continues his prayer, it is in different terms, which suggests he now acknowledges the facts of urban reality. He addresses her bluntly as an "old harlot of greatest lusting," granting her her place in modernity as a goddess not of beauty but of erotic vitality. Knowledge—and poetry—are to be gained through intimate experience; rather than the freshness of air and sun, he now asks her to "give me, / Them and me, always a new marriage," be it as anonymous and fleeting as the coupling of a Broadway john with a city whore. But as he continues his prayer, he undoes it, asking her, "May I be lifted up and out of terror, / Up from the death living around me!" He asks to be carried by her whim, not admitting that she has brought him to Broadway to face down his fear. The vision abruptly closes with her saying nothing to his prayers; it will take a venture into another city to complete his initiation.

Paterson is that other city. There, Williams tells us, he makes contact with the urban world, which becomes his father and tosses him like a baby. Modernity in Paterson is constituted by the social strife of the 1913 textile strike. The "dusty fight" he witnesses is a suitable initiation rite for a poet who sees life as "subversive of life as it was the moment before" and wants to give his verse "a tincture of disestablishment" (SL, 24). However, the notion of political disestablishment expressed in the poem is far from that of the strikers, the I.W.W., or Village sympathizers like John Reed.

Despite the section's title, very little of "The Strike" itself makes its way into Williams's poem. Not a textile mill nor a union man nor even a mill worker is specifically mentioned. The men's arms "toss quartered beeves / And barrels," not bolts of died cloth or leaflets. Instead of a picket line, Williams sees a bread line in front of a teashop, a scene he more likely witnessed in the winter of 1913–14, a time of severe unemployment and hunger—and bread lines that did not stand patiently, as does Williams's. Shortly before Williams's poem was published, a young anarchist named Frank Tannenbaum led 189 jobless men into a Catholic church to demand food and shelter. Tannenbaum's arrest and trial became a new cause célèbre for Mabel Dodge Luhan's circle and triggered an "Unemployment Movement" of demonstrations and church occupations. Williams's use of the bread line in his poem strongly suggests that he did not visit Paterson during the strike.[17]

If Williams did not refer to "the dusty fight," one might never know that this section of the poem was about the strike. His political response to the strike is displaced by his aesthetic response; he merely enjoys watching the men and women, ugly as they are. "Nowhere the subtle! Everywhere the electric!" is his refrain. He sees Paterson and the strikers in the light of his concern to find beauty and delicacy, not in the light of their concern for economic justice. Williams's values as a poet displace the political themes that he professes to be writing about.

This displacement, however, is precisely Williams's political point. When he describes the people in the bread line, he asserts that the quest for beauty is the poet's primary social responsibility:

> No questions—all stood patiently,
> Dominated by one idea: something
> That carried them as they are always wanting to be carried,
> But what is it, I asked those nearest me,
> This thing heretofore unobtainable
> That they seem so clever to have put on now?
>
> Why since I have failed them can it be anything
> But their own brood? Can it be anything but brutality?
> On that at least they're united! That at least
> Is their bean soup, their calm bread and a few luxuries!

The poet, Williams asserts, is the "Atlas" of his community; he creates or presents the "thing" that unites the people of Paterson or Rutherford or the United States—the "thing" being, presumably, the value of beauty or charity. Since the poet has failed them, the people of Paterson have been left to their own imaginative devices, and Williams does not think much of these. Lacking the poet, the unifying principle of the Paterson community is only "brutality," and the workers "put on" a strike that can only express unimaginative, raw violence.

So this passage reads to me. Williams claims that the poet's relation to his people is absolutely essential, for he, and only he, conceives of their lives in terms that will confer on them the desire and the means to organize their life together so that they attain beauty and self-fulfillment. Williams refuses the terms of class conflict in which the I.W.W., or even the mill owners and the conservative press, speak of the strike, and he insists implicitly that all are to blame for the failure of imagination that the strike represents. And, blaming himself for abandoning them to their own inadequate imaginations, Williams radically displaces politics with poetry, just as he would in *In the American Grain* and *Paterson*.

Having witnessed the strike and become drunk with the experience, Williams has overcome the terror he felt on Broadway, and tells his muse, "I am at peace again, old queen, I listen clearer now." Now it seems he will be able to face the urban world of modernity, even if it is "ugly, venomous, gigantic," and fulfill his responsibility to his fellow citizens such as the mill owners and laborers of Paterson. He and his muse can leave the cities and head "Abroad" to the Jersey hills, where she instructs him in the values he must impart to his community.

But Williams's fear of the urban environment is not so much overcome as assuaged by their flight west. "You are safe here," she tells him, and the values she teaches him to teach may be anachronistic in a society of mass production, management, and advertisement:

> . . . look child, look open-mouth!
> The patch of road between precipitous bramble banks,
> The tree in the wind, the white house, the sky!
> Speak to them of these concerning me!
> For never while you permit them to ignore me
> In these shall the full of my freed voice
> Come grappling the ear with intent!

What can this rural order have to say to those who walk Broadway, those who dye fabric and speak no English in Paterson? The title of the section suggests that Williams was more concerned with literary politics than with politics per se. Unlike Pound, so doubtful of making art in America that he left for London, Williams would take his trip "abroad" a few miles from his house, and find possibilities for poetry that America held. But the scene does have a political dimension to it, implying that Williams is holding up the moral superiority of

Jefferson's yeoman farmer—drawing his virtue from his intimacy with nature—to the factory dwellers and the boulevardiers.[18] The poet's response to his muse's instructions is Emersonian, presuming that all have their individual spark of divinity within them, rather than seeing that spark as being generated by their social situation:

> At which I cried out with all the might I had,
> Waken! O people, to the boughs green
> With unripe fruit within you!
> Waken to the myriad cinquefoil
> In the waving grass of your minds!
> Waken to the silent Phoebe nest
> Under the eaves of your spirit!

As on Broadway, and between Broadway and Paterson, Williams must be told to look again. She points out a second farm scene, this one including farmers in an oat field. "The weight of the sky is upon them," she tells him, as the farmers contend with elemental natural forces against which "all roof-beams crumble" (in the 1917 version, the natural forces are internal as well: the farmers are "bowed down with their passions"). Williams shouts again and learns this lesson for himself: his voice this time is merely "a seed in the wind." He learns, finally, that a poet's values must transcend the immediately political; he must teach the universal and fundamental—and tragic—terms of the human condition.

After "Soothsay," the muse's prophecy that Williams will become that Atlas-like creator of society's values, holding them up in spirit and "for pride and for mockery," the poet's initiation is completed with his now-famous baptism in the "filthy Passaic" river. The pattern of his quest for a poetic identity appropriately ends in his home town of Rutherford, yet this pattern seems to interfere with Williams's intention to be the poet of modernity.

His actual community was a suburb, where until 1920 train passengers from Manhattan walked home past Peter Kipp's farm. Living in such a hybrid of urban and rural, Williams, as Louis Zukofsky advised him in 1931, could hang on to small-community values and Jeffersonian politics even as the growth of the urban, national society rendered them obsolete.[19] Even when one grants that Williams predicts "new wanderings" at the end of the poem, or acknowledges that initiation rites often require a temporary withdrawal from ordinary life and society, even if one argues that suburban life such as that of Rutherford's is as much a part of modernity as that of New York's, the biographical fact that Williams stayed in Rutherford casts an ironic light on the pattern of his "wanderings" in his poem of 1914.

Williams's ambivalence toward the modernity he sought to mirror, then, is expressed in the ambivalence of his view of the political and social function of the modern poet. Williams's distaste for the urban world, in fact, is part of a deeper desire to escape society and politics, even those of small-town Rutherford, altogether. So the closing section of the poem, "St. James' Grove," suggests.

The poet's baptism takes place in Santiago Grove, a wooded and in effect wild parcel of land that runs up to the banks of the Passaic River. To get there, Williams would have walked less than a mile north and west, "right past the houses / Of my friends" on West Passaic Avenue—away from the community, that is, and into nature. He walks as he does "on any usual day, any errand," as if to insist that the poet's sacred business is part of the mundane, common life of the town—and to emphasize with irony that it is not. For his baptism is a solitary ritual—none of those friends, no member of the community for whom he immerses himself attends the ceremony. Any tribal shaman's knowledge is a closely guarded secret, and Williams rightly goes to his knowledge alone.

His privacy here, however, is temperamental as well as ritual. Despite his recognition in the poem that "the novitiate was ended, / The ecstasy was over, the life begun," Williams would recurrently long to recover that state of ecstasy, the delight of simply drinking in such scenes as the Paterson strike. Of course, he did enter a life of responsibility and duty, which included the responsibilities of the poet to his community. Yet one of his aims as a socially concerned poet—namely, to free his readers' imaginations so that they could experience the world with sensual immediacy—is profoundly apolitical and even asocial. As his personal responsibilities pressed on him, and as modernity created a social world and mass culture repugnant to his faith in American democracy and the transcendence of art, he would turn for consolation to the image of the poet as another Daniel Boone, who, as Williams said in his 1925 *In the American Grain,* was a "great voluptuary" who solved the social problems of the New World by leaving them behind (AG, 130). But Williams bore resolutely, if with a chafing collar, the tension between his ideal world of imagination and the social world in which he lived. He was much like the George Washington he imagined in *The First President,* serving the young nation while aching to retire into his pastoral Mount Vernon landscape, or like Joe Stecher, working all the time while inside him a solitary "other man" moves through the woods.

The close of "The Wanderer" embodies this tension, expressing the ambivalence Williams felt about serving any community, much less the particular urban communities of Paterson and New York. After his baptism, his muse-mother tells his river-father that Santiago Grove is now consecrated to poetry:

> Here the most secluded spaces for miles
> For wide around, hallowed by a stench
> To be our joint solitude and temple,
> A memory of this clear marriage
> And the child I have brought you in the late years!

The grove, Williams says here, is consecrated to modern poetry with modern means: the hallowing stench rises from the effluents dumped in the Passaic by the factories in Paterson. Poetry, he asserts, cannot remain isolated from modernity, however much its traditional value of connecting man to a pure nature, a pure solitude and beauty may be threatened. And yet the tone of the hag-muse's closing benediction implies how keenly Williams regretted giving up the older, "purer" aesthetic.

However much of modernity that Williams managed to mirror in the scenes and language of "The Wanderer," and however comically he may have intended his revulsions and exclamations, the close of the poem cannot but make us wonder if he had in fact given up an outmoded aesthetic—and if he committed himself completely to performing the function of the poet responsible for his community's social unity. If the grove is hallowed by the stench from the waste from the Paterson mills, it still is placed well away from them—and even from farm-hearted Rutherford.

But if poetry's realm remains separate from modernity in the poem, in history modernity came to Santiago Grove. Some time between 1915 and 1918 Rutherford voters defeated a proposal—initiated by petitions passed around by members of what a local historian called the "park movement"—to have the borough purchase the land and make it a park. This institutionalization of the wild was the best accommodation between nature and modernity that one could hope for, but by the 1930s, Santiago Grove had been sold off in parcels. In an unfinished poem of late in that decade, Williams celebrated the persistence of the natural forces from which he tried to draw the strength to create a more urban poetry, but this time he acknowledged that modernization spelled the grove's doom:

Santiago Grove/The Old Trees

The scar[r]ed hulks
of the old pine trees
of Santiago Grove

To which the building
development has
almost penetrated

High against the cold
still wave their ragged green
feathery green top branches[20]

Today the old pine trees are gone; all that is left of the grove is its signifier, applied to Santiago Avenue near the original site.

Thus "The Wanderer" is full of conflicts: between Williams's intention to create an aesthetic appropriate to modernity and his wish to preserve the values of his Keatsian conception of poetry; between his wish to speak to the modern world and his wish to preserve the values of the America that modernity was erasing; and, finally, between the aesthetic values and the political function of his poetry.

Keats found himself in a similar dilemma, as Williams may well have realized as he wrestled with his precursor in "The Wanderer," and memorialized his first hero's struggle with the relation of beauty to truth and the power to transform reality. For if the source of Williams's flight over the skyline early in "The Wanderer" is Whitman's city-celebrating "Crossing Brooklyn Ferry," the source of his image of poetry as the polluted Passaic in which he is ambivalently baptized is Keats's "Sleep and Poetry," where a "muddy stream" signifies the purity and transcendence of art that its subject matter—the present—has debased:

> The visions all are fled—the car is fled
> Into the light of heaven, and in their stead
> A sense of real things comes doubly strong,
> And, like a muddy stream, would bear along
> My soul to nothingness: but I will strive
> Against all doubtings, and will keep alive
> The thought of that same chariot, and the strange
> Journey it went.

Keats, like his American descendant, came to want his poetry to face those real things and somehow improve them. But "The Fall of Hyperion" shows how troubled he was by the paradox that his sensitivity to others' misery leads him to write poems that help no one—dreams of feasts of which he alone partakes. He asks his muse why others who "labour for mortal good," as he feels he does, are not there on the heights of vision with him. She answers him in the harshest terms:

> "Those whom thou spakest of are no visionaries,"
> Rejoin'd that voice; "they are no dreamers weak;
> They seek no wonder but the human face,
> No music but a happy-noted voice:
> They come not here, they have no thought to come;
> And thou art here, for thou art less than they.
> What benefit canst thou do, or all thy tribe,
> To the great world? Thou art a dreaming thing,
> A fever of thyself: think of the earth;
> What bliss, even in hope, is there for thee?"

Keats plainly intended to argue that there was hope for dreamers who wanted to move the earth; unfinished as it is, "The Fall of Hyperion" only states superbly the dilemma of the poet committed to both ideal beauty and earthly action. In "The Wanderer," Williams affirmed that he had worked through Keats's—and all bourgeois poets'—dilemma. He would seek no wonder but the face of modernity, no music but that of his townspeople's voices; he would reveal to them the cinquefoil within them, the Adamic freshness of the world without, a beauty in history. That, he insisted, was the essential benefit he could do for the world. But more than once in "The Wanderer," and more than once in his subsequent poetry, Williams fell back sickened by the sight of the modern world he sought to celebrate—and his revulsion brought on a relapse of the banished poet's dream of another beauty, the poet's fever of the self.

"My Name's Brobitza!" Egoism and Poems for *The Masses*

Williams may have suffered from that "fever of the self" which Keats's muse Moneta imputed to the socially concerned poet, but he did not willingly keep his art hidden in Santiago Grove. Although he wrote little poetry about specific major political or social issues and events until the end of the 1910s (and did not discuss them in the surviving letters of this period), he did write the series of "townspeople" poems, and commented on poverty, immigration, and education— not as national or abstract social issues, however, but as they touched him personally and locally. Throughout the 1910s he tried to perform his self-imposed duty of being the Atlas of his community and shaping its values.

But Williams's individualism and iconoclasm were intensified by his contact with the proto-dadaists and aesthetes of the Arensberg circle and the vaguely socialist and literary nationalist members of the *Others* group. From Grantwood and 67th Street he brought home some "pagan" morality and proclaimed it in his poems, if not his way of life. New York iconoclasm, of course, celebrated the individual's defiance of social convention. Williams's individualism was further honed, moreover, on a particularly abrasive whetstone from across the Atlantic; with that sharpened sense of self, he slashed not only at small-town social conformity, but at vaguer threats to autonomy made by modernity.

One of Williams's few references to larger political principles, made in his school inspection notebook in the fall of 1914, provides us with a clue to his leanings: "Surely there is no country," he wrote sardonically, "where I am freer to bludgeon any man—hurt him than here." That so much American talk of liberty cloaked one's self-interest rankled the Williams devoted to an idealistic ethic of service. However, the Williams who enjoyed Wilde's notion of the artist as the most highly developed Individual, and balked at restrictions placed on his urge to self-expression by his conventional life in Rutherford, was attracted by his own overstatement; he ended his note saying, "I desire such freedom" (LRN, 27). Such extremely individualist sentiments are the dominant note of *The Comic Life of Elia Brobitza*—and of *The Egoist*.

Mike Weaver was the first to point out how attracted Williams was to the philosophy of *The Egoist*, especially to the writings of editorialist and essayist Dora Marsden, noting Williams's interest in her writings on "lingual psychology," about which he published two letters in the journal in 1917. However, Williams's interest ranged beyond the questions of sexuality, language, and creativity Marsden raised. Her radically individualist philosophy of "egoism" provided him with support for his undoctrinaire individualist politics as an individualist artist.[1]

Williams started reading the London-based biweekly at Pound's urging, probably soon after it changed its name from *The New Freewoman* in January 1914. Over the next five years he published 19 poems in it (including "The "Wanderer"), three letter-essays, and an improvisation. He read it carefully enough to defend it to Viola Baxter Jordan and explain to her, "An Egoist is simply a person who owns himself to bestow himself perfectly." Williams said little else about the philosophy, but probably refreshed his interest in discussions with Marsden Hartley, who also read the magazine, after they met in 1916.[2]

As Dora Marsden defined it in commentaries on events and issues of the winter and spring of 1914 such as the suffragist movement, the Dublin general strike, democracy and morality, social reformers, and the war, egoism was a political philosophy to end politics: "The satisfaction of individual wants is the only authority we respect." Her tart editorials exposed the means by which other political philosophies and movements blinded their adherents to the brute fact that life was really lived "according to power":

> That there is one law for the rich and another law for the poor is a very inadequate way of putting the matter: there is a law for each man individually, be he rich or poor, which is the resultant of all his powers: his strength, charm, skill, intelligence, daring: the sum of his total worth and what it secures is a man's just dues.

Demands for liberty, for example, were "merely the appeal of the weak to authority to coerce the strong," a deluded plea to get another to do what only could be done by one's self.[3]

Such self-delusions, Marsden reiterated, were caused by the human habit of living "life according to concept," by granting too much power to verbal abstractions such as democracy or morality. To her, "Society is not based on any Conception whatsoever, it is based on the inborn predilections and instincts of individuals. . . . Whatever these instincts are Society is and will be." Social change was a matter of letting one's own instincts "break through the overlying verbiage" and asserting one's own will in action. As Marsden said of the Dublin general strike:

> Labor unrest . . . is a matter of temper: not of social arrangement.
> The poor will cease to be poor when they refuse to be: the downtrodden will disappear when they decide to stand up: the hungry will have bread when they take it. What will happen after is a matter of chance and circumstance. . . .[4]

As one may gather from Marsden's last remark, egoism was not exactly a "constructive" political praxis. Consistent with her philosophy, she refused to invent or impose another concept of society on others; however, there was little talk of live-and-let-live in her work. Glorifying the individual will, mainly by pointing out others' failure to use theirs, Marsden finally glorified force in the abstract with little concern for its concrete consequences, foreshadowing the fascism of the 1920s and 1930s.

The literary historian must take egoism seriously not only for what followed it but also because of its appeal to the 1910s artists who published in Weaver's and Marsden's magazine. The two men who wrote regularly on aesthetics and art for it, Huntley Carter and Ezra Pound, both implied their sympathy for egoism with their protests against "the de-individualization of the artist," in Carter's words, by mercantile culture—in Pound's more pungent terms, by "the rabble and the bureaucracy" whose god is "Mediocrity."[5]

Marsden herself wrote little specifically about art and artists in *The Egoist,* though in *The New Freewoman* she had defined art as "the highest manifestation of self-recognized emotion." But in her 1916–17 essays on "lingual psychology," she placed the imagination at the center of individual consciousness as the creator of a Berkeleyan, concrete "world" of perceived images. The priority she gave to the individual consciousness over material conditions naturally appealed to artists' desire for power over the world and assuaged their sense of powerlessness in the modern social order. That Pound, H.D., and Richard Aldington—all of whom published work in *The Egoist* asserting or assuming their superiority to the average soul—should edit the magazine's poetry is not surprising, no matter what dismissals of its political commentary they made.[6]

And Williams? Despite his enthusiasm to Viola Baxter Jordan about egoism in 1914, he was as undoctrinaire about it as he was with most other isms and followed the spirit rather than the letter. In fact, he may not have read all of the letter; in his reply to Marsden's essays on lingual psychology, he addressed only the first one, published in the July 1, 1916, *Egoist.*[7] And he followed the spirit only to a point. In *Spring and All* he celebrated the imagination's nature and power in terms similar to Marsden's, but he refers to her "philosophical algebra" (I, 97) only to point up the futility of philosophy—and the success of art—in answering life's fundamental questions.

In fact, the notion that an egoist "owned" himself in order "to bestow himself perfectly" on others is not Marsden's idea at all, but Williams's. Marsden viewed the ethic of service as a tool of the powerful, which led weaker people to form the habits of dependence and self-abasement. The Unitarianism that Williams grew up with, though, laid equal emphasis on individualism and the service ethic, and Williams evidently viewed egoism by its lights. And so, while he could say of the bread-line strikers in "The Wanderer" that they were "carried as they are always wanting to be carried," he proceeded to offer to bestow himself on them.

Egoism, then, consoled the poet whose townspeople did not recognize him or his work's value, but it did not breed in him the deep contempt for ordinary people implicit in the doctrine. His egoist heroine was not Dora Marsden but "a Polish woman, cook of the [Ivison] Castle," who became the speaker of his poem, "Portrait of a Woman in Bed," and the protagonist of his 1919 play, *The Comic Life of Elia Brobitza,* into which he incorporated the poem.[8] In the poem and play he honored a poor woman's fierce freedom from conventional morals; in posing Brobitza's strong sense of herself against official representatives of that morality, Williams also continued the uneasy dialogue with modernity that he began in "The Wanderer."

During an inspection of Rutherford's Washington elementary school on October 6, 1914, Williams "sent home for uncleanliness" a student named Rosa Robitza (LRN, 7). Some time that fall he may have visited the student's mother to discuss such health problems and heard the defiant words that eventually became the "Portrait" (in which the woman's name is Robitza). Another notebook entry contains the germ of the poem and play:

> Laugh at our-
> selves-we make
> serious things of
> her staying in
> bed + she triump[h]s
> over us + makes
> us ridiculo[us]
> −funny. (LRN, 23)

Rutherford's school physician was sufficiently detached from the values of his civic office to laugh at himself for making a "serious thing" out of her daughter's unscrubbed ears. Robitza reminded him of his grandmother Wellcome, the fierce outcast who figured as his hag-muse in "The Wanderer." So, when Williams's townspeople "were trying to kick her out of the house and she wouldn't go," he told John Thirlwall in 1953, "I wanted to throw her in the face of the town. The whores are better than my townspeople."[9]

What the biographical Mrs. Robitza was really like is not known. The Elia Brobitza of Williams's poem offends community morality on every front in defense of her self: work, sexual expression, property, education, and motherhood catch hell from her in 55 lines. She has no income, no jewelry to pawn like a respectable woman, but she will not work; she could not care less about wearing a corset or even drawers. She is happy to let "the rich lady" (Mrs. Ivison, one presumes) provide for her two sons, but hardly because she, as a good mother, wants them to have an Alger's chance in life: "let them go to the gutter," she says, if they do not "beat the school" with their own wits ("They're keen!" she says proudly). She claims title, as it were, to an abandoned house on the egoist grounds of desire and will: "It's mine because I need it."

Above all these pieties, Brobitza offends middle-class notions of Christian charity. She is willing to exploit them: "Oh, I won't starve while there's the / Bible to make them feed me." But she refuses to give up her self-respect by flattering her benefactors with gratitude. She owns nothing:

> But I've my two eyes and a
> smooth face and here's this, look!
> it's high! There's brains and blood in there!
> my name's Brobitza!

Nothing, that is, but what an egoist like Dora Marsden would call her property or her own: "instincts, family, grace, beauty, manner, brains, and the original dower of power which we have which puts them in evidence."[10] Brobitza insists on being dealt with according to her egoist sense of "charity": "Try to help me if you want trouble / or leave me alone, that ends trouble."

For Williams, the root of Brobitza's trouble is middle-class morality, but he also identifies her enemies as products of modernization. The main conflict in the play is between the autonomous Brobitza and the Poor Master, who comes to put her under the care of the state and to institutionalize her against her will. However, she and the Poor Master clash explicitly over questions of morality: he imposes the standards of the middle-class agency he represents upon this poor, immigrant woman, and tells her, "You oughta been kept in jail / while they had you there." Brobitza calls him a drunk and underscores his hypocrisy.

Yet Williams does imply that the hypocrisy and dehumanizing condescension are not the Poor Master's alone but are inherent in the social forces of which he is an agent. Contrasted to him is George, who, cowed by Brobitza, brings her an iron cot; when the Poor Master glowers at him, he explains, "Aw," he is "just trying to help / the old lady" like a good, old-fashioned neighbor. George pleads with her to "let 'em send you / to the old lady's home the way they / want to." "They got a swell place up there," he adds—but he also tries to help her remain independent.

Finally, though, Williams's criticism of such institutionalization is made implicitly, through Brobitza's character and her defense of her moral autonomy and, faintly, through the contrast between the Poor Master and George. In his own life Williams seems to have despised the moralizing that accompanied the development of such agencies of the state as "poorhouses," but did not question too strongly the process of their development. In 1921, when he replied to Harriet Monroe's appeal for support for his ill poet friend Emanuel Carnevali, he explained his suspicion of charity, but evaded discussing it in social terms. Instead he used the mystifying language of "fate":

> I am sorry for Em, as of course you are also, but I begin to see the impossibility of charity: one always does when he has a little himself. Give all your goods to feed the poor! It is a subtle

hypocrisy which the world has not yet exploded. I myself have been the subject of charity in small ways, the charity of fate, etc. that were it not for a yellow dog's constitution I would be all dead instead of moribund. Bah.[11]

Ironically, when Williams wrote this freewheeling indictment of such personal modes of charity as giving out one's own goods, he was serving Bergen County as the physician to its Children's Home (he also helped Carnevali, sending him money as late as 1932).

Just as Williams deflected the question of charity from social to personal circumstances in his letter to Monroe, so he focused in his play on the character of Elia Brobitza at the expense of the questions he raised about the character of the society that seeks to control her. Fate, and not society, Williams suggests, has been wholly uncharitable to Brobitza, and finally, despite her yellow dog's constitution, kills her. Ironically, the source of her independence is her having given herself up in love to two different men, both of whom deserted her. The opening of the play is a flashback to her encounter with her husband, Jim; she begs him to come back to her, even offering to turn over her children to the "the Sisters" if he does not want them around. And as she lies on the cot George has brought her, Flavi, her lover in the old country, calls her. She is so shaken that she denies the identity she is trying to preserve: "That ain't my name."

She recovers and Flavi appears to her, coming home at last from the fair. The scene between them is Brobitza's fantasy of revenge on her fate, but it includes compensation for her treatment by middle-class moralists as well. Her lover returns with riches from the fair (which, with "the crowds—the gifts to buy," resembles a Rutherford commuter's vision of New York). He never delivered them in real life, we discover, because he spent all his money on them: "Elia, I tell you, a fair eats up the cash. . . ." To earn cash for the trip home, he and a companion hired themselves out to a miller, who shortchanged them at the end of the month with hidden charges of room and board; they owe their persons, if not their souls, to the one-man company store. Denied cash, Flavi and his companion take their pay in flesh, bedding the miller's wife and daughter while he is drunk; thus Brobitza, who laughs to hear Flavi tell of catching the miller's wife, is vicariously repaid the insults to her morals from the Poor Master in the appropriate coin of sex.

But at midnight Flavi disappears, and three men come in to carry Brobitza, cot and all, to the poorhouse; laughing, she calls them fools, and dies. The core of Brobitza was her passion for Flavi; her defiant individualism, her very identity, was constituted by her despair at fulfilling it. Her death cheats the society concerned with her welfare but indifferent to—in fact shocked by—her self. Inevitably (and fortunately for the Poor Master), death takes her away before "they" can.

Elia Brobitza, then, argues for the complete recognition of the individual standing before you, as opposed to the partial and self-interested views of officialdom, the Church and the talk of the town. Williams did not have to read *The Egoist* to express such views—he had read Wilde and Ibsen and, of course, grew up in a milieu steeped in American individualist ideology—but the journal, one of the few concerned with philosophy and politics that we know he read with interest at this time, could only have pushed him further into forming a party of one.

Not only *The Egoist,* of course, but the culture of Greenwich Village, with its credo of self-expression in defiance of outmoded truths and moral codes, gave Williams plenty of support for his belief in the necessity of the artist's individualism. His first prose statement about the nature of the artist did not come until 1919, but it is safe to assume that he had held to the assumptions he made then for several years before. In "Notes from a Talk on Poetry," he stated premises about the nature of knowledge and the self from which the "essential individualism" of the artist—and the artist's refusal of ideological commitment—inevitably followed. And Williams wrote several poems apparently intended to demonstrate to the committed poets of the 1910s just how their cries against social injustice were failing the art, and, by implication, the people.

As he implied in *The Comic Life of Elia Brobitza,* Williams in his "Notes" defined the core of the self as the emotions: "the world of the senses lies unintelligible on all sides. It is only interpretable by the emotions." Desire drove the scientist to his logic and method, and Williams found more truth in the desire that drove Hilda Doolittle's astronomer father to sit with his eye to his telescope until his beard froze to the metal than in the calculations such patience yielded. Those numbers, in fact, only proved "the fundamental emotional basis of all knowledge": they were discovered—created, actually—in the encounter of Professor Doolittle's passion with the world. The scientific law he might have formulated was in a pale sense true, but if he applied it a priori to his next encounter with the stars, it would falsify the deeper truth of his experience and would eventually prove superficially false as well. Echoing Ibsen, Jefferson, and his own 1913 letter to Harriet Monroe, Williams added, "a truth twenty years old is a lie because the emotion has gone out of it."[12]

The poet, however, tried to smash "life's lies," those rigidified "truths" of science, morality, sight, and the worn-out language in which they were expressed. By expressing his responses to the world before him, the poet recreated the world with the plenitude of meaning that only the individual's experience could confer: "It [the world] only exists when emotion is fastened to it. This is artistic creation." And this world is one of unique particulars, each expressed in terms unique to it: "To each thing its special quality, its special value that will enable it to stand alone. When each poem has achieved its particular form, unlike any other, when it shall stand alone—then we will have achieved our language."[13]

Out of such individualism, and out of Williams's inconoclasm, came his ambiguous claim that the poet was a "revolutionist." On the one hand, as Williams said, the poet "is out for truth," clearing away the clichés from the language and the view; on the other hand, that truth may be reached only by getting outside the social order and staying there. A poet out for truth and outside the social order might change individual readers, if not the social order itself. "Get wise, that's all," is what Williams wanted to say to them.[14]

But get wise to what? Not, certainly, to any one creed of church or state. By expressing his own emotions, Williams believed he was expressing fundamental truths about the human condition, truths obscured by circumstance and history rather than constituted by them. In his 1917 essay, "America, Whitman, and the Art of Poetry," he implicitly identified the quest for such timeless truths with a democratic poetics:

> But back of these aristocratic forms lies the democratic groundwork of all forms, basic elements that can be comprehended and used with new force. Being far back in the psychic history of all races no flavor of any certain civilization clings to them, they remain and will remain forever universal, to be built with freely by him who can into whatever perfections he is conscious of.[15]

Before psychic history, all psyches were identical and equal. Somewhere in our bodies, no matter how scarred by our own histories, there remain those timeless universals that for Williams are our humanity. "My name's Brobitza!"

Thus poetry, by awakening the reader to fundamentals obscured beneath cliché, was for Williams by nature democratic. The poetry conventionally called political might indeed include the particulars of contemporary experience, but the presentation of them from a partisan point of view would be superficial, neglecting the deeper causes. "I am not one damned bit interested in socialism or anarchy," Williams wrote in 1919, "but I am interested and deeply interested in the brain that requires socialism and anarchy and brings it on, just as I am interested in morbidity. . . ." Williams's anti-ideological poetics of political poetry inspired in the 1910s one of his few political gestures with his poetry and one of his few poems on a political theme.[16]

The gesture took the form of two poems submitted to *The Masses*. Williams evidently read the poetry in *The Masses,* if not the rest of the magazine, and in "America, Whitman and the Art of Poetry" he caught the editors in a double bind caused by their commitment to both revolutionary socialism and art:

> [The] Masses cares little for poetry unless it has some beer stenches upon it—but it must not be beer stench. It must be beer stench—but not beer stench, it must be an odor of hops and malt and alcohol blended to please whom it is meant to please. Oh hell![17]

That is, the editors wanted poetry either written by members of the working class or which spoke for them, but wanted it to be poetry of the genteel sort as well. Williams resented the editors both for presuming to speak truly for and about workers—on his rounds, after all, *he* went "poking into negro houses / with their gloom and smell"—and for publishing some truly feeble *vers libre*. (Despite editor

Max Eastman's injunctions against such "lazy verse," *The Masses* published some in later years.) So Williams submitted two demonstration pieces, which were published in the January 1917 issue—two free-verse poems about the lower-class Americans he knew, stressing their characters rather than their emblematic power. "Sick African" runs in full:

> Wm. Yates, colored,
> Lies in bed reading
> The Bible—
> And recovering from
> A dose of epididymitis
> Contracted while Grace
> Was pregnant with
> The twelve day old
> Baby:
> There sits Grace, laughing,
> Too weak to stand. (CP, 59)

Unless the poem is a racist joke playing on the stereotype of the potent and rampant black male, which I very much doubt, it is about power relations within a marriage, and mostly about the folly of maintaining conventional moral proprieties when something funny happens to one's body. Mr. Yates's scrotum is as swollen and tender as his wife's birth organs, and he has to do the lying-in after the birth (bed rest is the prescribed treatment of epididymitis). He retreats into Bible reading, perhaps taking his affliction as a sign from the Lord about having more children. Grace, whose affliction is not a disease but a part of life, sees the joke in his being confined for a relatively minor ailment; after going through labor, she must find his solemn response to his illness a bit silly. Whether Grace is "too weak to stand" because of her recent delivery or from laughing, she for Williams is the stronger of the couple.

In "Sick African," then, Williams refuses to make commentary or allegory about the "woman question," race, or economic class. (If the Yateses lived in Rutherford, they were probably part of the small group of lower-middle-class blacks who found jobs as servants and menials around town. Williams's son William Eric used to play with some of their children.) Instead, he presents a concrete moment in a particular couple's life, the significance of which Williams refuses to comment on. It becomes a political poem, or rather a comment on political poetry, through Williams's gesture of submitting it to *The Masses*.

His second submission, "Chinese Nightingale," is less successful:

> Long before dawn your light
> Shone in the window, Sam Wu;
> You were at your trade. (CP, 59)

Williams clearly respects this hard-working Chinese immigrant, whose diligent "trade" is his song, but the slightness of the lyric begs some questions. Granted, not every worker in America was a "Caliban in the Coal Mines," as Louis Untermeyer put it in one of his poems, and Williams was right to remind readers and writers of *The Masses* of that, but to compare a man with a trade and skills and in a service industry to the proles of the mine or mill is to match apples with oranges. If Williams intended to comment on *The Masses*'s poetry about workers with this poem, his white-collar professionalism, with its assumptions about the mobility of the individual, obscured his vision.

That Williams had a bone to pick with the political poets of the mid-1910s is clearly implied in one of his most explicitly political poems, "Libertad! Igualidad! Fraternidad!" published in *Al Que Quiere!* in late 1917. In the poem, Williams parodies the easy identification with "the worker" of a poet such as Lola Ridge, and then proceeds to make an identification of his own, for him a deeper one than the accidents of wage and social class.

The poem opens with the speaker, whom we may safely presume is Williams, insulting an ash-man:

> You sullen pig of a man
> you force me into the mud
> with your stinking ash-cart!

The two men may share the same sidewalk, but they are not alike in social status; Williams acts as if he should have the sidewalk to himself. Yet Williams, to judge from his tone, is as sullen as the ash-man; the parody is of his own middle-class fastidiousness. Perhaps Williams recognizes his own sullenness, for he turns the confrontation into an assertion of solidarity, erasing whatever differences exist because of unequal economic or social status:

> Brother!
>   —if we were rich
> we'd stick our chests out
> and hold our heads high!
> It is dreams that have destroyed us.

Just what their dreams are about is unclear: American opportunity and wealth? Perhaps so, to judge from Williams's last exclamation. More likely, as the rest of the poem implies, they are simply whatever dreams they had when young that have gone unfulfilled.

Williams and his version of the Leech-Gatherer then "sit hunched together brooding / on our fate" in a tableau of loss. The destroyer, the poem makes clear, is time and change: "There is no more pride / in horses or in rein holding," laments the owner of a Model T. He then concludes this moment of recollection with a reaffirmation of his and the ash-man's equality:

> Well—
> all things turn bitter in the end
> whether you choose the right
> or the left way
> and—
> dreams are not a bad thing. (CP, 77)

Whichever of the two men is forced off the sidewalk, both will end up in the mud. Regardless of the class or status of the dreamers, their dreams are finally all the same.

Whether Williams's emphasis on the democratic universals of human experience can produce a poetry satisfactorily committed to transforming the particulars of history will be answered according to one's own politics and aesthetics. Viewing things as "standing alone" and people as self-reliant "dowers of power," Williams found allies in the pages of *The Egoist* rather than *The Masses,* a choice of bedfellows that may be hard to countenance. However, given the inadequacy of Village radicals' aesthetic responses—and some of their political responses as well—Williams's commitment to the individual he saw threatened by abstractions, whether from left or right, seems as laudable as it is questionable.

8

The Town and the "Townspeople" Poems

The next time William Carlos Williams crossed the Hudson in his poetry—in "January Morning," published in 1917—he presented only one glimpse of the city, from the distance of the river, as he dances "alone / at the prow of the ferry" (CP, 102). In effect, he remained safe in a grove—the ferry is even named Arden. We have seen how Williams's sense of the threats to the autonomy of the individual and the artist from the urban world, industrial politics, and politically radical poets fed his ambivalence about fulfilling his vow to be a poet of the people. His remaining in Rutherford both in life and in imagination was in some sense a retreat from the modernity he hoped to mirror to a more familiar social world, one in which he could encounter people as individuals who could be judged by moral character rather than as strangers or abstractions.

But if he did not confront modernity as directly as he had vowed, he did make his art intrinsic to his everyday life in a community that was in many ways as modern, if less urban, than Manhattan. Although Williams often wrote in the 1910s as if he were trying to prove something to Pound in London, to the New York sophisticates in the *Others* crowd, and to the radicals of the Village, he had another audience in mind: his townspeople in Rutherford, especially the respectable, white-collar Republicans who should have been able to appreciate both his art and their own vitality. Williams's persistent attempts to address his suburban audience, in fact, grant him qualifications as a poet of democracy which are the equal of those of Carl Sandburg or Edgar Lee Masters.

His townspeople still made him feel as if he lived as an artist *"sub terra,"* but now, armed with the iconoclastic attitudes of the Village and the "naked" expression of vitality in the speech and lives of lower-class town residents like Elia Brobitza, Williams set out both to defy and to conquer them, challenging their status-conscious stiffness and their indifference to the presence of an artist in their midst. In 1909, he had decorously alluded to them as entombed pharaohs, but now he was blunter: "If I talk to things / Do not flatter yourself / That I am mad / Rather realize yourself to be deaf," begins a poem he started in the fall of 1914 (CP,45).

As aberrant as the young doctor may have seemed, however, he shared many values with the "progressive," leading citizens of his town, and politically Williams remained much the same liberal at the Union Club who wrote *Sauerkraut to the Cultured* to mock their status-bred hypocrisies, *Betty Putnam* to challenge their greed-bred insensitivity to art and self-expression, and *A September Afternoon* to stir them into taking responsibility for their own civic affairs.

Before considering several of the "townspeople" poems in detail, we should consider the town for which Williams wrote them, so we can understand just how intrinsic the poems are to the community for whom he wrote them.

Rutherford continued its build-up into what its leaders hoped would be a haven for the right sort of white-collar professionals and entrepreneurs who took one of 63 passenger trains a day home from their jobs or businesses in Manhattan to rest in what they (and Williams in "The Wanderer") felt was a pastoral middle ground between the untamed Jersey hills and the city. As *Rutherford Illustrated* put it in 1892, "Rutherford is nearly all one vast park whose primitive charms are enhanced rather than marred by the macadamized roads and pretty cottages."

Of course, Rutherford had never quite been a small town with its life contained entirely within its boundaries. From its founding it had been tied by the umbilical Erie line to New York. But if proximity to the city made it easier for residents to view their community as comparatively pastoral, the progress-minded among them, even in 1892, foreshadowed the contradiction inherent in such rhetoric, as they, like *Rutherford Illustrated,* eyed Peter Kipp's farmland as "the highest, driest, and most desirable building property in the whole town."

Twenty years of improvements created conditions that further strained the credibility of the idyll. Rutherford did grow more slowly between 1910 and 1920 than in the previous decade, when its population had jumped by 60 percent. But the borough's 35 percent population increase in the 1910s, from 7,000 to 9,500, was hardly a lull in its growth; 101 building permits were issued in 1913.[1] By 1915, the previously cordial entry for Rutherford in the *Industrial Directory of New Jersey* told prospective manufacturers that "no desire is expressed" to invite them in. In fact, it said, "many residents prefer to emphasize its many attractions for purely residence purposes." But limiting industry to the four firms then in the borough was only a symptom of the sheer growth in residents (including many of the "not-quite-right" people filling up the West End of town) that, with or without industry and a laboring population threatened to mar its primitive charms.

Rutherford tried to control this growth and change in nature of its population and preserve its self-image as a pastoral community governed by small-community values and middle-class respectability and refinement. As its self-appointed poet, Williams urged the townspeople to make another kind of progress, casting off respectability for the sake of the intimacy greater than that of any small town. But he also contributed a good deal of time and energy to efforts to harness and humanize the growth, using his civic capacities to meliorate the effects of modernization.

By 1913, most of Rutherford's municipal plant had been built and the government's offices and functions established. Rather than pioneer and found, borough leaders administered, maintaining roads and shade trees and trying to expand such services as the police and fire department while balancing the budget. Town government was still largely free of federal or state involvement in its affairs (though Bergen County's services were expanding significantly), and citizen initiative still played an important role in civic affairs. Modernity came to Rutherford in forms other than government: the Criterion motion picture theater opened in 1912, and an "Isle of Safety" for pedestrians was set at a three-road intersection in 1915.[2]

Rutherford's middling style of urbanization is illustrated by details such as a proposed ordinance in 1915 to regulate the keeping of chickens, and by one of the more important local issues of the decade, the "playground movement." The very concept of a playground, a specialized space for children's fun, is completely urban, a world away from Kipp's woods and the meadowlands Williams roamed as a boy. In the summer of 1914, some townspeople started an association and set up playgrounds in two school yards, the popularity of which led the borough council to establish a playground commission empowered to purchase land for municipally owned playgrounds and parks.

But although the ad hoc association developed into a commission, at least some officials disliked extending the borough government's domain, and the association carried on a campaign of appeals for several years with constant resistance. In his annual message in January 1916, Mayor William C. Black flatly opposed playgrounds. To him, they were "a needless expense, as the population of Rutherford is not sufficiently dense to require these city ideas."[3]

Williams recurrently longed for a world without cities, but he could see the value of some "city ideas"—particularly those that would preserve health and aesthetics in a growing community. Back in 1910, he and his brother had made "many plans" to create "a beauty spot" on one plot close to town (which was made into a park); in July 1914, Dr. William C. Williams, school medical inspector, was present at the opening ceremonies of the two improvised playgrounds, and as a member of the association's executive committee he signed "A Playground Appeal" for contributions.[4]

When it came to other city ideas that concerned his own profession, Williams was a dedicated professional man. As the school medical inspector, he was an enforcer of the community's largely unwritten health standards. On his own he followed up cases he diagnosed in school, whether by sharing his knowledge of scarlet fever with parents, warning them to end their indifference or carelessness about their childrens' problems, or quietly passing word of their poverty to the ladies of the Town Improvement Association, who quietly solicited and administered private charity. When in late 1914 help presented itself in the form of a district nurse, who would be urged on the borough and paid for in part by the state, her appointment met a great deal of resistance from local residents, probably from those who, as Williams said, "are not paupers but are too poor to do what they would like but are too proud to seek aid."

This description comes from a long, early 1915 letter to the *Republican* with which Williams opened his campaign to get Rutherfordians used to the idea that the government, at least in this case, was intruding on them for their own good. He went on to say that although "the aid must seek [the needy] . . . it never fails to find them when the people are interested and work with modern methods." Those methods included Miss Lucey's making "thorough investigations" of potential charity cases, attending patients in their homes at lower rates than private nurses charged, and holding a clinic once a week with a volunteer doctor for those who could not afford a regular house call.

All of this meant admitting publicly that one was not one of "the better class of people," or, if one were of the better sort, acknowledging that Rutherford was not just "an ideal suburban place of residence" for "the New York business man of family," as the mayor put it in 1916. Williams acknowledged that "at the start, Miss Lucey's position will not be an enviable one . . . as it will be a new institution in Rutherford and as such it is bound to pass through the stage of misunderstanding and mistakes that all new things encounter," but he pressed for "official recognition" from the borough council—which had refused his request to use the council's large chambers as the clinic examination room—and invited surrounding towns to support the nurse, as they "ultimately" would have to anyway.[5]

A petition from the hospital committee of the Town Improvement Association helped the board of health to allow Miss Lucey to use the board office for her part-time work; presumably the townspeople got used to her. There were no further stories in the paper, so one cannot say for sure; perhaps she did not have enough time to calm down the generic citizen whom Williams quoted as threatening, "If she comes to my house, I'll kick her out." Williams himself had already spent five years representing community authority as school physician and dealing with the pride of the less well-off, and by now he was sure that he was intruding on them for their own good. Four years later, in 1919, he published a parable on "The Poor" that summed up his satisfaction with this city idea—and made it clear that the concrete nature of his "administration" of the body heavily qualified his abstract urban professionalism with the intimacy of the small community:

> By constantly tormenting them
> with reminders of the lice in
> their children's hair, the
> School Physician first

brought their hatred down on him.
But by this familiarity
they grew used to him, and so,
at last,
took him for their friend and adviser. (CP, 159)

"By all means use "The Poor," he told Harriet Monroe. "I like it among the [group of poems] first of all. Do not fail to use that poem."[6] She did, in the next issue.

A most eloquent sign of the tension caused by Rutherford's desire to have both progress and the pastoral also concerned the needs of children: it was the question of expanding the school system. Between 1902 and 1912, the school-age population had doubled, and even with the opening of two new elementary schools in 1913 (making five in all), every school building in the borough was badly overcrowded. Rutherford's voters were reluctant to spend money on still more schools—"there's lots of things we need before that," as one character in *The Build-Up* says—but they always eventually had to (BU, 90). In May 1915 they defeated a proposal to build an elementary school to replace the outdated Sylvan School, only to have Sylvan torn down and rebuilt in 1917.

Also defeated in 1915 was a plan for a $100,000 high school. But the 15-room Park School, a model building when it opened in 1901, could no longer hold all of the elementary school students funneling into it, even with every inch of basement and attic space converted for classroom use. Pressure to build a new high school was exerted for the rest of the decade, especially by the newer, younger, and rather less affluent residents of the West End section of town; the older, "better" sort of East End residents resisted these newcomers as firmly as the Dutch farmers had resisted them. Not until 1921 was the by-then annual proposition to build a high school approved, after the mayor was forced to insist at one stormy meeting, "I am not in favor of the east side or the west side."[7]

Williams, his older son coming of school age in 1919, took an active part in the fight. Making his weekly inspections of classroom conditions, he knew the overcrowding problem early on: "1st grade / Washington 46," he wrote in his pocket notebook in the fall of 1914; "31 in Wash. kindergarten / *too many*." One case of measles or scarlet fever in that packed kindergarten could infect the whole borough—so he had to "Report" young "Sheverman, 70 Morse Ave.," to the board of health (LRN, 11, 3, 4).

In neither of the notebooks he kept in 1910 and 1914 did Williams draw connections between overcrowding and the teaching of "obedience to convention" that he despised. Given his hatred for such teaching, though, feelings which accorded well with progressive education's rhetoric about educating the whole child and nurturing the capacity for self-expression, it would be surprising if he had not seen a relation. Whether he saw the problem in sectional, sociological, or strictly medical terms, when the town approved what he and many others felt were plans for a bad building in 1921, he put his by-then well-established standing as a concerned professional behind the push for a roomier, healthier site and building.

The school fight would be Williams's most dramatic effort in over a decade of local civic activity, most of which was rather more mundane than the speech-making of 1921. Besides continuing as school physician through 1925, he was appointed police surgeon in 1917, and encountered at the railroad the wild, drunken, farmer woman he remembered in *The Build-Up*. In July 1916 he was appointed to the Bergen County mosquito commission, which put to use the knowledge gained in the construction of the Panama Canal to drain lowlands and fought to overcome public resistance to its efforts to rid the county of "Jersey birds." During the war, he served in several public posts, and later, from 1920 to 1922, was physician for the county children's home.[8]

Little of this civil service had much to do with politics, neither to Dr. Williams nor to the Rutherford mind. As a professional man, Williams felt he was simply rendering disinterested service. Of course Williams took public stands to benefit "the people"—but he did so with both diffidence and impatience. He could not see why he had to take the time to convince people of what was to him the obvious truth about the high school. His fight for the town nurse yielded a wonderful letter to the *Republican* with a brisk, tart put-down of the borough council—the fight itself reveals how Williams was unwittingly participating in the very institutionalization of private or local concerns he would mock in *The Comic Life of Elia Brobitza* and oppose with the very structure of *In the American Grain* and his poetics of "contact."

But in the mid-1910s, even as state governments acquired the power to urge nurses on towns, as both federal and state governments came to shape individual life and opinion more extensively than ever before, Rutherford looked away from playgrounds, mosquito control, and other costs of the growth it boasted of; the borough categorized politics as another city idea, connoting the unseemly interests of a machine or a local faction. As Williams put it in his 1917 prose improvisation, "The Delicacies," politics meant the kind of intimate involvement with local concerns that he shares at a dinner party with a friend, the chairman of the borough streets committee, who "has spent the whole day studying automobile fire-engines in neighbouring towns in view of purchase" (CP, 156).[9]

But for Williams, beyond the health inspections, mosquito surveys, school board speeches, and after-dinner talk, there was the making of poems out of the details of life in Rutherford. To him, that was the most important civic function he performed, the means to fulfill his desire "to do some deed of great love for humanity," as he told his mother in 1916.[10] As a poet, and a most unconventional poet, his work was hardly as visible in Rutherford as that of his architect brother Edgar, who went from advocating borough beauty spots to designing the post office, the library, and the war memorial that replaced the "Isle of Safety." But as

Williams later told Edgar in "The Basis of Faith in Art," from the start he meant his writing to be as useful to others as his brother's blueprints: "it had to be useful. You ought to know. . . . You build houses, for people. Poems are the same" (SE, 177–78).

Williams's desire to address his poetry specifically to his townspeople seems to have been greatest just after publishing "The Wanderer" in March 1914. By the summer of 1915, he had joined a community of his own kind—the *Others* group of poets—and was so intent on claiming that their American work was equal to that of Pound and his new London circle that he insisted on his art's freedom from any specific locality. But he left his imitation of Gaudier-Brzeska's essay in *Blast*, "Vortex," unpublished (RI, 57–59). The idea that art transcended the mundane accidents always appealed to his deepest longings—"God knows I'm tired of it all," he said in December 1914—but he knew that mundane happenings such as the sight of the strong-haunched woman who sold him eggs were what he had to work with.[11] He published the best of his addresses to Rutherfordians, "Tract," in early 1916, and the last of them, "Riposte," in *Al Que Quiere!* in the fall of 1917. By then his sense of his audience had broadened, and he published his first critical essay on the relationship between "America, Whitman, and the Art of Poetry"; he also considered making the local details of the *Al Que Quiere!* poems into synecdoches of America by subtitling the volume "The Pleasures of Democracy."[12]

Three years before, he was searching for a way to represent "The Spectacle of Life" that was his community. In the fall of 1914, a trip through downtown with glimpses of people (and "an auto truck full of merchandise") inspired him to jot down details in the "Little Red Notebook" he used for school inspections, resolving to use the details to forge the uncreated conscience of his townspeople: "Take them to show it in this and that phase—explain how it comes about then bring in examples—H Jacks—Miss Herald—link them up according to true nature" (LRN, 26). Perhaps he could train his eyes to read the signs of class or social position, individual personality, intellect, and style: "The dress of the people on the streets so that one tells by it where each stands—and who they are—walking the street what they think of and do—how it shows differently in each what this means" (24)

No such telling detail, however, informs the vignettes of downtown life that he jotted down on the next pages: a girl, "rather well shaped neatly dressed," coming out of a bakery, a "colored man" pointing out someone to a "colored boy," the enigmatic looks on two faces (25)—all were guesses at "what they think of and do" rather than "where each stands" (24) in the local social scale (LRN, 24, 25). With few exceptions, Williams's presentations of particular townspeople in the 1910s foregrounded no explicit markers of economic or even social status; when he speaks of social distinctions, as when he juxtaposes the Episcopal minister with the "old man who goes about / gathering dog-lime" in "Pastoral" (CP, 42), he does

so to assert the equality of poor citizens' moral character against the pretensions of
Rutherford's upper crust to moral superiority. Not until his short stories of the
1930s did he question their right to the profits that led them to put on such airs.[13]

The "true nature" by which Williams linked up his townspeople, then, was
their individual moral character and their aesthetic concerns. He did not, as he did
for Paterson in "The Wanderer," identify "the thing" constituting the
community—"brutality"—in a single word. However, as he did with the strikers
in the "Abroad" section of "The Wanderer," he challenged Rutherfordians with a
call for moral regeneration, especially through their appreciation of art—and of
their very own artist.

Williams's first political poem, the "Hymn to Fraternal Love" in his 1909
Poems, made moral and cultural criticisms of the well-to-do, contrasting the
sincere, "naked" love of poor shepherds with the insincere "cloak" of flattery of a
dead pharaoh. In his "townspeople" poems, Williams repeated the same criticism
in similar terms, demanding that the pharaohs among them learn from the
shepherds to express themselves more fully, honestly, and nakedly, stripped of
pretensions to social superiority that denied the equality of human emotion and
experience. To express fully one's fundamental concerns to another, to listen to
another speak his or hers, implies that one belongs to a most ideal community of
equals. Although instead of shepherds and pharaohs Williams now used sparrows,
rumsoaks, and a young man with a bad heart, and although his voice now
completely threw over iambic piety for the rhythms of what Kitty Hoagland called
a "cultured New Jersey" tone,[14] Williams's moral vision was still at heart one of
fraternal love unqualified by irony. He had, of course, learned how, unlike
quarreling sparrows, Rutherford's citizens unfairly kept silent:

> . . . we who are wiser
> shut ourselves in
> on either hand
> and no one knows
> whether we think good
> or evil. (CP, 70–71)

But as a poet he had to open the windows. "We have looked out through glass /
long enough, my song," he had said in August of 1914 (CP, 36); in December, he
invited his townspeople to open their windows in the first of the poems addressed
to them: "Let us be conscious and talk of these things" (CP, 40).

"Tract" is the richest of the "townspeople" poems, in fact among the best of
all his early poems. His criticism of Rutherford values in "Tract" is more compre-
hensive than in the others. In "Apology," for instance, the reasons for his being
inspired differently by the faces of the town's "nonentities"—"colored women /
day workers"—and its "leading citizens" are coyly hinted at but barely developed
(CP, 70). As in "Pastoral" ("When I was younger"), where he stated his preference

for noting the colors of the "very poor" section of town to trying to "make something of myself," Williams asserts the "vast import" of his aesthetically dominated vision without articulating very specifically how it counts (CP, 64–65).

"Tract" (CP, 72–74) is more didactic than those two brief imagist lyrics, and therefore more articulate, but the poem works particularly well because of Williams's choice of image. The poem's subject is the proper conduct of a local funeral procession—a public ritual, that is, every gesture of which is by definition charged with social signification. Williams's often overriding concern with aesthetics becomes here a community concern as well. By questioning the aesthetics of the funeral procession, Williams challenges the basis of Rutherford's, or rather its "leading citizens'," moral judgment of the late, anonymous (and therefore generic) member of the community.

What makes Williams's moral criticisms convincing, however, is the voice in which he delivers them. Terse, impatient, spare of figures, it violates the proprieties of both conventional poetry and the poem's occasion. Read against these conventions, the poem embodies the virtues of honesty and open expression of emotion that it preaches. Williams had written nothing so clearly based on speech before and nothing that brought out so clearly the moral and social dimension of his new poetics.

For through this voice, as well as its instructions, Williams takes a stance within and against Rutherford's heirarchy of social status. He addresses not all of his townspeople, but only the borough's upper crust, the inhabitants of Ivison's mansion, the owners of stores on Park Avenue and the members of the Union and the Fortnightly Clubs. They were the ones who could afford to hire the upholstered wagon with glassed-in enclosure and silk-hatted driver. Williams, speaking for the rest of Rutherford, teaches them to make a work of art out of the procession that expresses their grief rather than their social station, and by doing so to admit that they are part of a community of equals.

Williams's "design" for a hearse appropriate to Rutherford emphasizes openness "to the weather as to grief," an intimacy with the physical fact of death and with the deceased, and the social intimacy of the small town that Rutherford already no longer was. The hearse should not be a painted coach but a wagon "weathered" like a farmer's, as if to commemorate Rutherford's rural origins (now sophisticated like the hearse-wagon's wheels, with gilt "applied fresh at small expense"). Or, Williams suggests, it should be even rougher, a "dray" bumping the coffin over the road. The coffin should not be protected from the elements by glass—Williams mocks the absurdity of doing so to remind the bereaved that they cannot shield themselves from their loss. To be sure that they feel it, he denies them even the aid that "little brass rollers" set in the hearse's floor would give in loading and unloading the coffin. It must lie, Williams says pregnantly, "by its own weight."

The next two parts of Williams's design stress the need to express one's sense of loss by expressing whom one has lost. No flowers, he warns, especially not the ostentation of glassed-in, protected, "hothouse flowers" such as orchids from Edward Roeher's greenhouse in East Rutherford—unless, Williams says, the deceased "had come to that," and the conventional symbol becomes that of the individual. The most appropriate memento, says Williams, is something the deceased is "prized and is known by"; to choose such an item is to respect him for who he was and what he felt for, and to respect the community's understanding of him.

Toward the driver of the hearse Williams has a particular animus, for he is the most visible image of the hypocrisy of an elaborate funeral. Seated high in the hearse in his silk hat, he in effect presides over the procession (no minister is referred to in the poem). Yet the driver has no personal relation to the deceased and no right to his position; he presides only because he has been hired to play the role (worse still, his authority is doubly sham, borrowed from the undertaker whose "understrapper" he is). He is a representative of the kind of human relationships being created by modernization, and Williams will have no market-generated alienation in this ritual of small-town friendship. The driver must walk "low and inconspicuous"; for him to assume his place on the wagon would be "unceremonious."

However concealed the mourners' grief is, in the procession they are exposed to the gaze and judgment of the rest of the community, which, Williams's commentary should remind them, watches as they go by. The rest of the townspeople, Williams emphasizes, are not fooled by trappings that divert one's attention from grief to wealth and power. In the closing lines of the poem, Williams identifies himself with those less well-off in Rutherford (though frankly qualifying his identification with a "perhaps"), and expresses a populist's faith that the common people of the community have the "ground sense necessary" that the better-off have tried to deny:

> Or so you think you can shut grief in?
> What—from us? We who have perhaps
> nothing to lose? Share with us
> share with us—it will be money
> in your pockets.

Here Williams articulated the social criticism implicit in his poetics that he left unelaborated in many of his 1910s poems. Punning on financial terms, he makes political comment on his community. As in *Sauerkraut to the Cultured,* he identifies certain aesthetic values with a social class—the "progressive" business-men of Rutherford—and then challenges their validity on moral grounds.

He and his less well-off townspeople have comparatively few material riches, but as is implied by the idiom, "nothing to lose," with its connotations of being willing to risk one's self, they have ample reserves of emotion and the capacity to respond to another's grief. If the mourners invest, not their cash in displays to the community, but their sorrow, they will get the kind of return, their fellows' sympathy, that will console them more than a false sense of power over others in town.

To share their grief would mean acknowledging their common humanity with the rest of town, a kind of democratic understanding that Williams always insisted on. The faint taunt in Williams's tone at the close here reminds the well-to-do mourners that in "the ground sense" they are only equal to those who watch them. Opposing true feeling to business values, Williams puts them in a double bind: they can strip their ceremony of pretensions or not, but if they do not, the commoners have seen through them anyway. To drive home the fact that the mourners are trapped, Williams plays on their faith in the financial: if they simplify the procession, they will keep the "money in their pockets" they would have spent; they also will keep the goodwill of others in town, upon whom, perhaps, their business depends.

Williams's poem would be only another of the many indictments made by artists in the 1910s of the wealthy's "refined insulation," as Max Eastman put it, "from real contacts with the matter of life"[15] were it not for its formal inventiveness and, most important, Williams's willingness to acknowledge the wealthy as members of his community. Obviously, few of Rutherford's well-to-do were quite as remote as those living in mansions on Park Avenue; moreover, Williams was in Rutherford and knew them. Unlike the members of the hermetic artists' community of Greenwich Village, or anywhere else in the anonymous city, Williams could not simply rule them out of his town. He had "real contacts" with them.

Furthermore, if Williams was speaking for the commoners of Rutherford in "Tract," he was speaking *to* those from whom he had the best hope of being recognized as an artist. He could pun about money on behalf of his patients, his fishman, and Elia Brobitza, but only the "leading citizens" would get the joke. His deep-seated need to be recognized by them, born out of his young faith in the "gentlemanly," cultured status of art and his self-consciousness about being the son of foreigners, led Williams to question ambivalently the basis on which they assumed the right to lead. The intelligence he valued so highly, upon which depended his being recognized as a poet as well as the solution of the world's problems, was to be found in the better-off, even though the virtues he exhorted them to live by, the "ground sense necessary," resided in the poor. This divorce embodied in the structure of "Tract" appears over and over in his social commentary.

Given this reservation about Williams's political terms, "Tract" succeeds, I think, as a political poem. Certainly it is a more effective argument that the poet plays an important role in shaping the values of his community than the vows and rhetoric of "The Wanderer." Rather than discussing his role, Williams performs it. Moreover, he does not just legislate aesthetic values, he shows that they are moral and social values.

Nearly all of the other poems he addressed specifically to his townspeople make the same case for the poet as "Tract": Rutherford should recognize the moral function that poetry performs for them and give Williams the poet his place as Atlas in the community. Of this group, however, only "Apology," "Pastoral" ("The little sparrows"), and "Pastoral" ("When I was younger") attack conventional standards of status in the name of moral character and measure such character by the beauty created by vitality and experience. Two of them, "Invitation" and "Riposte" (CP, 95–96), concern themselves with the basis of the Rutherford community. "Invitation" asks why "we" live in Rutherford and not New York, and "Riposte" implies that the answer ought to be for love. All of these assert or self-reflexively enact the main theme of the other four "townspeople" poems, "Gulls," "Naked" (54), "Epigramme" and "Stillness" (52): the need of the community for Williams the poet.[16]

All of these poems play some kind of joke on those townspeople to demonstrate the insufficiency of their perception (and their need of the poet's keener eye) and fool them into accepting the validity of the poet's vision even as they ignore or condemn it. Four of the poems ("Invitation," "Apology," and the two "Pastorals") close with assertions of meaningfulness or importance, the precise nature of which Williams rather coyly refuses to explain. In "Invitation," for example, he asks the townspeople why "we do not all leave this place" for the "smoke-grey towers" of the city. Instead of answering for them, he asks them to share what must be, he says, "a noteworthy wisdom": "Let us be conscious and talk of these things."

The joke of "Invitation" is that Williams is the one townsman dissatisfied enough to be "conscious" of the attractions of the city, one of which is the existence there of a community that values poetry. "Do you think I like to practice medicine here in Rutherford," he had asked Viola Baxter Jordan in June of 1914, six months before he published "Invitation," "and see others skipping over the face of the globe from the two pole[s] to London, New York, Hoboken + Pekin?"[17] By asking Rutherfordians to share their wisdom, Williams hopes to stir them into questioning their values; at the least, by talking about "these things" they will make a place for the poet in the community, debating his question, "consciously" and openly expressing what they feel.

In "Gulls," as in "Naked" and "Riposte," Williams's strategy is not so much to withhold his meaning as to surprise his townspeople into accepting it. By "gulling" them with the image of the three gulls, Williams shows them that their religious dogmatism has made them intolerant of "strange birds" such as Unitarians and poets and has so rigidified their habits of mind that they are unable to discover the very truth they think they already know.

Williams begins "Gulls" (CP, 67–68) by warning his townspeople that despite the substantial temptation to leave Rutherford for "the great world," he stays. Whether they (or he) like it or not, he is their "singer." The first thing he sings to them is another of his riddles:

> . . . you have seen the strange birds,
> have you not, that sometimes
> rest upon our river in winter?
> Let them cause you to think well then of the storms
> that drive many to shelter. These things
> do not happen without reason.

One reason is given by Williams, but in the form of a second riddle about seeing an eagle and three gulls in the sky over one of Rutherford's "principal churches" (the Episcopal church across the street from his parents' home on West Passaic Avenue) on Easter Sunday.[18] Williams ecstatically describes his sighting of the birds and then swiftly turns to comment, "Oh I know you have your own hymns." Although the townspeople's hymns are not sung to this world, as Williams's hymn to the birds is, he can respect the impulse that makes his fellows sing:

> and because I knew they invoked some great protector
> I could not be angry with you, no matter
> how much they outraged true music—

If the townspeople could quell their feeling that Williams's poetry outrages "true music," perhaps they would respect the impulse behind his invocation to eagles and gulls. They might even come to wonder at the birds themselves, and at the poet—that is, if they catch the analogy between hymn writers, poets, and the "strange birds" seeking shelter from the storm. All hope for protection; all are strange birds. The townspeople's tolerance, then, will lead them to see the nature they miss while sitting in church and hear the "true music" of Williams's poetry. Perhaps, then, they will not provoke him into calling them "deaf" for thinking him "mad."

Williams is more gracious in "Gulls" than in "Pastoral 2": "You see, it is not necessary for us to leap at each other." But just as the conflict between the tolerant poet and his now-less-intolerant townspeople seems to be resolved, Williams, still gracious, starts it up again:

> You see, it is not necessary for us to leap at each other,
> and, as I told you, in the end
> the gulls moved seaward very quietly.

These things, the townspeople know by now, do not happen without reason. But the reason? After all this, no certain meaning can be assigned to the three gulls.

Are they the birds that in the opening of the poem call Williams away from Rutherford, or some of the strange birds that seek shelter? If the former, we should note they leave quietly, perhaps signifying that Williams is indeed resolved to stay; if the latter, then we have to note that they need no shelter on a fine spring day. Perhaps their quiet departure, not outraging the churchgoers' hymns with their high cries, implies nature's respect for the invocations to protectors other than herself. Perhaps, after all, Williams was less concerned with its specific meaning than with its satisfying tone of closure.

The action does end and the quarrel calms, but whatever it may mean, the final image does something unsettling. Williams tells the townspeople about seeing the gulls, but immediately shifts their attention away from the birds and their meaning to discuss hymns and the relationship between poet and townspeople. At the close, he suddenly returns to the gulls as if they were significant (as his saying "as I told you" emphasizes). But the townspeople did not notice them much, being too distracted by Williams's shift of focus. The moral: they still need Williams to point out to them the things they miss while in church and to show what the things signify.

Rhetorical strategies such as the one Williams uses at the close of "Gulls" occur in nearly all of the "townspeople" poems and contribute to what readers from out of town may feel is a coyness that only adds to the poems' slightness. I have gone into them at such length in a discussion of Williams's political poetry and poetics because they reveal to me rather more desperation than coyness—a sign of how seriously Williams intended these brief lyrics. Throughout the 1910s, Williams sought not merely a voice in which to speak of the dignity of common things and people, of the sheer wonder, exclamation points and all, of seeing as Adam saw. He was trying to find a voice that a specific audience, the leading citizens of his hometown, would acknowledge. That he resorted to riddles in "Gulls" is a sign of how difficult it was to tell the truth "nakedly" to a group of the unconverted, or, at best, offended; that he dropped all such convolutions and spoke so directly in "Tract" was small consolation. Soon after he found that voice, Rutherford, and the rest of America, were captivated by voices urging them to prepare for war.

9

Postwar Williams

In the first fall of World War I, William Carlos Williams wrote a poem called "Peace." In it he dedicated himself to fight—but only in "another greater" war for personal freedom. To substitute "war with mud" for "war with fire," he gamely asserted, would be "the vilest deception." True peace, he added, was equally rigorous, so much so that it "requires genius to be preached" (CP, 41–42). But the world made just such debasing substitutions. By the time Congress was debating Wilson's kind of peace, Williams, like so many Progressive-era artists and intellectuals, had lost his kind of war.

The idealist in him embraced the idea of America's making the world safe for democracy, but the atavism of war patriots and postwar "hundred-per-centers," and the machinations of politicians, diplomats, and employers made the gap between the interests of a wartime people and the moral terms used to justify them too wide for him to talk anymore about "our wonderful future." He willingly served government institutions that regimented America into what was called "war socialism," but after the war he celebrated the individualism of Elia Brobitza, John Coffey, Daniel Boone, and Aaron Burr, and spoke, more and more shrilly, of the loss of individual liberties.

The freedom that in "Peace" he said he would fight for was the individual's freedom to work at what satisfied him the most—for Williams, of course, the freedom to be an artist. For the poet who had hoped to waken its citizens to the "myriad cinquefoil" within their souls, the America that castrated Wobblies and voted down the League of Nations was an ugly foe. Nevertheless, his greatest enemy was his own cynicism. War and postwar society tried Williams's faith both in America and in poetry's power to change it. In spite of his own despair, however, he clung to the possibility of making art out of, and for, an America that had become "a bastard country where decomposition is the prevalent spectacle."[1]

As was the case for most Americans, at first the war touched Williams only in the form of "a few futile arguments" about it on a vacation. However, he despised the German militarism he had encountered in Leipzig in 1909; his sympathies were, he said later, "pro-French if not pro-British" (A, 154). Writing to his publisher Edmund Brown a few weeks after America finally openly declared war, he apologized for a tirade in a previous letter, blaming it in part on his anti-German feelings: "I was so god damned sick + tired of a pro-German atmosphere—I was so convinced of the inevitability of a triumph of the German idea of brute force in the world . . . that I wrote that blasting letter."[2]

Rutherford boasted a propreparedness newspaper, a chapter of the National Security League, a Home Guard that drilled with a borough-purchased machine gun, and few German-American residents. Williams encountered pro-German sentiment mainly in the home of his Bavarian father-in-law, who was ostracized in 1916 for refusing to make unanimous a resolution of the Fortnightly Club urging Wilson to aid Britain; soon after, Paul Herman moved out of town in disgust (A, 154–56). Williams himself became the subject of innuendo: the week after he apologized to Brown for sounding off against the Germans, he made a public denial in the *Republican* of rumors (spread, he said later, by another doctor) that he was pro-Kaiser: "I am quite passionately opposed," he said, "to the undemocratic principles which seem to underlie German force"—though some of his best friends, he added, were German.[3]

Williams refrained from volunteering only because his father was terminally ill (A, 159); he would always wish, his son Paul recalls, that he had served overseas. At home, though, he conscientiously did his part. Besides examining draftees, he got as involved in civic affairs as he ever would. In addition to continuing as the school medical inspector and a member of the county mosquito commission, in January 1918 he became president of the borough board of health. In August he became a government bureaucrat: he was appointed head of the local office of the Food Administration, enforcing the new federal agency's regulations and relieving women volunteers of the task of keeping track of every pound of sugar and flour sold in Rutherford. In October, something like war—the influenza epidemic—hit the northeast United States, and Williams had to issue and enforce the board of health's strict quarantine regulations while making up to 60 house calls a day. His duty on the home front ended in May 1920, when he served on the emergency committee for Rutherford's Memorial Day services, which culminated in the dedication of the borough war monument that his brother Edgar designed.[4]

The armistice brought the war home to America on several fronts. Politically, the war-induced and propaganda-enforced consensus on American ideals and duties vanished. Woodrow Wilson and Henry Cabot Lodge and each man's followers fought an often ad hominem battle over the peace treaty and the League of Nations. The tone was exceptionally sour; just before the 1920 presidential elections, the *Republican* predicted that the country would "cure its universal present sickness" by voting against the "idealism and clap-trap of the school master and the demagogues." When Warren G. Harding beat James M. Cox, the *Republican* smugly headlined the election returns, "Wilson, That's All." Williams put a chip on his shoulder about Wilson's aura of rectitude, referring to him shortly after he sailed for the peace conference as the "Sedately-Impetuous"; however, Williams soon held the view that J.M. Keynes took in *The Economic Consequences of the Peace* of Wilson as a New World *naif* outfoxed by David Lloyd George and Georges Clemenceau.[5]

The country's "sickness" arose in no small part from economic ills. In 1919 alone, over four million workers took up the weapon they had agreed to lay down in wartime and struck for a chance to catch up with the "High Cost of Living," as the war-induced inflation was called. Middle-class people complained that only "salaried" people had not received pay increases, and they snarled at the greed of both "profiteers" and unions. One *Republican* columnist groused in May 1920, "It would seem that the actual President of the United States for some months past, and right now, is the Honorable Samuel Gompers." Rutherford's mayor Fred Sheaf, a friend of Williams's, organized crews of citizens to deliver milk and run commuter trains during strikes in 1920. The borough council accused landlords of being "rent profiteers," and the Town Improvement Association promoted vegetable gardening on vacant lots as a way to cut out one of the middlemen. Williams, whose Polytopic Club held an evening on the high cost of living in 1919, used his stature as ex officio food administrator to urge the borough council to buy up surplus sugar offered by the federal government.[6]

"World Not Yet Normal in 1920" was the headline on the Rutherford *Republican*'s chronicle of that year's events; it was an understatement. The energy and idealism frustrated by the war's sudden end and the many relatively sordid problems of the peace were projected on to a bogey, and chasing the bogey turned the United States into the beast it feared. Lenin's "Letter to American Workingmen," smuggled into the country (reportedly by Carl Sandburg) and published in *The Liberator* in 1919, called on them to make the Bolsheviks' revolution international; two tiny American Communist parties were formed in the fall of 1919. The fear of Bolshevism was exacerbated by the strikes (among them an ominous I.W.W.-led general strike in Seattle and the Coolidge-making strike "against the public safety" by the Boston police), by employers who saw the chance to break the newly recognized unions, by a series of "anarchist" bombings, and by Attorney General A. Mitchell Palmer's political ambitions. From this fuel burst the "Red Scare" in the fall of 1919.[7]

Just as Williams had kept his distance from political radicals before the war, so now he did not protest this government-approved violation of civil rights (and more) by ex-servicemen, American Legionnaires, the New York State Senate, and the attorney general. However, the Red Scare resonates throughout *In the American Grain,* particularly in its verbatim chapter from Cotton Mather on the Salem witchcraft trials. In January 1921 Williams told Harriet Monroe that Eugene V. Debs, who had just polled a million votes for president while serving a jail term for obstruction of the draft, "was the only hero," although the "A-a-a-a-a-men etc."

Williams added suggests that he was mocking the way Debs was being canonized.[8] But Williams was probably mocking himself as well; in 1939, telling the *Partisan Review* that a writer in wartime must not become "a liar for propaganda's sake," he toasted Debs's memory (Int, 80).

Nor did he ever comment directly on the howl for "one hundred per cent Americanism" that he heard in his local paper long after the immigration restrictions of 1921. He did attack xenophobia obliquely in *In the American Grain* by reproducing Benjamin Franklin's letter, "Information to Those Who Would Remove to America." By placing it in the context of the 1920s, particularly with Franklin's prophecy of industrialization's stimulation of immigration, Williams made every line of it ring hollow with irony. As for Russia, in 1922, after American troops sent in to support the White Army had been withdrawn and the Red Scare had died down, Williams praised a company of Russian dancers appearing in New York for translating into art the beauty of the peasant, which in life was made "mercenary to the landlord / who kills the splendour of national character / by his demands for rent" (CP, 247–48). For the rest of his life Williams wished the Russian *people* well in achieving what he imagined was a grassroots, democratic revolution—but he never praised the Bolsheviks.

The general distemper of the moment gave Williams a case of what Robert McAlmon called "afterwar" or "post-war despairing."[9] As Williams told John Thirlwall in 1954,

> I lost faith in what can happen in the world—no specific betrayal. It was pretty obvious that the world wasn't going to right itself after World War I. We kept hoping that something would happen. It is the idealist who is finally thrown for a loss. I was thoroughly disillusioned. I was full of ideals, whatever they are. (Int, 78)

Williams's political ideals, of course, were determined by one ideal: a world in which art could flourish. He had seen signs of this world's arrival in the prewar talk of world peace, the prosperity and cultural maturity implied by the New York skyline, the "can-do" aura given off by Progressive reform, and his discovery of the *Others* group. But the war and the war's aftermath cancelled that millenial sense. As Williams recalled, the daily prose improvisations of 1917 that became *Kora in Hell* were his way of going underground:

> Damn it, the freshness, the newness of a springtime which I had sensed . . . a reawakening of letters, all that delight which in making a world to match the supremacies of the past could mean was being blotted out by the war. The stupidity, the calculated viciousness of a money-grubbing society such as I knew and violently wrote against; everything I wanted to see live and thrive was being murdered in the name of church and state. (A, 158)[10]

Nowhere in *Kora* does Williams explicitly protest the war or its effects on American life or "church and state"; perhaps he regarded the violence that the improvisations' language commits on ordinary perception as such a protest. Just as his retreat into Santiago Grove in "The Wanderer" rendered ambiguous his professions of desire to affect the world, so here his withdrawal from the hell of the United States in 1917 to the Hades of language's potentialities make the work seem an act of private "relief"—"to keep myself from planning and thinking at all" (A, 158) and protect his own Kora, his imagination.

There are suggestions that he blamed the war on the "money-grubbing" of "business civilization." He owned a copy of John Kenneth Turner's *Shall It Be Again?*, which argued that a "financial oligarchy" started the war for profit and that Wilson's rhetoric fooled the American people into believing that they, and not a few men on Wall Street, had the say about fighting. Williams also printed Ezra Pound's first notice of Clifford H. Douglas's *Credit Power and Democracy*, in which Pound announced that "In a world governed by imbeciles and knaves, there remain two classes of people responsible: the financial powers and those who can think with some clarity." Williams said little in the 1920s about one of these classes, but quite a lot about the other, as he tried to establish the poet's credentials as the man of "clarity."[11]

In Williams's most detailed comments on the war, in "Four Foreigners" and "More Swill" of 1919 and "Glorious Weather" of 1923, his desire to assert the poet's qualifications as clarifier overwhelmed his views on the subject. In "Four Foreigners," he unfavorably reviewed war poems by D.H. Lawrence and Richard Aldington that appeared in the July 1919 issue of *Poetry*: "No poet was able to exist during and in the war as far as I have been able to find out." Neither Lawrence nor Aldington—the former writing as a pacifist during the war, the latter writing in the trenches—"mounted to the impossible height of housing a war in their hearts equal to the hellish filthiness of a war of tedium and ennui such as we knew." The failure of the two Britons, Williams acknowledged, raised the disturbing possibility that poetry itself failed: "If no human mechanism is strong enough . . . then indeed we had better know it [at] once in all its terrible significance and kill ourselves or murder the cannon makers."[12]

The demands Williams made upon war poets are appropriate enough, and after the next war, he himself tried to meet them, seeking words for "the Jew in the pit" and the atom bomb. However, he went on in "Four Foreigners" to praise James Joyce and Dorothy Richardson for their "war" to invent a new form for the novel. In "More Swill," published in the October 1919 *Little Review*, Williams used the idea that non-combatants could not comprehend soldiers' combat experience to draw an analogy between soliders and avant-garde artists: neither group could be addressed in the old terms (RI, 60–61). The analogy only diminishes the moral force of his criticism. Apparently his need for self-justification overrode his concern with war poetry and war. He, too, longed for a "normalcy" in which the avant-garde could function as before.

Throughout the 1920s, Williams tried to use an ostensibly neutral discourse both to place the artist above politics and to claim some special insight and power for him. In his 1923 essay, "Glorious Weather," he condemned war for its "stupidities" and argued that "no amount of . . . packing it with new meanings will save it," but his calculus of efficiency undercuts his sardonic tone: when the percentage of "stupidities" such as unemployment or maiming, which act as "a drain upon [war's] resources and a deterrent to its freedom of action," becomes "sufficiently high, war has become—obsolete, until new MEANS or a better use of MATERIALS has been discovered."[13] He was more direct about war when he was less articulate; "It Is a Living Coral," published in 1924, ends its parodic catalogue of the "official" American art hanging in the Capitol with "The Battle of Lake Erie": "Perry / in a rowboat on Lake / Erie / changing ships the / dead / among the wreckage / sickly green" (CP, 258).

The possibility of making "a world to match the supremacies of the past" had hardly been Williams's alone. However, the artistic community in Greenwich Village lost a good deal of its prewar missionary fervor and optimism, thanks to the chills of the war and the Red Scare, the inevitable aging of the subculture into a style for consumption by the larger "uptown" culture, the arrival on the scene of a demi-generation of new bohemians, and the eventual expatriation of old and young.

All of this also altered the artists' relations with political radicals—whose own community was not just altered, but shattered by events abroad and arrests at home—and the artists' sense of the social and political function of their work. They found that their prewar assumptions—especially about a congruence of interests between radicals and bohemians, and the corollary that their new art was both sign and agent of some sort of new American society—had been shown up as callow by the successes of both Bolshevik dogma and American capital. Shorn of their optimism and sense of belonging to a larger, revolutionary movement, the New York artists as a group did not, however, give up the old terms of their commitment but tried to find ways to sustain them.

At first Williams kept up his prewar optimism. "We are only beginning," he wrote Harriet Monroe in April 1919; "I feel that barring death, I shall see some work done in the next five years that will be unrivalled anywhere at any time. We are at the opening of a golden age of poetry HERE."[14] However, by the early 1920s he was deprecating such expectations, as if guarding himself against another defeat.

His hopes were diminished especially by the breakdown of the artistic community he relied on for support. The would-be archindividualist, who conceived of that community as a group of simple, separate persons, "each thinking his own thoughts, driving his own designs toward his self's objectives" (A, 138), needed to feel teamed up with others; if he had to go underground, then he wanted to share the bunker. But with whom?

The Stieglitz circle, with its commitments to both European experimentation and American expression, had been in centrifugal motion since the Armory Show, as the photographer withdrew from the growing public for modern art and his disciples left to start galleries and magazines of their own. He closed 291 in June 1917 and had no gallery until he opened An American Place in 1925. Williams got to know him around 1917, but they remained distant. Williams's oldest painter friend, Charles Demuth, was having difficulties with his diabetes and was away from New York much of the time from 1917 on, either at his mother's in Lancaster, Pennsylvania or at a clinic in Morristown, New Jersey.[15]

The mind-play of the dadaists who gathered from afternoon through the night at Walter Arensberg's peaked in 1917—the year of *The Blind Man* and *Rongwrong,* Arthur Cravan's drunken, striptease "lecture" at the Independents Exhibition, and the rejection of the urinal *Fountain* by "R. Mutt" (Marcel Duchamp). Williams's work from *Kora in Hell* on was strongly influenced by New York dada. Unlike the Berlin and Zurich versions, though, New York's dada was far more verbal than political, focused more on subverting the institution of Art than that of the bourgeois State.

At Arensberg's, Williams watched presiding spirit Marcel Duchamp work one paradox after another into his *Large Glass*; the Frenchman's project of "meta-irony," as Octavio Paz calls it, frightened Williams as much as it freed him. Duchamp's ruthlessly intellectual approach yielded ruthlessly undecidable propositions, and by temperament Williams wished to decide and affirm. He could regard one of Duchamp's central questions—"Can one make works which are not works of 'art'?"—as a challenge to reduce Poetry to poems, but he would not go as far as Duchamp to assert that to question the former inevitably questioned the latter.[16]

Williams also felt nonplussed and patronized by Arensberg's coterie, and seems not to have visited as often after the war as before. The fact that Williams did not meet Charles Sheeler, an Arensberg regular in 1917 and 1918, until 1923, suggests how much distance he kept. But although Williams later made out his resentment to be personal (A, 137), one suspects that it was as much the group's contempt for "art" as their condescension to an American Adam that bothered him.

Williams's reply to them came after most of the French painters had left New York and the Arensbergs had abruptly moved to Los Angeles, even after Duchamp made his most radical gesture, completing-by-abandoning his *Large Glass* in 1923 and giving up art, reportedly, for chess. Williams, about to publish his prophecy of the death of Art and the rebirth of poems, replied to "Marcel's intelligent and devastating silence" with an energetic "if you do, you do / if you don't, you don't / and that's all there is to it."[17]

By 1922, when the new little magazines *Broom* and *Secession* began a two-year-long quarrel about dada's usefulness to American artists, Williams was already tired of the argument. More congenial to Williams than dadaists of any nation was Marsden Hartley, with whom he became close friends during the postwar period. The two shared an interest in egoism, and Hartley, too, saw dada through American eyes, calling it "the newest and most admirable reclaimer of art in that it offers at last a release for the expression of natural sensibilities." Williams, saying in *Spring and All* that the effect of the imagination is "to free the world of fact from the impositions of 'art,'" told his readers to "see Hartley's last chapter" (I, 150).

The two men were allies especially in emphasizing the creation of an indigenous American art, starting a quarrel in the summer of 1919 with the editors of *The Little Review* over the merits of Maine poet Wallace Gould. Hartley also introduced Williams to the young midwesterner, Robert McAlmon, with whom Williams would publish *Contact* and articulate his notions of American art. But Williams and Hartley could not settle on the terms of their intimacy, and the two cooled to each other in the summer of 1920 when Hartley detected glibness in Williams's gossip.[18]

The painters whose work so puzzled and excited Williams were finally less important to him than writers and places in which writing could be stimulated and published. But the poets with whom he had collaborated were failing and scattering. *Others* died from bickering and lack of funds with the July 1919 issue, in which Williams, in "Belly Music," pronounced a dyspeptic coroner's verdict on the circle of writers—Kreymborg, Maxwell Bodenheim, Arensberg, Stevens, and himself—that it had brought together: like all avant-gardes, they, their work, and their magazine had calcified into rituals of middle age.

None of the magazines that survived or started after the war satisfied the criteria Williams had developed when working on *Others*: openness to formally innovative work from anywhere for use by Americans, and judgment of work by artists themselves or editors sympathetic to innovation and literary quality.

The Little Review came closest. Although it presented itself as "a magazine of Art and Revolution," its publisher, the remarkable Margaret Anderson, promptly added, "If you ask me which it believes in most I shall have to say—Art. Because there is no real revolution unless it is born of the same spirit which produces real art." She stayed faithful to "the beautiful and simple tenets . . . of anarchism" until they became "quite uninteresting," and then converted to an egoist view of art as absolute self-expression. "Only sensibility matters," she pronounced, and made sure that her magazine lived up to its motto, "MAKING NO COMPROMISE WITH THE PUBLIC TASTE." Emma Goldman noted drily that her comrade's magazine "lacked clarity in social questions"—Anderson's protest of the Mooney bombing arrest began, "I really must say what I think about this ridiculous bomb business"—but Goldman admired her as a "strongly individualized" rebel "for [her] own liberation." Anderson and editor Jane Heap published whatever they (and foreign editor Pound) felt expressed individual "sensibility." They printed work by every major English and American modernist, including *Ulysses* and Wyndham Lewis's story, "Cantleman's Spring Mate," each of which garnered a prosecution for obscenity.[19]

Williams said in 1919 that he, like Anderson, was "not one damned bit interested in socialism or anarchy" compared to art. He also respected Anderson's editing *The Little Review* with personal taste alone (even though she had, he said, "a complete lack of judgment in literary matters"); in it he published much of *Kora in Hell* and his important self-portrait, "Three Professional Studies." And in Anderson and Heap's office he encountered a sculpture with chicken heads by the Baroness Elsa Freytag von Loringhoven, which led to his encounter with the walking dada woman he called "America personified in the filth of its own imagination."[20]

Although Anderson's airiness sometimes infuriated him, Williams got along very well with her and Jane Heap and praised them twice in their own pages, once in 1919 for respecting artists' freedom and consequently being "far more important than the United States senate," and again in 1922 for their special issue on Francis Picabia, which proved them to be "American": "It is the only important reaction to the American environment."[21]

Besides *The Little Review*, however, few of the literary magazines started after the war pleased Williams. He took no interest in *The Liberator*, the successor to *The Masses*; he despised associate editor Floyd Dell, though because Dell disliked Kenneth Burke and advocated psychoanalysis and not for Dell's still-socialist politics. When former *Liberator* editor Mike Gold and others started *The New Masses* in 1926, Williams contributed to the first issue a short story, "The Five Dollar Guy," which was the same sort of demonstration to radicals of how to write about America as the poems he had published in *The Masses* in 1917. But he knew none of the people who worked on the new magazine.[22]

When Scofield Thayer took over *The Dial* in 1919, he shifted its emphasis from John Dewey's and Thorstein Veblen's "reconstruction program" for American society to literary concerns. Despite the change, which boded well for poets like Marianne Moore (who became an editor) and a new star, e.e. cummings, Williams disliked the tenor of discussion in the magazine, and the fact that discussion took up space that could have been used for poems. He later recalled that when *The Dial* "set up shop . . . as usual the intellectuals began to intrude upon the terrain opened by the lunatic fringe of three years before" (A, 171). (Certainly the fact that *The Dial* published *The Waste Land* in 1923 had much to do with this judgment.) He did become close friends with one of those "intellectuals," Kenneth Burke, and relished the opportunity to discuss art with him, but when it came to writing he constantly admonished Burke not to let "cerebral brick-brack"—morals, ideas, theories—take priority over the words and form of his fiction.[23]

And despite his charge that Dewey's program was deeply flawed because it neglected "the interdependence of thought and art," Williams did profit from some of the cerebrations in *The Dial*. Dewey's essay, "Americanism and Localism," in the June 1920 issue, was crucial to Williams's notion of "contact" and its political dimension. While he named none of Veblen's *Dial* essays (and probably did not read *The Theory of the Leisure Class* until the 1930s), Williams echoed one Veblenesque editorial of 1919, "The High Cost of Waste," in *The Great American Novel*. The editorial dismissed the postwar hue and cry against profiteers to attack the "waste, social and economic" caused by running a society according to the profit motive rather than "to satisfy social needs."[24] In his novel, Williams foregrounds the face of "the lady of my dreams" against "the complicated affairs of the town" which "twitter toward the open sewer in the meadows by the Button Factory [in East Rutherford]," and comments, "Supreme in a fog of stupidity and waste, profit in what is left. Oh what delectable morsel is left" (I, 163–64).

The idea of "efficiency" greatly attracted Williams through the Twenties and into the Thirties, but he did not trust the Progressive means of achieving it through government control. He was more attracted to the nostalgic mélange of single-tax economics and philosophical anarchism espoused by *The Freeman,* which Albert Jay Nock and Francis Neilson published between March 1920 and March 1924. It was an appropriate place for Williams to publish his defense of the "naked" human presence against institutions, "A Man versus the Law."[25] Although he had acquiesced in silence to the Red Scare of the past six months, a test of justice by an idiosyncratic political radical named John Coffey provoked him to speak out—though not for Coffey's politics, but his own.

Coffey was a young Irish tough who was close to the young poets Louis Grudin and Louise Bogan, and to Maxwell Bodenheim, who modeled the protagonist of his 1924 novel, *Crazy Man,* after him. With a compound of anarchism, egoism, and Christianity that he called "Trusteeship," Coffey hoped to break the hold of the concepts of bourgeois property and Christian sin. If people thought and acted for themselves instead of relying on God, he felt, they would see that ownership was "an illusion invented by the weakness of men's imaginations" and accept their "Trusteeship" of material objects. By accepting their own capacities, they would escape this "unreal trap that seeks to mangle their expression" of themselves.[26]

To make people realize this, Coffey set out to become, as Bodenheim put it, "an intellectual Christ" by stealing furs from department stores, informing the police, and submitting himself to arrest and trial, all to demonstrate the law's fundamental invalidity. When he was finally tried, the court evaded the challenge by declaring him a paranoiac with delusions of grandeur and sentencing him to Ward's Island hospital. He escaped with Bodenheim's help, but was rearrested in the spring of 1920 and committed to a more secure hospital, from which he eventually was released when it became overcrowded. He "came to realize," Williams said, "that no matter how good his idea was, it wouldn't work" (IWWP, 56). As Williams put it in "The Suckers": "They 'cured' him all / right" (CP, 377).[27]

In 1919, Williams, rushing to a mosquito commission meeting, had been summonsed by an East Rutherford cop for not buying tickets to a charity entertainment (A, 267–68). Williams also had stronger evidence of "the law's fundamental weakness as a human instrument," as he made clear in "To a Friend of Mine," published in 1919 in *Poetry*:

> Well, Lizzie Anderson! seventeen men—and
> the baby hard to find a father for!
>
> What will the good Father in Heaven say
> to the local judge if he do not solve this problem?
> Does one with a little two-pointed smile
> Change the law—pouff!—into a mouthful of phrases?[28]

Indeed, Prohibition debased the law into mere phrases for millions of Americans on January 16, 1920. For Williams, the most visible postwar attempt to legislate hitherto private matters became a symbol of less obvious intrusions.

In "A Man versus the Law," however, Williams played down the political implications of Coffey's challenge, taking "the present code regarding property ownership" at face value. Instead, he argued that Coffey sought something more neutral: "definition, a light in the dark, a diagnosis, without which no advance of knowledge is possible." What political rebellion he did see in the visionary fur thief was the same ambiguous sort he celebrated in Elia Brobitza and Lizzie Anderson—the challenge to abstract and abstracting categories like social institutions by the actuality of a human being: "What Coffey was attempting was an investigation into the nature of the law with his own body at stake, his body against the body of the law. Humanly taken, there could be only one answer: the man must win."[29]

Coffey himself refused to protest the sentence he received, which allowed Williams to do the same. "His satisfaction," Williams said, "is in the sheer logic of his existence with its unassailable humanity." And so was Williams's. He saluted Coffey's "logic and human devotion," reducing a political act to a rhetorical gesture—a quixotic piece of performance art, perhaps, the significance of which its author and especially its critic diminished.[30]

With this limited protest, Williams once again played the "liberal at the Union Club," one of the perpetual minority whose political actions were moral signs rather than practical acts. This sign had a long half-life, however; Williams maintained an abiding sullenness about the law's claims to authority. In 1951, he wrote in "The Desert Music," "The law is based on murder and confinement, / long delayed, / but this, following the insensate music, / is based on the dance" (PB, 109). Underlying all this protest was a nostalgia for a "sheer humanity" lost, he felt, in urban modernity. And the logic of this nostalgia seemed impeccable: if the authority of the law should be based on the "truth" of the human presence, then by rights that authority was the artist's. Throughout the 1920s, Williams, facing Prohibition, censorship, and neglect, tended to see himself more and more as a John Coffey.

Williams did not feel quite so isolated right after the war. Besides new magazines, there were fresh writers to get to know in 1919, such as the newer *Others* poets William Saphier, Evelyn Scott, and Lola Ridge, and the circle formed by Grudin, Bogan, Emanuel Carnevali, and Isidore Schneider. However, most of them were too young for Williams to feel with them the kinship he had had with Kreymborg, Orrick Johns, and Marianne Moore. Besides, they hung around with self-proclaimed "decadent" Bodenheim, with whom Williams—and eventually these writers, too—did not get along (Bodenheim told him off in a letter just before sailing for England in 1920). His relations with another group of younger writers, Malcolm Cowley, Matthew Josephson, and Burke, were cordial but paternal. For Williams, there was nothing like the group of equals that began meeting at the shacks in Grantwood in 1915.

The closest thing to Grantwood were afternoon teas and evening parties and readings hosted by Lola Ridge, the rail-thin Irish-Australian who, since her arrival in New York in 1907, had lived wholly for art and social revolution. Twelve years older than Williams, she unified her passions more resolutely than almost anyone of the old Village and kept the old community's apocalyptic spirit alive well into the decade of the Lost Generation. For those who knew her, old and young, she was a mirror in which they read their own expectations for art and social change. To Emma Goldman, with whom Ridge started the Ferrer School early in the 1910s, and for whom she read a tribute at a farewell dinner shortly before Goldman's deportation to Russia in December of 1919, she was simply "our gifted rebel poet." To Emanuel Carnevali:

> This rebellion of hers is pure beauty. . . . It is no longer the particular fact of the revolt against actual social conditions. . . . It is an eternal thing, the thing that caused Prometheus to be bound. It's the fire of heaven burning in this wonderful woman's blood.[31]

Kay Boyle helped Ridge edit *Broom* in 1922 and 1923 and, a little awe-struck, served the tea and lemon cake at the Thursday afternoon open house. Although their guests included both artists such as Marianne Moore and Williams and radical writers such as John Dos Passos and Mary Heaton Vorse, the conversation was not like that ten years before at Mabel Dodge Luhan's. Boyle, herself then a passionate supporter of the Irish rebellion and for a while an acolyte of Ridge's poetry and social vision, recalls hearing no strictly political discussions: "I think we all quite simply took for granted that we shared the same convictions." Nor was Williams often there on Thursdays, she adds, because of his heavy schedule.[32]

But because his Fridays in the late 1910s consisted of lectures at two New York clinics, Williams was able to get to Ridge's postwar evening parties at her East 14th Street apartment about every two or three weeks, according to Floss. There he met Carnevali and McAlmon; there, some time between April 1918 and September 1919, he talked with John Reed. In 1913 both Williams and Reed had taken an alliance between poetry and revolution for granted, though with a difference in emphasis that five years of history had turned into an unbridgeable communications gap. Recalling their meeting, Williams said, rather slightingly, that Reed "played with the poem but was not primarily interested in writing." Reed—then struggling to take time away from organization and propaganda to write some poetry—"looked at us as if he couldn't quite make out what we were up to, half-amused, half puzzled" (A, 142). The two men now stood far apart on once-common ground.

Williams's encounter with the man about to found the first American Communist party (and find out that "this class struggle plays hell with your poetry!") represents the change in general relations between artists and social revolutionaries caused especially by the Bolshevik Revolution. No longer could anyone assume, as Maurice Aisen had in 1913, that a revolution in one phase of life simply reflected all the others. Government pressure widened lines already drawn into cracks. In 1917 the editors of *The Masses* went on trial for urging draft resistance and soon had to pack in the magazine, and the patron of *The Seven Arts* bowed to warnings about Randolph Bourne's antiwar articles and withdrew support ("You add politics" to the arts, kidded Robert Frost to Louis Untermeyer in a limerick, "and the Seven will all die a-Bourning").[33]

Artists, including Williams, also feared losing their mailing privileges during wartime, though for obscenity rather than sedition. In the hysteria of 1919, however, with the *Saturday Evening Post* painting every unconventional practice of the Village red, they were understandably nervous. When Malcom Cowley returned from the war in 1919, he found that the Village "was full of plain-clothes dicks from the Vice Squad and the Bomb Squad," raiding tearooms and harrassing women who smoked on the street. Government archives indicate, though inconclusively, that the Bureau of Investigation cast at least a glance at Village artists and editors as well as radicals during the Red Scare.[34]

While the government forced one to define just what kind of revolution one supported, the followers of Lenin and Trotsky did the same, demanding a more concrete commitment than those who sympathized but did not subscribe were prepared to make. In early 1920 Dell made "A Psycho-Analytic Confession," a dialogue between the two parts of his psyche, in which his Unconscious admitted that the notion of "revolution" was looking more and more like plain reality and hard work. And there was the problem of working for someone else. Not long after Reed and Williams met, *The Liberator* took Romaine Rolland and Henri Barbusse to task for calling on authors to write for the sake of "humanity" without subordinating themselves to the Third International. Even though *Liberator* editor Max Eastman tried to continue to believe in both the scientific truth of Marxism and the bohemian freedom of the artist, Village prewar notions of revolution now lay in sectarian fragments.[35]

The pro-Bolsheviks and Communists demanded that one subordinate sensibility to praxis; the American government and people had become ogres of conformity. What were individualists committed to evolutionary, legalistic socialism or to the salvation of democracy through moral regeneration to do? What were the artists, whose self-expressions would waken the American from the sleep of his machine heart and crude business soul, or at least save themselves, to do? There was psychoanalysis or expatriation or, after the turn of the decade, consumerism and a suburban home; but for a while there was confusion and disillusion. To younger bohemians like Malcolm Cowley, the Greenwich Village he came home to from France in 1920 "was like a conquered country," and the older bohemians a lost generation:

> "They" had been rebels; they wanted to change the world, be leaders in the fight for justice and art, help to create a society in which individuals could express themselves. "We" were convinced at the time that society could never be changed by an effort of the will. . . .
> Now, with illusions shattered, they were cynics. . . . We were content to build our modest happiness in the wreck of "their" lost illusions, a cottage in the ruins of a palace. . . .
> The truth is that "we," the newcomers to the village, were not bohemians. We lived in top-floor tenements along the Sixth Avenue Elevated because we couldn't afford to live elsewhere. Either we thought of our real home as existing in the insubstantial world of art, or else we were simply young men on the make, the humble citizens not of bohemia but of Grub Street.[36]

Williams's friends among the *Others* crowd, like those Villagers described here by Cowley, had been progressive or bohemian in their politics, and after the war, Williams found himself on neither side of the generations' quarrel about politics and art. His closest literary associate after 1919, Robert McAlmon, stood apart from the question of poetry and politics altogether. The young midwesterner, who arrived from Los Angeles by way of Chicago in 1919, hated abstractions of any sort; they obscured his individual responses, he felt, and he made their direct expression a social imperative as well as a literary virtue. He parodied one of Ridge's parties, given for a woman poet he called "Vere St. Vitus," in his 1923 novel *Post-Adolescence* and rudely questioned Ridge's sincerity: "Damned little had he and she to say to each other; poor old thing, pretending to be revolutionary and flaming with passion when a few good meals would change all of that perhaps, except that she'd still be pathetic." In the scene, he rescues Jim Boyle (Williams) from a woman telling him he would be a greater poet if he would put more "social content" into his work, and the two go off with Brander Ogden (Marsden Hartley) in tow to mull over an idea for a magazine. Once outside the party, Boyle bums a cigarette and says, "I wish I could be a truck driver."

Williams himself was of two minds about Ridge's commitments, to judge from the two different tones of voice in which he spoke of her in his autobiography. On the one hand, he was terse and, echoing McAlmon, dismissive: "She made a religion of it" (A, 136), when for him, as the cover of the first issue of *Contact* said, the worship of Art was "the supreme hypocrisy" of a merely "information-cultured," vicariously experiencing people.[37] But remembering the epiphanic night in 1925 at Ridge's when he heard Vladimir Mayakovsky boom out in Russian his poem about Willie the Havana Street Cleaner, Williams more respectfully referred to her as "that Vestal of the Arts, a devout believer in the humanity of letters" (A, 163).

For the rest of Williams's life Mayakovsky was for him the figure of the real thing, the "poet of the people" that Carl Sandburg, as Williams charged in 1929, only pretended to be. Williams may have suspected the sincerity or, more likely, the aesthetic intelligence of committed poets like Sandburg or Ridge, but he remained no less committed than they, no matter how embarrassed he might have been to express it in the late 1910s. In fact, his devotion to art is what made him loathe most theory or prescription about it, for it all had become a dead language blocking the actual invention of new work; for him, true thought about art was achieved only while one worked hands-on.

Williams's idealism about art's power was bloodied but unbowed by "postwar." The government—the "state" from which he had half-hoped to liberate his townspeople with poems such as "The Wanderer" and "Portrait of an Old Woman in Bed"—had clamped down on and silenced, if not the artists, the milieu of free expression in which such hopes of revelation could be spoken, shared, and perhaps even fulfilled. "The church" of moral and social conformity, out of whose stifling shelter he had tried to tease his townspeople in "Gulls," now had sealed their lips. And his townspeople had for the most part gone right along. When they spoke now, it was to bray about an "Americanism" that erased all difference, whether moral, political, or ethnic, and confused democratic "liberty" with social egalitarianism or economic self-interest.

The difference that art might make seemed trifling to them, if they considered it at all. After the Red Scare passed, the distractions of the new mass culture, such as those that drew the baseball- and movie-goers whom Williams ambivalently portrayed in the 1923 poems "Light Becomes Darkness" and "At the Ball Game," quashed his faint but persistent hope that Americans might become a mass audience for poetry. Worse still, the practitioners of the art themselves seemed silent or in despair. But even as he wrote his harshest criticism of American life, or of poets such as Ridge who persisted in the older aesthetics of radicalism, even as his letters to other poets bespoke cynicism, Williams, in the next line or the next poem, reaffirmed his desire to be "The Wanderer" who rooted his community.

He had told Edmund Brown in 1916 that he couldn't stomach the idea of creating "brotherhood" through poetry, but went on to say how the rhythms of everyday speech in Rutherford drove him mad to write. In 1921, after telling Kenneth Burke, "You tire me with your Whitman guff," he parodied his own aspirations to be a poet of democracy with a cartoon of himself bearded, with a little naked man standing on the beard, and captioned "The American ideal!" "Postwar" made him sick and tired of calls from *The Seven Arts* or Lola Ridge's guests to feel responsible for a people who had rejected his offer, or who failed to understand that to be responsible to them he first had to be responsible to his art. When Monroe Wheeler wrote him in 1923 to discuss his plans for continuing Williams's magazine *Contact,* Williams congratulated him for wanting to focus only on the literary quality of work and not expecting great things to come of that: "Glad to see you are planning no revolution."[38]

Williams may have torn at his good gray beard, but it simply grew back to nest that homunculus. For every denial of the poet's dependence on society he issued in the 1920s, there is an assertion that the autonomous artist performs an essential function for that culture. His vitriol about America and democracy increased in proportion to its neglect of him; so, portentously, did his overamplification of the poet's power. One's "townspeople," he consoled himself, were inevitably threatened by genius, but genius was magnanimous because of its superior understanding.

Thus Williams consoled Alva Turner, telling him he was "a wreck" because he was "a normal man adrift in a pack of lunatics."[39] Indeed, Turner was one of the pure products of America Williams mourned. A small-town minister in Texas and Illinois, he was hospitalized several times in mid-life for nervous breakdowns. He recovered sufficiently to be a painter on state crews, a village board member, mayor, and "the poet of Ina," Illinois. In the fall of 1920, Williams defined for Turner the poet's "relation to [his] environment":

> You are so far beyond your environment by sheer instinct that the community you live in would be destroyed by your mere presence did it not make an example of you, keep you subdued. These are the fools and their breed is unnumbered. Yet you love them because you can understand what they are, the good that they generate among them. (SL, 46)

Williams's own place in Rutherford seemed little better. In "Portrait of the Author," he, maddened by the spring, pleads with a local audience of a single townsperson: "We are alone in this terror, alone, / face to face on this road, you and I, / Wrapped by this flame! . . . Tell me the commonest thing that is in your mind to say, / say anything. I will understand you!" (CP, 172–73). In the heat of composing in Rome in 1924, this isolation ballooned into paranoia: "Why do I write. . . . I know they hate me and will kill—if they can. . . .They'll rob me in a minute if I confess my happiness" (*Rome,* 41, 45).

Williams's case of "postwar," then, was at times most severe. As a member of the older, Progressive-era generation of bohemians, radicals, and artists, he had as an integral part of his self-definition as an artist a sense of social responsibility, however unsophisticated it might now seem. The war and postwar, with all their betrayals, did not erase Williams's sense of duty, a sense that Cowley's generation did not acquire until the Depression. Nor did they cause him to question the terms in which he intended to fufill that duty. On the contrary, the harder the world pressed its thumb on the scale of politics or social messages, the harder Williams pressed his on the scale of art and form.

In *Post-Adolescence,* Peter and Jim Boyle—McAlmon and Williams—have a brief exchange that neatly expresses the divided nature of Williams's disillusionment, and the difference between the older and younger poets' values. Peter expresses the quintessential Lost Generation cynicism about ultimate values when he tells Boyle, "I know only individuals and what they do, and if it doesn't matter then to the devil with it. We haven't a religion any more; we don't accept scholastic or esthetic standards, or the old ideas of morality any longer, so we must recognize individual qualities more." Boyle's reponse is at once an agreement and a refusal: "That's too little," he says; "I want something inclusive."[40]

Williams had never been keen to speak as straightforwardly as Boyle does to Peter about the social responsibility he felt as a poet. Yet during postwar, when older artists tried to save appearances that seemed suspect to younger artists such as McAlmon, Williams began to assert more openly and loudly than ever that the poet, above all other members of the intelligentsia, had the key to the new social values that would replace the shell-shocked old. In the fall of 1921, with the economy stalled in a depression, Williams wrote *The Great American Novel* about a Ford in a fog-ridden land, parodying with the novel's careering juxtapositions the notion of narrative—and American—progress. One of those juxtapositions, a dialogue with a voice of postwar cocktail skepticism, insisted:

> Do you mean to say that—O ha, ha. Do you mean to say that art—O ha ha. Well spit it out. Do you mean to say that art is SERIOUS?—Yes. Do you mean to say that art does any WORK?—Yes. Do you mean—? Revolution. Russia. Kropotkin. Farm, Factory, and Field. —CRRRRRRASH. Down comes the world. There you are, gentlemen, I am an artist. (I, 170)

While he may have craved nicotine and tough-guy talk when such a question came up at Ridge's, Williams harked back to and drew strength from the hope he had in 1913, and sometimes "spit it out."

In the spring of 1919, a 21-year-old Italian reminded him of what the prewar faith in poetry had meant. Emanuel Carnevali, "the hurried man that has no direction," was prodigal in all he did and felt, whether washing piles of plates at Mouquin's or rifling through a stack of submissions to *Poetry,* telling his friends how much he loved or hated them. He embodied the spirit of 1913. His brief friendship with Williams roused the older poet by showing him the self he had wanted to be but had never quite been: "wide, Wide, WIDE open."[41]

The precocious son of a broken bourgeois home who promenaded in Bologna at 16 in the flowing tie of a futurist and anarchist, Carnevali emigrated to the United States in 1914 after being expelled from the boarding school to which he had won a scholarship. While surviving a series of dishwashing, table waiting, and editorial jobs, he learned English quickly enough to write *vers libre* acceptable to

The Seven Arts and *Poetry*. He became close friends with Louis Grudin, and together they scouted editorial offices for publications and work, in the process meeting Kreymborg and through him the New York poets.

The America of the Woolworth Building, to which his friend Grudin tipped his hat each time they passed it, almost crushed him, Carnevali said. "I was coupled with misery, like two dogs on a street corner. But there was something else. There was always a little light shining that guided me through this country of America, this black country: I knew I was a poet and I had in my soul the desire to write."[42]

As for his poetics, Carnevali shared Williams's prewar ideal of "nakedness." "To be a man of honor," he wrote, "is to tell everything. . . . For the truth of one single human being would be enough to horrify the most ferocious Kraft-Ebbing imaginable." For him, however, that truth had a social dimension more explicit than to Williams. "Because I am poor," he wrote in one poem, "no ceremony will clean me." Crushing poverty, though, was less painful than the fact of being an immigrant. He felt excluded by bourgeois America in a way that rebels from Iowa did not; moreover, he felt bereft in New York, "this awful network of fire escapes," where he had exchanged a furnished room—a "transitory institution in the transitory New World"—for the Italian social networks of family and town. He wanted to write not just to express himself, but also to speak for hyphenated others: "There were millions like me, of course, millions; and if these millions had a voice it would be the voice of God. . . ."[43]

How would he achieve that voice, and what would it say for those millions? "I chose revolution." However, although he often put his misery in social terms, he did not go the way of his anarchist countrymen Carlo Tresca, Nicola Sacco, and Bartolomeo Vanzetti; he put his millenial fervor into art. His was the revolution of the visionary poet, whose "domain is emptiness, his empire muteness, his regime disorder, his dance dislocation," whose desire would dynamite the language (and thus the world) of the bourgeoisie. As he wrote in an essay on his hero Arthur Rimbaud:

> I know from Carlyle that revolution is sometimes the people producing poetry en masse. Clear as the fire of even the things most rotten is revolution in the pure vision of the seer, the inspired man who wants revolution for the beauty of his eyes, for the beauty of his limbs, for the beauty of his heart—who wants and has long wanted the world to be his own body, cast infinitely, speaking.[44]

Once Williams and the *Others* crowd were such poets, Carnevali told them one night at Lola Ridge's in the spring of 1919, but now their talk of "new expressions" and new technique was mere cage rattling: "The fight you started in the beginning has you exhausted." He also accused them of trying to separate their art from common life and warned them that, though they might escape "the mob," they could not rise above "the world":

For what does the expression "to create" mean? It means "To hell with the mob, who will always understand?" Yes, but then let us speak what we have to speak, in our language no matter how the mob has warped, stumped, and minced that language. You pure artists, you non-utilitarians, you half-and-half, you socialists, you souls of serenity, let us see supreme serenity, the last indifference, the highest pride, that of the man who, even if alone in the world, talks the world's language. Let us see you brave the danger which brings insanity and damnation to an artist, the danger of being taken for a megaphone of all the filthy symbols of death and the rest which wear such shining names as god, life, beauty, liberty, democracy, and peace along the ash-can-guarded streets of the mob. That is art, its fight, its bitterness, its curse and its uselessness. If you want art to be absurd, what greater absurdity than to stand against millions.[45]

Hearing this Italian half his age electrified Williams, reconfirming his ideals—he had just been to Chicago and, feeling his old fire before an audience of peers, called the poet a "revolutionist . . . out for truth"—even though Carnevali accused him of only pretending to live up to them.[46] Carnevali's view of the relation between poetry and politics roused Williams as well. His view of the nature and risks of the poet's engagement with the world challenged Williams to answer for his own aim to make poetry out of the rhythms of contemporary speech that would awaken the ash-can-guarded mob to their own values.

The nearly lapsed rebel and the hurried man became friends that night, and Carnevali became the first of the sons of Pater-son. Williams dedicated the last issue of *Others* to him in July 1919, and in an essay called "Gloria!" passed him the baton: "It was for you we went out, old men in the dark." But in a second essay in the issue, "Belly Music," Williams parried and thrust back:

I deny that one writes because he cannot live. Carnevali is wrong. . . . An artist is NOT forced out of life, he refuses it. He does so wilfully. He writes in order to escape the mechanical perfection of sheer existence. He writes to assert himself above every machine and every mechanical conception that seeks to bind him. He writes to free himself, to annihilate every machine, every science, to escape defiant through consciousness and accuracy of emotional expression. And this can never occur until he is conscious of and takes discriminating grips upon the first brains of his generation.[47]

Williams took back here nearly everything he conceded to Carnevali in "Gloria!" He admitted in "Gloria!" that he and his contemporaries were seeking "the seclusion of a style": "we make replicas of the world we live in and we live in them and not the world." In "Belly Music," however, he asserted that he did so precisely to engage "life": his concern with technique (a concern he faulted Carnevali for not having) was the same quest for truth that "first brains" such as John Dewey were undertaking. "The mark of a great poet," Williams said, "is the extent to which he is aware of his time and NOT, unless I be a fool, the weight of loveliness in his meters."

But it was Carnevali's fatalism that especially bothered Williams. Although in "Gloria!" he had conceded that art had been defeated by the environment ("Who can write a poem complete in every part surrounded by this mess we live in?"), he deflected his own surrender on to Carnevali, who, he lamented, had been "smashed to pieces by the stupidity of a city of s**tas**s." As for himself, he spoke in "Belly Music" as a stalwart egoist: what looked like defeat was a willful refusal, and correct strategy at that.[48]

Williams's aesthetic duel with Carnevali was sparked by differences in generation and temperament and by social differences as well—the middle-class doctor was freer to feel one had choices to make than the immigrant struggling to hold on to "these scanty rights to live." But there was no difference in the intensity of their faith in poetry. Carnevali was Williams's own young passion for poetry in the flesh, the most uncanny of the things that stirred Williams to a renewed fervor in the early 1920s. When Williams came to write *Spring and All* the year after Carnevali, trembling with encephalitis, sailed back to Italy, he celebrated the imagination with the extravagance of "the unfinished god in the unfinished divinity which is the world." In her review of the book, Marjorie Allen Sieffert aptly noted that it was written "Against the Middle-Aged Mind."[49]

Williams and Carnevali's exchange prefigured the quarrels Williams had in the early 1920s and ever after with conventionally committed writers like John Gould Fletcher of *The Freeman,* who mistook him for a "decadent," "disillusioned" aesthete. (He took Fletcher's misconception of his commitment to form in *Kora*—"Literature, however, depends not on the kind but on the degree of statement"—headed it, "The Italics Are God's," and printed it in *Contact* with Fletcher's name upside-down underneath.) The point of inventing new form, Williams asserted in the last issue of *Contact* in 1923, was to record "the best sense of the time." This was a "practical attitude toward writing," he insisted, "as against the front of 'pure aesthetics.' " More important, in "Belly Music" he made his first specific challenge to the priority of social, political, and philosophical thought, calling John Dewey one of the "hard thinkers" but complaining that the social philosopher's "reconstruction program" neglected "the interdependence of thought and art."[50] Williams repeated this challenge for the rest of his life.

In the spring of 1923, as the American economy bolted out of its depression, Williams began to parody the sour spirit of Versailles, Centralia, and the recent layoffs ("O meagre times, so fat in everything imaginable!"). He metamorphosed the war into the destruction by the imagination of the world—which resulted in its re-creation "afresh in the likeness of what it was." For suffering postwar, the human race was granted "strange recompense": "in the depths of our despair at the unfathomable mist into which all mankind is plunging, a curious force awakens." Wilson, postwar's great failure, became the figure of that force:

> It is HOPE, long asleep, aroused once more. Wilson has taken an army of advisers and sailed for England. The ship has sunk. But the men are all good swimmers. They take the women on their shoulders and buoyed by the inspiration of the moment they churn the free seas with their sinewy arms, like Ulysses, landing all along the European seaboard. (I, 97)

When Harold Stearns said in *The Freeman* in 1921 that an artist was in such thrall to his environment that American art was entering "a fallow period," Williams retorted that art was "a self-related" activity and could be created at any time, in any society (RI, 62–63).[51] Unlike Ulysses—and the expatriates— Williams found his hope at home, in the form of the ex-president secluded in his home by a stroke and his disgrace.

For by the early 1920s, Williams was sure he had found that "inclusive" value he was seeking, a poetics that would ground American society and culture upon the values—moral, epistemological, aesthetic, religious, and even political—that he thought America was all about. Williams distanced himself from conventional notions of social purpose and content to achieve what he felt was the social purpose of art: contact with the realities of the present and a clarity of consciousness that would renew the individual reader.

Ironically, at the moment Williams discovered his inclusive values, they were losing force in American culture. By the early 1920s, the individual's autonomy was dissipated by the forces of modernity, the locality was being overshadowed by things national, and art's power was being usurped by mass culture. Even as Williams found the voice in which he could speak to America, he found himself with no command of the nation's attention. Thus he found himself defending his politics of "the local" and asserting their corollary: "Poetry restores authority to man by grace of the imagination."[52]

10

Zoning the Sacred Wood:
The Politics of the Local

As America learned to shout a new language of modern prosperity in the 1920s, William Carlos Williams raged in his widest-ranging criticism yet against the materialism he felt was leading Americans to create a second-rate culture and art of their own. Much of his hostility was an artist's self-defense, but no small part of it was the anger of a citizen of the smaller-scaled world that modernity had displaced, a world in which "the regular Fourth of July stuff" of local independence and concrete personal relationships had once held good. Not only did the transformation of American society disperse his cherished community of avant-garde artists who, like him, were committed to the "naked" expression of a full personality, it significantly altered the small American community in which one's "personality" was self-contained and social life was a matter of concrete, immediate relationships. But modernity, ironically, left Williams the modernist artist bereft of a vocabulary for either art or politics, putting him in the position in which his own radical poetry put conventionally minded readers of *Spring and All:* "You have robbed me," they cry. "God, I am naked. What shall I do?" (I, 89).

He did what most Americans did, sticking to the discourse of individual liberty. Even though Americans became (willingly) the mass consumers and (less willingly) the producers required by the new industrial order, they were, as economics writer Walton H. Hamilton noted in 1922, "far from ready to surrender" the "inherited belief in an individualistic theory of the common good," despite the obvious disappearance of the economy, culture, and small community in which the belief made sense. Hamilton hoped Americans would develop a "common-sense appreciation" of the industrial order, but despite their willingness to have the federal government restrict the intake of alcohol, immigrants, and leftist politics, most Americans clung to the inherited faith. While the air filled with Jeffersonian-toned rhetoric (from businessmen pursuing Hamiltonian interests) about minimal government and individual freedom, people paid through installment plans for ubiquitously advertised goods, and the federal government, in spite of all that Harding, Calvin Coolidge, and Herbert Hoover would say or not do, multiplied, divided, and expanded its control.[1]

Williams lived the same contradiction as his countrymen. Paralleling his efforts to recover power for poetry were his defenses of the whole self, the autonomous individual of premodern American society. When Williams wrote about poetics, poetry, American culture, American history, or American politics, he started not from abstract principles but from the individual, asking what kind of large-scale structure would enable an American to make contact with his immediate environment. By experiencing his world with his own senses and intelligence, the individual could take responsibility for his own character and behavior again and thus, Williams believed, accomplish "the restoration of democracy on another plan" than the intrusive, abstracting plan full of "prohibitions" that modernity was inexorably imposing on America. Government, in a sense more radical than any Progressive-era call for "direct elections" and the like, was a matter of direct involvement of the individual—and of leaving him alone to exercise his modicum of power responsibly.

Thus Williams came to articulate his defensive politics of the local, an antifederalism so strong that he called the "Salvation of the Union" in the Civil War "a disastrous error."[2] His assumptions about individual autonomy shaped his poetics of contact as well, but before discussing how they shaped his defense of the imagination in *Spring and All,* let us examine his more straightforward responses to modernity, namely his criticism of American culture in *The Great American Novel* and of the American character in *In the American Grain,* and his assertions about the virtues of local government. And let us place these in the locality where he confronted modernity, Rutherford in the early 1920s.

In January 1921, seven months after Peter Kipp was laid to rest, the ghost of the old gentleman with the farm in the heart of town appeared in the pages of the Rutherford *Republican* to damn his townspeople for thinking him a selfish old crank and trampling his wheat. Stung by their disrespect for his property and his way of life, he told them to "get back to work in the ground" instead of letting "young supper snappers" ride around in unearned automobiles.

But the ghost's jeremiad served only to signify his quaintness. As he went on, the shade of the borough physiocrat—actually the persona of some clever partisan in the current fight to change the site of the planned new high school—was made to capitulate to modernity. "Mebbe" after all, he admitted, he should have willed a few acres to Rutherford, seeing how the town's growth and not his cultivation of his land had driven up its dollar value. His heirs, the ghost was made to suggest, could make amends for him by giving the borough a few acres for the new high school, allowing those youngsters to get "plenty of fresh air and sunshine"—if not while digging dirt with their hands, at least while they sat daydreaming in class of Dodges and Rudolph Valentino.[3]

The author of the ghost's jeremiad had a real point to make. Rutherford's present high school had no gymnasium and sometimes filled up with fumes rising from the chemistry laboratories crammed down in the basement; a new building was imperative.[4] The site on Park Avenue proposed by the board of education verged on the ever-busier downtown; a larger building on a bit of as-yet-undeveloped farmland would indeed be healthier.

However sound his point, though, this suburbanite's sales strategy was as ironic as it was appropriate, a local instance of how, as William H. Leuchtenberg says, Americans in the 1920s "sought security by incanting their allegiance to the older virtues at the same time they were abandoning them."[5] The symbol of the rural past is dead, but long live the rural past, somehow, while we build the up-to-date future over it. For although the author of the ghost's jeremiad mocked Kipp's quaintness, he appealed to local belief in some magical property of Kipp's land: setting the school—a quintessentially urban, regimented space—on Kipp's property would somehow keep the essence of ruralness in the air and light of the classrooms.

The ghost-writer spoke for those in town, many of whom had recently moved into the West End, who wanted to have the best of both city and country in what still seemed like the "one vast park" touted in the real estate brochures of the Nineties. Besides Kipp's open property, many still-wooded acres dotted the borough in 1921, and one could hope that some of this land would remain undeveloped—but not for long. Some of Rutherford's leading citizens did not care to wave in the rearview mirror at all and were bent on further "progress." A December 10, 1921, *Republican* editorial which celebrated the "wonderful possibilities Rutherford has in the way of future growth" made no obeisance to the ancestral spirit. "A farm in the center of our borough," the paper warned, "does not show an especial wide-awakeness and alertness on the part of our citizens."

But the new suburbanites dedicated to saving something of Kipp's rural virtue for their children had saved some old-fashioned community spirit and organized to force a vote on a new high school site after the Park Avenue site had been approved. One of those who pitched in to help air and exercise and public good prevail over private profit was school physician Dr. William Carlos Williams. He wrote a letter to the *Republican* against the Park Avenue site before the election, served as secretary of a committee of eight local doctors which pronounced the Park Avenue site unhealthy, and overcame his admitted "diffidence" about civic activity to write another letter to the paper and speak at what the *Republican* called the "Greatest Mass Meeting Ever Held in [the] Borough." In his second letter, he bluntly charged that the town "real estate interests" were greedily blocking the move. To Kenneth Burke, he was blunter: he was "fighting the town," he said, "in order to get the shitasses to take their hands off the lid long enough to get a new high school built."[6]

The boroughwide fight was the bitterest since incorporation, full of sectional antagonism, charges like Williams's, and at least one near-fight at a public meeting. The usually genial *Republican* even called the new-site movement "damnable nonsense, detrimental to the community and to American interests."[7] But Williams's side carried the new vote, and the high school—built for 350 but housing 437 in its first year—was built on a piece of the farm land, which Kipp's heirs, ignoring the ersatz voice of their forebear, sold to the borough for $29,000.

But the forces of "progress" won the war. In March 1922, Kipp's ghost was made to walk again, this time to plead to have the rest of his fields made into a municipal park. But he was only a shade of the earlier playground movement. Now the cost was much greater, the number of people needed to support the movement was huge, and the town was exhausted from the school fight. Two weeks later in the *Republican,* the two unnamed "shades" who had appeared with Kipp's in all the previous stories waited again for him. To kill time, they suggested to readers that the borough's civic organizations—now 33 in number—could pitch in and raise the money to buy the land from the heirs. But the ghost of Peter Kipp never showed up.[8]

The *Republican*'s editorial on "especial alertness" heralded the arrival of modernity in Rutherford. It was part of a campaign by a loose alliance of municipal officials, real estate agents, and the chamber of commerce to step up the pace of progress in Bergen County to the fondly remembered tempo of wartime production, and it worked. The prospect of soon being able to drive an automobile to Manhattan over a bridge or through a tunnel was much ballyhooed, and sparked a county-wide real estate boom. Although the Holland Tunnel was not completed until 1927 (and the George Washington Bridge not until 1931), and the boom fell short of its boosters' expectations, Bergen County's population nevertheless swelled at a rate of 73 percent between 1920 and 1930, and the size and functions of county and municipal governments multiplied accordingly.[9]

Thanks to its location on the Erie Railroad line, Rutherford was already well settled and well organized. And thanks to the better-than-average incomes of its residents, it was already much more "improved" than many other communities, which now had to organize sufficiently to dig, pave, build, and bond a town. Nevertheless, Rutherford's rate of growth from 1920 to the mid-1930s was its fastest ever. The borough population grew from about 9,500 to 15,000, and its leaders now had to take frankly "modern" measures to preserve even a dim glow of the pastoral aura.[10]

In 1921 Rutherford's first zoning ordinance was passed, stirring fears that the sanctity of private property would be profaned. The *Republican* assured readers that although the law read "like a Chinese puzzle," it would only prevent "unsightly tenement houses and disreputable-looking shacks" from being built, particularly on the highly visible Kipp property. After a weekly campaign to get people used to the idea, late that year the paper even called for "More Zoning"—out-and-out municipal and regional planning, and all the government control that it implied.[11]

Progress, as Rutherford's early farmers well knew, meant letting the community spend one's money. By 1921, borough taxes had doubled from prewar rates, mostly because of rising local school and county road expenditures, and for the next decade Rutherford's middle class was as crusty about government spending as were the old farmers. As usual, local politicians promised fiscal conservatism, but now they added that modern life had to be paid for and started speaking openly of Rutherford in urban terms. Ezra Kennedy, a long-time councilman up for reelection in the fall of 1922, reminded voters that they had to meet "demands that were non-existent when I first landed in the borough 25 years ago," and warned that "our present rapid growth" would require yet more spending. By 1928, the mayor was justifying expenditures to a restive taxpayers' association by pointing out that the borough had to meet "the demand for improved and extended services caused by the increasing complexity of our city life."[12]

Rutherford probably shifted to city government and city life more easily than many other American communities, especially more rural ones. When 29 Ku Klux Klansmen from the Bergen County chapter appeared in Rutherford at the funeral of one of their fellows in May 1922, the *Republican* treated it as a distasteful intrusion.[13] Nevertheless, no matter how sophisticated Rutherford's commuting residents were, the shift in the community's center of gravity from local to national culture took some getting used to—especially if one were a civic-minded artist like William Carlos Williams.

The automobile, and the new strategies for stimulating consumption of the extraordinary numbers of them that could now be produced, made America fully modern in the 1920s, and prosperous Rutherford was just ahead of the times. The *Republican* was already filled with advertisements for Dodges, Fords, and Standard Oil products when the borough got its own automobile license bureau in late 1920. (The local Buick dealer still used small-town-style peer pressure to sell his modern products: in 1922 he advertised by publishing a list, increasing a half-dozen a week, of the names of his customers.) The borough also licensed bus lines in the fall of 1920, and soon the "Trolley Fare Fight" over rate increases in late 1920 and 1921—to which Williams referred in *The Great American Novel* (I, 222) by reprinting part of an open letter from the franchise owners (the ironically named Public Service Corporation)—was a moot issue.[14]

Buicks and buses were a mixed blessing. Accidents and automobile thefts were now common enough to become local news, though uncommon enough to make the front page. Pedestrians and drivers alike had a dangerous time navigating the four-street Union Square across from the railroad station, which had no "Isle of Safety" at the time. The marking of lines for pedestrian crosswalks there in late 1922 won the gratitude of the *Republican,* a cartoon mocking both pedestrians and motorists bewildered by the numerous signs and directions in the square, and inclusion in Williams's 1923 poem "Rapid Transit" as the "Careful Crossing Campaign" (I, 146).[15]

Williams was making serious fun of this particular local crusade, but he was not joking when, in June 1921, he and other residents of the section of town called "The Terrace" fought a nearby automobile supply store's request to the borough council to install gasoline tanks, arguing that the danger of fire spreading to wooden homes on Ridge Road (of which Williams's was one) should outweigh the area's need for more gas pumps. The automobile in itself was an ambivalent boon to the poet's imagination as well. As a doctor, Williams, a car owner since 1913, spent a good part of his time in rapid-transit motion, and, as Cecelia Tichi has noted, his paratactic poetics of "the stop-action immediate" are a product of this quintessentially modern experience.[16] The irony that undercut his delight at speeding around is evident in his poem, "The Right of Way."

The car was modernity's most powerful force, but the new "consumer durables" available had nearly as much impact. Rutherford was an ideal market for modern, time-saving goods such as the A B C Super Electric Washer, which turned doing laundry into "little more than supervising a most obedient servant," or a gas range, so convenient "for the man whose family is away" and has to keep "'Bachelor's Hall.'" Some Rutherford consumers probably got letters like the one Williams inserted in *The Great American Novel* (203) from the Retail Credit Men's National Association, which threatened to notify banks and other lending institutions that they had not paid their last few installments. Newly extended means of credit such as buying on time, the Lynds noted, replaced the town banker's personal opinion as the enforcer of social conformity and political conservatism.[17]

Also becoming more impersonal were the social relations embedded in "culture" itself. Rutherford's aspirations to high culture continued to be at least partially fulfilled, mainly through the Reading Club and other women's groups, which over the years occasionally gave Williams a chance to perplex them with readings and discussions of modern poetry. But the drama productions which Williams's father managed ended after his death in 1918, and references in the paper to singing and playing music at home grew fewer and fewer. People were now watching and listening to strangers from far away perform, and both high culture and the idea that any sort of culture should be self-produced now had competition.

Ironically, the borough council voted in April 1920 not to let a Chautauqua Club hold its old-fashioned open meetings, but allowed newer forms of mass culture to proceed apace. Advertisements for vaudeville acts and motion pictures had been growing more frequent since 1917, and now the *Republican* sold several half-page displays each week for performances at the Criterion, the new Rivoli, and theaters in nearby towns. Just six months after public broadcasting began in the fall of 1920, Rutherford had a radio club and weekly features on radio in its newspaper. The theater in Williams's backyard, for which he planned productions as late as 1919, was an anachronism.[18]

The shift from local to national culture in Rutherford was most visible in the

Republican itself. John Dewey could have had a copy of it on his desk when he wrote in his 1920 essay, "Americanism and Localism":

> Of course, the paper has the Associated Press service or some other service of which it brags. As a newspaper which knows its business, it prints "national" news, and strives assiduously for "national" advertisements. . . . But somehow all this wears a thin and apologetic air. The very style of the national news reminds one of his childhood text-book in history, or of the cyclopaedia that he is sometimes regretfully obliged to consult. . . . How different the local news. Even in the most woodenly treated item there is flavour, even if only of the desire to say something and still avoid a libel suit.[19]

By the end of the war, the *Republican* was carrying syndicated columns and features which spoke "thinly" to Rutherfordians on national issues such as the high cost of living. By the early 1920s, brand-name advertisements appeared in full force. One of them is a parable of modernity's arrival: a large advertisement for Du Pont "Prepared Paint," featuring the company logo up top, a huge can of the paint pouring rays of light on a house at the bottom, and two inches of copy about the paint in between. Tucked between the copy and the house, a third of the size of the Du Pont logo, were the name and address of the local painter and decorator from whom one could buy the Du Pont product. The proportions between national brand name and local man were now completely reversed from those in advertisements before the war.[20]

It is impossible to tell from the *Republican* how Rutherford was affected by what is universally considered a "revolution in manners and morals" in the postwar era. One of the new syndicated stories, complete with statistical survey, did announce in the May 1, 1920, issue that "More Than One-Half of Adults in U.S. Lack Church Influence," and the Reverend Mr. Clee, the local Baptist minister, preached on the present "Glaring Denial of Faith" in March 1922, but no public discussion of the changes in private relations made its way into local print—not even a letter decrying the new depravity of Rutherford youth. The closest the paper came to an acknowledgment of the young people's growing "speed" was its claim in January 1922 that some local girls had begun a national fad for "knickerbocker" skirts. But forces ranging from the experience of wartime freedoms to the impossible-to-chaperone automobile to the vogue of pseudo-Freudianism— and particularly the entrance of many women into the work force— were weakening family ties and authority and undercutting traditional attitudes toward sex, marriage and divorce, and gender roles, so that many middle-class Americans now sometimes acted like prewar bohemians.[21]

In Rutherford, however, they certainly did not sound like prewar bohemians. To judge from the *Republican*'s silence, the town tried to keep private freedoms private, maintaining a furtiveness that made the poet who urged nakedness of feeling on his townspeople furious. In *The Great American Novel*, Williams implied that at least some town youth were "flaming," though hardly from sexual activity: a middle-class voice tut-tuts over a "well-built" girl who "will never finish school" and whose younger brother has already outgrown her, apparently because she is masturbating—while her younger brothers sit by the Episcopal church devising sadistic tortures for the suitor who might save her from the virginity that is driving her crazy (I, 204–5).

In his own voice in his *Rome* journal, Williams bluntly scored the hypocrisy of such repression: "The blond flapper that in high school lies and is fucked—gives twins—is the one whom we bury in shit to . . . wreck—[but] it is ours. . . . The Board of Education is eating shit for her" (53). The poet of erotic contact with immediate experience despised the silences and evasions with which he was surrounded. Williams never told the board of education in public what he thought of their sexual morality, but he continued to give his townspeople broad hints in charged poems such as "The Lonely Street" (CP, 174). And in *In the American Grain* he accused the whole nation of mass hypocrisy, of generating out of its repressions a culture of hysterical titillation that brought millions to the movies every week.

Mass-produced, consumer-cultured, urban-governed modernity citified the suburb out of much of its original pretension to being a park or a small town. The borough government used some of its new powers to zone industry out of town, but the new homeowners who built on old farmland had their kitchens stocked with appliances, their driveway curb cuts approved by the borough council, and their payments for all of it generously deferred and closely watched. They joined a community with a more impersonal means of conducting civic affairs, a checkered culture of notices of meetings of the Reading Club tucked above advertisements for a showing of *Queen of Sheba,* and with, perhaps, the temptation from a slight new sense of anonymity to defy public morals, starting with a few cocktails.

Whether life in Rutherford came to seem as thin as the syndicated stories John Dewey bemoaned, or whether by contrast experience in the town felt richer, is a crucial but unanswerable question. It is perhaps significant that after 1917 no Rutherford resident wrote to the *Republican* to lament his no longer knowing everyone on Park Avenue or the train platform by name. Even if by a commuter's comparison with Fifth Avenue and Grand Central Station Rutherford still seemed like a pastoral haven or a hick town, its residents no longer expected to know all of their neighbors.

Such was the progress trumpeted all over town by the real estate men who eyed the late Kipp's fields. But despite their jibes about farms and being forward-looking, Rutherford's "men on the make" drove ahead with an eye on the rearview mirror. Their ideology of progress, ironically, was the unwitting swan song of old-fashioned, entrepreneurial individualism, which they chanted as they helped along the transformation of the economy that made them obsolete. It consoled them as it drove them: "We all possess perceptions and faculties that have the capacity of lifting us into supermen," intoned a *Republican* column filler. "The rub is, we do not suspect our own powers or exert ourselves sufficiently to bring them to the surface." The next item recounted making a slick sale on the train in to work.[22]

The salesman who read this homily needed to hear some self-congratulation after the squeeze of the government-managed war years and the unsettling of moral certainties. Politicians, ministers, intellectuals, and radicals—not to mention artists—were all now discredited as leaders, and businessmen stepped into the vacuum to claim the role. "The most potent constructive influence in a community," said the speaker at the first meeting of Rutherford's chamber of commerce in April 1922, "is a body of business and professional men banded together for the purpose of improving the citizenship."[23]

Businessmen identified both their own communities' interests and the nation's interests with their own, legitimating their version of America by proclaiming Alexander Hamilton as the genius among the founding fathers (and Secretary of the Treasury Andrew Mellon as his heir) and through such means as the series of advertisements for the Rutherford National Bank, which presented highlights of New Jersey history "to unite more closely the residents of this and neighboring towns in a spirit of community pride and to promote a cordial relationship with our bank." The advertisement's twin intentions—the latter commercial and the former either cynical or nostalgic—sum up the American businessman's relation to the past he helped erase. Such transparent appropriations of history formed one layer of the "chaos of borrowed titles" which Williams tried to clear away from American history in *In the American Grain*.[24]

As for the American character, that "superman" of perception and "faculties" which a salesman could become with self-confidence and exertion: if the old-fashioned individual was to feel whole and free from the spreading net of impersonal regulations, he had to revise his sense of autonomy or withdraw still further into private depths—or parody himself, like the salesman using those unsuspected powers to make big deals, buy a new Hoover vacuum and think himself the captain of his fate. Another commuter-targeted homily from the *Republican* rings an astonishing change on America's quintessential individualist and sums up the dominant ideology of the American 1920s: "The courage given us by our work is like the self-reliance which Emerson has made forever glorious. Like self-reliance, courage is ultimately a reliance on widening concentric circles of property which reach to God."[25]

"Progress is to get" was how William Carlos Williams replied to such mystifications (I, 159). *The Great American Novel,* in which he said that, is packed with signs drawn from his own environment of America's betrayal of his kind of transcendentalism, which wanted to see those "concentric circles of property" not in terms of titles and tax rates, but as occasions for quite another kind of "especial wide awakeness and alertness" than the *Republican* called for. The immediate perception he called "contact," which reached from and to a more properly Emersonian self-reliance: he wanted "men intact—with all their senses waking," who out of their embattled autonomy would create an authentically American art, culture, and democracy (AG, 206).

But the *Nuevo Mundo* he had envisioned in "The Wanderer" was turning out to be a parody of his ideals of community, the individual, culture, and liberty. America's amazing "profusion"—not of money, but of "freedom, a loosened desire running free in plenty, tempered instinctively to beauty," was being debased into a pursuit of the merest material sort of wealth.[26] The community of articulate and honest townspeople for which he had hoped in the 1910s had been debased into a consumer culture, united not by honesty and beauty but by a powerhouse on a side street off Park Avenue:

> In rows sat the great black machines saying vrummmmmmmmmmmmmm. Stately in the great hall they sat and generated electricity to light the cellar stairs with. To warm the pad on Mrs. Voorman's belly. To cook supper by and iron Abie's pyjamas. Here was democracy. Here is progress—here is the substance of words—UMMMMM: that is to say meat or linen or belly ache. (I, 163)

The dynamo democracy generated a culture valuing quantity over quality, foisting on the public Congoleum and "shoddy," a wool cloth ingeniously but carelessly made out of recycled rags (I, 227). It honored immigrants such as Louis Horowitz, the errand boy who built the Woolworth Building—proof that America grants "genius" the freedom to express itself (while Claude Monet, who Williams mischievously claims was "born in Columbia, Ohio," leaves to be able to paint) (220–21). Such a culture, Williams warned again and again in the early 1920s, was nothing but "an unconscious porkyard and oilhole for those, more able, who will fasten themselves on us" (AG, 109).

How could an American artist make art out of a culture indifferent to the kind of progress that a Monet made? In *The Great American Novel*, Williams, like Van Wyck Brooks in *The Freeman*, exhorted American culture to free itself of its colonial mentality toward European art, lamenting America's having no true "words" of its own: "Every word we have must be broken off from the European mass" (I, 175).

Unlike Brooks, however, Williams insisted, "FIRST let the words be free" rather than somehow allying them with the proletariat (172). In *Spring and All*, he even divided society into classes according to their relation to the imagination; in Russia, the "social class" (of workers and peasants) was "ebullient now . . . because of the force of the imagination energizing them." But that class was "without the power of expression" and needed the poet—who was not one of them (I, 134–35). "There are moments," he told Edmund Brown in 1921, "when I could be one of the proletariat—if the P[roletariat] were all as I could wish it. . . . Forty thousand million men all—myself."[27]

Also unlike Brooks, Williams emphasized the difficulty of having the immediate experience of America which he felt was essential to making one's words one's own. For modernity was as powerful an enemy of such experience as European form. Not only did the copy of the Seville church tower on Madison Square Garden threaten American art (168), so did the stone-and-steel Garden itself: "I turn [the words] over in my mind and look at them but they mean little that is clean. They are plastered with muck out of the cities" (175).

Williams articulated his hostility to the urban world with the help of John Dewey, whose pronouncements on the virtues of the locality became one of Williams's touchstones. In "Americanism and Localism," Dewey made the observations cited above about how "thin and apologetic" "national" news was to support his assertion that "the country is a spread of localities, while the nation is something that exists in Washington and other seats of government."

Dewey blamed this thinking in national terms for the failure of American literature. The lack of vivid and particular presences in the " 'serious novel' " in America, said Dewey, was caused by the same absence of the local as in the new newspapers: the novelist, like a well-meaning bureaucrat, "aims at universality and attains technique." For Dewey, the failure was more than the novelist's or even the city's: in America, local culture was too often stillborn or forgotten, and so "there is no background" with which the characters might interact. By "background," Dewey meant more than local color; he defined it as "tradition, the descent of forces," which formed a part of the social environment in which an individual became himself, and which produced the distinctive "manners" and values of a locality.[28]

Williams took Dewey's observations to heart when he wrote his serious parody of the American " 'serious novel.' " In it he announces his intention to set down "the American background," even though a voice warns him, "You will go mad" (196). Indeed it was a quixotic quest: American high culture was entirely derivative of European forms, and there had never been any truly local culture. As for contemporary mass culture, it was as remote from local experience as the newspapers that described it: "jazz, the Follies, the flapper in orange and green gown and war-paint of rouge," the movies—all were "impossible frenzies of color" that people used to compensate for "not living impassioned lives" of their own, mistakenly trying "to find these things outside themselves; a futile, often a destructive quest" (200).

It was the same criticism that Williams made in the 1910s when he scored Rutherford's "leading citizens" for insulating themselves from the kind of real experience that the underclass had, though in the *Novel* he expanded his scale from a local class to a culture. He had to do so, for that culture was invading his locality. Williams found it on the floor of his car, as a newspaper opened to advertisements offering clothing as a self: "Pisek-designed Personality Modes" that are "genuine inspirations of individual styling," bearing "the unmistakable stamp of individuality" and inspiring admiration for their "differentness" (190–91). He found it in his mailbox, in which he found the promise of "real" experience debased into a form letter: if he was one of those "who think of life as the supreme adventure," he could "safely" subscribe to the *Atlantic Monthly* (221–22). He found it in his bedroom, where his wife read *Vanity Fair* while waiting for him to come home (161).

Could one transform or break through or get clear of this pervasive mediation by the "information culture," recover immediate experience, and thus recover one's individuality and build a local culture?[29] Williams kept his faith that an "eternal moment" existed behind America's façade of culture and progress. Americans were currently devouring popular science and history books like H.G. Wells's *Outline of History* and flattering themselves that by buying a gas range they had progressed up the ladder of natural selection. But behind this "obscure" biological evolution, Williams argued, there was "a compensatory involution" that canceled time; he proposed to write its "natural history" and expose both the lie and the truth of the "fad of evolution":

> Borne on the foamy crest of involution, like Venus on her wave . . . it is the return: See they return! From savages in quest of a bear we are come upon rifles, cannon. From Chaldeans solving the stars we have fallen into the bellies of the telescopes. From great runners we have evolved into speeches sent over a wire.
> But our spirits, our spirits have prospered! Boom, boom. Oh yes, our spirits have grown—
> (215)

Although the return of the gods that Pound heralded in the poem Williams alludes to here had been reduced by modernity to mere spectacle ("Eric the Red landed in Providence, Rhode Island, and was put in a cage so everyone could see him") (210), everyone was still Eric, capable of discovering a "new world" with his own faculties.

One solution, then, was individual and moral: if that salesman would exert himself sufficiently to put his untapped "perceptions and faculties" to proper use, his spirit rather than his company's accounts would prosper. If enough Americans did so, they could rid their faculties of both the European-bound past and the modern present and bring themselves back to an "American situation" prior to culture and history:

> We are only children when we acknowledge ourselves to be children. Weight of culture, weight of learning, weight of everything such as abandon in any sense has nothing to do with it. We must first isolate ourselves. Free ourselves even more than we have. Let us learn the essentials of the American situation.
> . . . We too are free. Free! We too, with paddles instead of turbines will discover the new world. We are able. We are kings in our own right. (211)

But early on in the *Novel*, Williams expressed one powerful moment of doubt which resonates through all of his subsequent exhortations. He passes by a group of children "released from school" who, lying in the gutter and covering themselves with leaves, look out for a moment of freedom and discovery "on the new world." Facing the difficulty of his quest to isolate himself and free his words from Europe and modern America, Williams wonders "if it were too late to be Eric" (182).

This anxiety underlies most of Williams's social and political criticism of the early 1920s; it was caused, I think, by his uneasy awareness that there was no way for him to beat modernity unless he played its game—which would mean that he, the autonomous individual and artist in concrete touch with his locality and his words, would cease to exist as such. If as an individual he felt his life was being thinned by modernity, as an artist he was having trouble competing with the discourses of modernity—of progress, science, philosophy, and politics—which, he felt, were displacing art as the highest mode of experience.

He persisted, however, in trying to remain an Eric, and in the *Novel* he found a way to attack the discourses of modernity with the discourse of art, by investing his formal experiments with a dimension of social commentary that allowed the *Novel* to remain a novel: "If there is progress then there is a novel," the book self-reflexively begins. "Without progress there is nothing." However, says the very next sentence, "Everything exists from the beginning" (158). By identifying conventional narrative progress with the culture's debased value of progress—"to get"—he hoped to shatter the hold on his reader of both.

Late in life Williams recalled that "the heroine" of his *Novel* "is a little Ford car—she was very passionate—a hot little baby" (IWWP, 39), and what narrative line there is follows the car as Williams drives it about in a fog—a fog of corrupted words at one point, a "fog of waste" soon after (I, 159, 163). This fog dissolves—or thickens—into a collage of scenes and voices from past and present, of narrative moments, dialogue, disquisitions on art, advertisements, overheard conversations. The organization of the book thus challenges the notion of progress from past to present, and the myth of material progress founded on it.

In associating linear time with material progress, Williams verged on naming what Marshall Berman calls "the tragedy of development" of modern capitalism: the twin ironies that capitalism's drive to build the economy requires that it tear that economy down as it goes, and that as fast as such development opens possibilities for human development it closes them off.[30] Williams might well have agreed with Berman, but he would have resisted using Berman's language, suspecting that both its abstraction and its implicit privileging of economics would prevent the concrete experience necessary for his own priority, art. Williams meant his formal strategies in the *Novel* to reach through history to that prehistorical moment of the *Nuevo Mundo:* the novel must progress not through linear time but toward "a word" (165), a name for experience "freed" from the muck of cities, the inappropriate values that kill it, so that it can both describe and embody that no-time when "everything exists from the beginning."

Satire does not necessarily propose a remedy for the defects it excoriates, but it often implies a positive norm through its choice of objects for criticism. Did Williams write such a norm for social or political organization in between the lines of *The Great American Novel*? He later got in the habit of asserting a direct analogy between the government of words and the government of men, and he seems to do so in the *Novel;* however, he hesitated before the evident difficulty of describing a government that enables one to have immediate experience and create art.

The novel's linearity-shattering form implicitly argues for the kind of progress a culture makes when it roots itself in a place and in a pure present—a preindustrial culture, such as the local culture of the Cumberland Mountains, the people of which are "untouched by modern life." They "have changed so little," in fact, "that they are the typical Americans" (220). Ma Duncan, a 55-year-old mountain woman whose neighbors send for her "in time of need," seems to speak for Williams. She lies on the ground "So as I can hear what the old earth has to say me," and, looking out at the stumps of trees cut for the nearby sawmills, she laments:

> If folks wasn't so mad for money they might be here and a preachin' the gospel of beauty. But folks is all for money and all for self. Some-day when they've cut off all the beauty that God planted to point us to him, folks will look round and wonder what us human bein's [*sic*] is here for— (219)

The preciosity of style in the passage on the mountain folk strongly suggests that Williams is mocking a popular magazine, perhaps *National Geographic*. But elsewhere in the *Novel* he expresses Ma Duncan's sentiments in his own voice, and we have noted his recurrence to peasant culture in *Rome*. Williams may be trying to have it both ways: by adopting such a tone, he can escape the embarrassment of being regarded as seriously proposing mountain culture as an alternative to a culture that, whatever its materialist horrors, offered too much to want to escape it. Yet by parodying the condescending attitude of the usual writer about folk culture, he deflects our laughter from Ma Duncan and her sentiments to modern culture's failure to take the "religion of beauty" seriously.

Williams was well aware that rural life was anything but paradise, but he could find no other image that embodied his ideals of immediacy, idealism, and poetry as a counter to the "information culture" of modernity. In his own local community only the children lay on the ground, and it was paved with bond issues. His only alternative, then, was to be a lonely Eric the Red—and modernity was building a cage for him. In one important sense, then, Willliams went "mad" trying to create the American background, for his *Great American Novel* could not be as comprehensive in its criticism as his ambitions demanded. It was a setback for art in its competition with the philosophy and science that explained, and hailed, progress and information.

Despite Williams's intentions, *The Great American Novel* is actually mostly foreground, a charting of the symptoms of contemporary culture. The full background waited until *In the American Grain,* in which Williams traced the "tradition, the descent of forces" that produced the psychology and morality of the generic American character that created the culture of shoddy progress and secondhand experience in which he and his Model T wandered. In *In the American Grain,* he also extrapolated from his analysis of that American character to articulate politics that he felt would allow one to experience one's locality as richly as did Ma Duncan. And his hostility to modern society's mediation of experience and encroachments on the individual intensified to the point that, in spite of his common sense, he envied those who defied or escaped society altogether.

In the American Grain is best read as Williams's version of Yeats's *A Vision,* also published in 1925, as poets' mythologies about the creation of poetry. Both works order history and personality (each is a typology of character), and thus ground the poet's aesthetics in a cosmos. Each yields not just "metaphors for poetry," as the spirits told Yeats they had come to give him, but the structure in which those metaphors have meaning—and the structure of the cosmos and the social order in which the poet's imagination may come into full play. Although *In the American Grain* was researched as meticulously as Williams could manage, even those chapters wholly comprising selections from documents take their meaning from being integrated into the structure of Williams's mythology: the individual's discovery of the *Nuevo Mundo.*

Williams was concerned to show that "there is a source in AMERICA for everything we think or do" (AG, 109), and by America he meant one's experience, immediate or not, of the actual continent. As he said of Daniel Boone, "Boone's genius was to recognize the difficulty [of making a culture appropriate to the New World] as neither material nor political but one purely moral and aesthetic" (AG, 136). Out of this epistemological core Williams elaborated a psychological (and moral) history of the American character, and even his politics. To understand the character of those politics, we have to understand Williams's narrative of plenitude and Puritanism.

Williams describes the central trope of this myth in a passage on Boone's genius:

> Filled with the wild beauty of the New World to overbrimming so long as he had what he desired, to bathe in, to explore always more deeply, to see, to feel, to touch—his instincts were contented. Sensing a limitless fortune which daring could make his own, he sought only with primal lust to grow close to it, to understand it and to be part of its mysterious movements—like an Indian. And among the colonists, like an Indian, the ecstasy of complete possession was his alone. (136–37)

Ideally, one's experience of the (female) New World is purely erotic, but ethically pure. Although primal lust drives the male discoverer, his complete possession of her comes not through rapine possession, or exploitation of a money-measured fortune, but through a "marriage" of equals requiring his surrender of attention to her actualities as a place. Doing so requires him to slough off past habits of mind—European habits—and make terms on the place's own terms. *Nuevo Mundo*, entails new experience, new man, new words, works, and culture. Daniel Boone was "Indian-like" in this perceptual sense, and so is each modern American—but Boone had been "robbed of his world" (128).

Boone's world—and self—were robbed by the Puritans, whose image of man as a weak sinner with no hope of salvation but from God's choice debased the individual's powers to match the New World's plentitude with a plentitude of his own. Practicing a scarcity economics of imaginative energy in an environment of sensory abundance, the Puritans accomplished "the secret inversion of loveliness." Perceiving only "a zero in themselves" (65), they saw only the devil in the landscape, and so "the emptiness [of the landscape] about them was sufficient terror for them not to look further" (63). Such a psychology, moreover, created a hypocritical democracy of utter conformity. They relied on "the weight of many to carry through the cold," and their "common wealth" was merely "common to all alike, and never the proud possession of any one." Their survival was endangered by any individual's yielding to his own impulses, Williams acknowledges, but such conformity was disastrous for art: "Each shrank from an imagination that would sever him from the rest" (65–66).

This fear of genuine contact with the American environment was transmitted by the Puritans down through the generations, and especially furthered by Benjamin Franklin, who translated the theology and morality of his predecessors into the Protestant ethic and the fear-born psychology of capitalism: manipulate the environment for the sake of thrift, not experience, and pretend that you are not touching. Franklin "was the full development of the timidity, the strength that denies itself. . . . He was the dike keeper, keeping out the wilderness with his wits. Fear drove his curiosity" into science (155).

This fear of contact—Williams calls it "delay"—is the root cause of contemporary American culture, a vast network of perversions and hysterias:

> The characteristic of American life is that it holds off from embraces, from impacts, gaining, by fear, safety and time in which to fortify its prolific carcass—while the spirit, with tongue hanging out, bites at its bars—its object just out of reach. (175)

This delay, "not of effort, but of touch," fosters Americans' obsession with the "game" of making money. "It is because we fear to wake up that we play so well" (179). The sneaking curiosity of Franklin's, in fact, motivates the finance capitalism of a J.P. Morgan, whose holding companies are the expression of the "acquisitive, but mediate" American character: "American lines but British ships. We own them. But who HAS them?" (175). The "machine civilization" of mass production and distribution riding on such financial structures is but another form of delay: "Yankee inventions. Machines were not so much to save time as to save dignity that fears the animate touch." The lust for "efficiency" that drives American workers and assembly lines is not even greed, but "fear that robs the emotions; a mechanism to increase the gap between touch and thing, not to have a contact" (177).

Like any people, Americans want to touch experience—in fact, Williams said, "the common people" were "lovers of the senses" (206)—but can get it only vicariously, from newspaper headlines about murders, the stands of college football stadiums, newsreels of bathing beauties on aquaplanes, "psuedo-naiads tasteless—wineless, wholesale" (183–84). Indeed, all of modern civilization, Williams asserted, is a prophylactic of Protestant morality:

> America adores violence, yes. It thrills at big fires and explosions. This approaches magnificence! We live not by having less fires but more, by the excitement of seeing torturing things done well, with light ease even. But we have violence *for service*, mark it. Battleships *for peace*. The force of enterprise *for bringing bananas* to the breakfast table. Massive mining operations to transport us—whither? Bathrooms, kitchens, hospitals with a maximum of physical convenience and a minimum of waste to spare us—for what? We never ask. It is all a bar to more intimate shocks. Everything is for "generosity" and "honor." *It has to be* for us to get away with it. (177)

Rather than face their fear of direct experience, Americans evaded both the fear and the experience by pretending that success was a sign only of salvation and moral worth, not of one's own skill or prowess. That need to believe in their own goodness, however, looked mighty hypocritical to foreigners and to Williams. In one of his more insightful criticisms, he scored such hypocrisy as it shaped American foreign policy. Americans needed to believe that such aid as Herbert Hoover delivered through the Relief Commission just after the war, or that "neutral" American advisors were currently giving to the European nations' conference on war reparations, was motivated by pure, disinterested generosity:

> It is this which makes us the flaming terror of the world, a Titan, stupid (as were all the giants), great, to be tricked or tripped (from terror of us) with hatred barking at us by every sea—and by those most to whom we give the most. In the midst of wealth, riches, we have the inevitable Coolidge platform: "poorstateish"—meek. THIS is his cure before the world: our goodness and industry. THIS will convince the world that we are RIGHT. It will not. Make a small mouth. It is the acme of shrewdness, of policy. It will work. We shall have more to give. Logical reasoning it is: Generous to save and give. It is bred of fear. It is as impossible for a rich nation to convince any one of its generosity as for a camel to pass through the eye of a needle. (175)

Williams also showed how the fear of complete possession and immediacy of experience was perverting American democratic politics. The Puritan-Franklinian tradition of self-degradation implied not trusting the individual to act responsibly on his own desires, but constraining and prohibiting such "liberty" in the false name of the good of the greater community. This is Williams's concept of democracy in *In the American Grain,* a benevolent libertarianism with a trust in the individual that would have appalled John Adams, who believed in original sin and wrote checks and balances accordingly. But given Williams's political education in Unitarianism and early muckraking Progressivism, and given his education in the nature of the poet—and given the threats from modernity to the autonomy of the individual, artist or not, and to art itself—Williams's extreme defense of his kind of liberty is understandable.

In its very structure *In the American Grain* was a defense of the individual, as Williams tried to recover the humanity of his subjects from historians, who imprison men "in generic patterns . . . which say nothing save, of such and such a man, that he is dead" (188). Indeed, he conceived the book as if he were revising his Unitarian Sunday School primer, *Noble Lives and Deeds,* with its 40 biographical illustrations that "religion," as the introduction said, "rests at last on the individual." Embedded in Williams's history was his argument that American democracy rested first and last on the individual. For him, the story of American democracy was the extremity—and ambiguity—of the resistance made by free individuals against the extreme constraints placed on them by the Puritan-Franklinian-Coolidge community.

Indeed, the relationship between the individual and his community was wrong from its mythic start. In the first words of the book, Red Eric, the father of Leif Ericsson, lays out the opposition that defines politics in *American Grain*: "Rather the ice than their way; to take what is mine by single strength, theirs by the crookedness of their law" (1). Eric is the primitive archetype of the whole individual who, to remain whole and achieve "complete possession," to remain true to his own desires, and to speak his self-interest openly without hypocritically masking it with a "crooked" law, must either defy or flee society.

Eric has killed a man and been outlawed from Iceland, which is coming to be dominated by Christianity spreading from Norway. He despises his "townspeople's" hypocrisy in sentencing him: after all, "one or the other of us had to die, under the natural circumstance." But they claim that "their way"— Christianity—"is the just way," when it is really the interest beneath their evangelism that is at stake. The man he killed was important to their "schemes": "They would have made him archbishop," Eric scoffs (1–2). The Norwegians are the archetype of all of the "schemers"—the fear-driven planners, manipulators, and moralists—in American history, from the federalist junto to 1920s reformers of morals and government (207).

Eric despises Christian law for the same reasons that he hates the Norwegians' "courts and soft ways": the values of both institutions conflict with those of his tribe. But worse still, they devalue the individual. The Norwegians are proto-Puritans, "weaklings holding together [through the court] to appear strong." Of Christianity, he says, "Promise the weak strength and have the strength of a thousand weak to do your bidding" (4). Pagan and proto-egoist Red Eric, however, is one of those "eager to lead" and, he asserts, worthy to do so, for "I am I, and remain so" even in exile (1).

But this leader pays a price—isolation from society. Even his wife and two sons have converted to Christianity and left him to hold to "the way of the kings and my father." Although he is proud to say, "What I suffer is myself," he acknowledges, "that it only should be mine, cuts deep. It is the half only" (3). Furthermore, although Eric glories in his "single strength," he knows his case is lost precisely because it comes down from right and law to strength. The Norwegians are "many in their act against his one" (2), and so "they in effect have the power, by hook or by crook." Remaining himself, he is forced into exile; choosing himself to colonize the new land of Greenland, he is made "their servant, in spite of myself" (1).

Eric's is the ironic fate of the autonomous self in America, the land of such selves: he could take "complete possession" of the place, but is constrained on the one hand by Christianity (and then by American Puritanism and Protestantism), and on the other by Norwegian royal authority (and then the Puritan commonwealth and American Federalism)—all powers having the strength of the weak many. He is also, of course, the archetype of the avant-garde poet, stronger in imagination than those who ostracize him, living like Boone by the higher law of an "aesthetic and moral" code and isolated because of it, stronger than any one person in the community, yet made its servant by virtue of his single strength. So Williams consoled Alva Turner (and himself) in 1920: Turner was "so far beyond your environment by sheer instinct that the community you live in would be destroyed by your mere presence did it not make an example of you, keep you subdued" (SL, 46).

Williams does qualify his veneration of American individualists, recognizing the inevitability of the constraints on the self that community survival requires. But his recognition is usually more grudging than the noblesse oblige of his letter to Turner. Although Williams tried to accommodate himself to such conflict by accepting that it was inherent in the situation of the poet and the individual citizen, it was a stormy resignation. All his work of the 1920s is a protest against the caging of the Eric in every man by modernity—and, at its most extreme, against the caging of the Eric within by any form of community.

For the means of accommodation he found in his historical examples were few and unsatisfactory, and the restraint chafed like the collar Williams wore when he addressed the stones and blue-gray moss in a 1914 poem (LRN, 29). One can submit to a complete "political conversion of the emotions," as did George Washington, and resist "a mad hell inside" (AG, 142). Yet by becoming "the typical sacrifice to the mob," Washington is for Williams "in a great many ways thoroughly disappointing" (143). Could Washington have avoided such a sublimating "conversion"? Daniel Boone did, but he "deliberately chose the peace of solitude, rather than to mingle in the wild wranglings and disputings of the society around him—from whom it was ever his first thought to be escaping." Had Boone not retreated, Williams maintains, he "would never have penetrated to those secret places where later his name became a talisman" (131). But Boone, like Eric, was an unwilling agent of the society he hoped to leave behind.

To leave society, then, is not to leave. To remain within it is to sacrifice one's self unhappily; to protest it is not to change it. Nevertheless, Williams maintained that there ought to be a way to allow such individual liberty within the social structure, and held up as his exemplar Aaron Burr. But Burr, more clearly than any other figure in *In the American Grain,* demonstrates the double bind of apposition and opposition in which Williams's individualist concept of liberty is constituted.

For Williams, the American War of Independence was not political but total revolution, much like that of 1913: "it was springtime in a new world where everything was possible" (193). However, in the inevitable moment after revolution, when a government must be constituted to replace the one overthrown, that spring died into winter: "The sense of the individual, the basis on which the war was fought, instantly the war was over began to be debauched. . . . The Federal Government was slipping in its fangs. The banks were being organized" (194, 197).

The chief agents of this tyranny were Federalist theorists, especially the proto-corporate capitalist Alexander Hamilton. Hamilton wanted

> to harness the whole, young, aspiring genius to a treadmill[.] Paterson he wished to make capital of the country because there was waterpower there which to his time and mind seemed colossal. And so here organized a company to hold the land thereabouts, with dams and sluices, the origin today of the vilest swillhole in Christendom, the Passaic River; impossible to remove the nuisance so tight had he, Hamilton, sewed up his privileges unto kingdom come, through his holding company, in the State legislature. *His* company. *His* United States: Hamiltonia—the land of the company. (195)

The "true element, liberty," reposed in Hamilton's enemy Aaron Burr (195). Burr, says Williams, "carried into politics . . . a humanity, his own, free and independent, unyielding to the herd, practical, direct. That was his violent party that, based on the rock, could not be moved" (204). Burr's kind of humanity—sensual, direct, refined—was in fact "an element of democratic government, even a major element, those times were slighting . . . an element so powerful and so rare that he was hated for it, feared—and loved" (190). For "a democracy must liberate," says Williams, "men intact—with all their senses waking"; Burr, like his partisan historian, had (though "raised to a different level") "the directness of 'common people' which reformers, that is to say, schemers, commonly neglect, misname, misapprehend as if it were anything but to touch, to hear, to see, to smell, to taste" (206).

Perhaps Burr's is an impossible individualism, a demand for freedom *from* rather than freedom *within* a social order, a willful refusal to accept as necessary the sacrifice of one's private desire for the public good. So thinks Williams's interlocutor (Floss, who according to Williams [A, 183] did the research for the chapter) in the dialogue that makes up the chapter on Burr. She charges that Burr "proposed nothing yet refused to abide loyally by the established order" (196). But according to Williams, the Federalists were the irresponsible ones. They tried to evade the responsibility for their selves that such liberty as Burr's assumes: "wanting to escape their load, each [of the Federalists] puts his harness on a lesser nag,—the government on top" (196). Burr opposed them for their own good, fearing "that they would only lock up themselves" inside their bad faith in fallen man (197).[31]

This question of who was irresponsible to the American community is unanswerable as long as Williams and his interlocutor refuse to negotiate their conceptions of the individual and liberty. She sees the founders' sacrifice of libido as "what they must give up of personal liberty for the general good." Williams, though, just cannot acknowledge that such surrender is inevitable; he does call it "What they must sacrifice of hard-won freedom," but immediately turns to its effects on the Federalists: "whittling themselves down—it was dispiriting—they realized with a nostalgic tremor that Burr KEPT. An unbecoming jealousy sprang up instanter, as pioneers in a bad country who know that one of them is hoarding up his sugar" (203).

Underlying their incompatible views are two different psychologies, hers presuming scarcity and his abundance. To Williams, the country is so full of sugar that it is blind meanness to hoard. "The world," he proclaims, "is made to eat, not leave, that the spirit may be full, not empty" (205). Burr was a precursor of an idea "only lately understood"—by Williams's collaborators and competitors in Greenwich Village in the 1910s and by the pioneers in mass advertising of consumer psychology—that one's pleasure can be more than "the acute delight Americans have always got from denying themselves joy and maiming others that they might be 'saved' from some obliquity of moral carriage" (205).[32]

But just as Village "paganism" and self-expression were transmuted by the larger culture into the purchase of a "Pisek-designed Personality Mode," (I, 190), so Williams's politics of individual liberty were contained within the politics of original sin and social order. Burr was indeed "the essence of the schemes the others made" (207) and posed the Federalists an intolerable conundrum: "They knew they must give up much, he refused—and demanded still a place for himself, whole" (204). But there is no scheme of government for Williams to name that could preserve whole the kind of humanity and individuality that Burr represents for him. He admits as much when he qualifies himself to say that "A country is not free, is not what it pretends to be, unless it leave a vantage open (in tradition) for that which Burr possessed in such remarkable degree" (197). For merely to leave a window open on the ambiguous historical fact of such freedom is only to incorporate it in the structure of the imagination, not that of institutions. Burr finally remains only a permanent disturber of an equally permanent peace.

Yet Williams persists in disturbing his interlocutor's peace until the end of the dialogue, demanding that government enable people to devote themselves to the "careless truth" of their own senses, "giving and receiving to the full of [their] instinctive nature[s]" from "the obscene flesh in which we dig for all our good, man and woman alike" (207). If democracy, or all forms of government, have so far failed to embody such liberty, it is only a question of time and individual will: "if it has not appeared in the great rulers of the world," Williams insists, "it is because they lack power of the spirit and it is yet to appear. It is difficult but it is IT" (206).

Thus the dialogue ends in stalemate. She says she will continue to think Burr "immoral, traitorous, and irregular," and he replies with a story about the aged Burr warning a young lady about those two little words "they say" (207). Williams's questions also leave themselves open to question. Just as Burr's function in our history is to remain an unresolvable quarrel over fact and fiction, so the place of the individual in his community is that of the inside agitator. As art, in Williams's words, is "apposed" to nature by being "opposed" to it (I, 121), so Burr and the erotic self are apposed by being opposed to society and government. They will never resolve the opposition, for the existence of Burr, the self, and their demands depend on the existence of government in whatever form. Neither the scheme nor its essence can do without the other. Each is the grit for the other's pearl.

Williams himself would not have been content to think of his attempt to carry over the essence of the individual into politics as grit for society's oyster; the image connotes too trivial a role for himself and his art. He wanted to unhinge the shell that he felt modernity had clamped shut over him, and he had a scheme in which he felt the essence of humanity could be preserved, if not entirely liberated: local government. Starting from the assumption that "'Morals and happiness will always be nearest to perfection in small communities'" (197), he identified Burr's fight for individual liberty with the struggle to preserve "'the original principle of state vitality, the most important element of our Constitution, and one steadily undermined by Federal encroachment'" (194).

Recounting in *In the American Grain* a discussion with French critic Valéry Larbaud of Puritanism and the French Jesuits, Williams elaborated on how he translated the basis of the American character—the individual's immediate experience of his locality—and its distortion into the basis of his politics of immediate personal participation and responsibility and its present debasement:

> From lack of touch, lack of belief. Steadily the individual loses caste, then the local government loses its authority; the head is more and more removed. Finally the center is reached—totally dehumanized, like a Protestant heaven. Everything is Federalized and all laws become prohibitive in essence.

Such, the trail of Puritanism, is the direct cause of the great growth of the Catholic Church with us today, this dehumanization. It offers to the headless mob a government, and THAT is its appeal (to take immediately the place of that lost local one that used to touch), a government in opposition to the general evil of our civil one; [Catholicism] is at least humane vs. the other (morally) that's merely stupid. . . . Catholicism gains in that it offers us ALLEVIATION from the dullness, the lack of touch incident upon the steady withdrawal of our liberty. (128–29)[33]

For Williams, Prohibition epitomized the government's encroachments on the private realm. His own locality had banned the sale of alcohol since its founding, but that was the local will. The Eighteenth Amendment, however, was "the very essence of all that contradicts the common sense of the democratic American," as he wrote in 1929.[34] Throughout the 1920s, "prohibitions" was his term for all restrictions of individual liberty by the Puritan heritage—"all the asininities of ignorant fear that forbid us to protect a doubtful freedom by employing it" (AG, 109).

But Prohibition, and "prohibitions" such as customs officials practiced on imported books and works of art, were not only a problem of the American character but of modern American government. In 1929, Williams answered a speech of President Hoover's for Philippe Soupault's magazine *Bifur* and wrote his most straightforward political commentary yet. Because it is so consistent with his brief comments on government in *In the American Grain*, "L'Illégalité aux Etats-Unis" may stand as Williams's political manifesto for the 1920s.

In "L'Illégalité," Williams called the disappearance of local government the "capital mistake" causing the widespread disrespect of the law that Hoover deplored. The disappearance of the American sense of responsibility had started with Hamilton, whose Federalism helped strip the individual of his "inmost rights." It was further weakened by the "disastrous error" of saving the Union in the Civil War; now, with the present government "an invisible, mysterious entity, impossible to place," and average citizens feeling "as remote from contact with [it] as we would with ancient Athens'," their representatives nothing but corrupt agents of party "blocs," and with laws "one on top of the other piled on our shoulders," they no longer felt any responsibility for the laws or those who violated them. Hoover's solution, Williams noted with wry exasperation, was to create more law enforcement specialists. But only when "local administration" was reestablished and the federal government "relegated to its function as a simple body of tax collectors" would men regard crime as "a personal insult to their community" again.[35]

Almost all of Williams's political education and experience—his Unitarianism, his idealism about American ideals, his friendship with Paul Herman, his coming of age in the Progressive era, and especially his growing up in Rutherford—led him to write "L'Illégalité." But perhaps even more than his politics, the aesthetics he learned from Oscar Wilde, Ezra Pound, the Village, his townspeople, and his values as an artist—the Individual with a capital I—drove him to rail against modern American "tyranny." Williams's defense of local government was in essence a variation on his myth of the lone explorer caught in wonder at the sheer sensation of standing in the *Nuevo Mundo*. In this version of his story, the discoverer turned pioneer and small-scale founding father, but, like Daniel Boone, had to light out for the territory when the settlement built up, always having to make another last-ditch defense of the now-zoned primal ground of William Carlos Williams's poetics.

There is a grain of history in all myth, however. Whether the Federalization of the individual and the prohibition of his desires began in the Federal period or in Iceland around A.D. 1000, Williams felt it going on all around him in the early 1920s. It has been the burden of this chapter to show how accurately, but also nostalgically, he responded to the modernity which made Rutherford feel like a city, the nation a network of factories and shipping routes, the federal government an octopus. Even if he never quite felt at home in Rutherford, Williams never lost his feel for the "country village" in which he grew up; in fact, he learned to thrive on his displacement. Nor did he ever stop wanting to share his knowledge of his townspeople with them. Yet the context in which such a relation between a poet and his community was truly possible—if it ever was—had long ago vanished.

In the 1920s the conditions in which he could produce his poetry were being erased, as the "information culture" forgot and tried to make one forget what pure experience was. But local government was finally a gesture of regret rather than a practical political program. Calling for such a politics was part of what anthropologists call "rites of intensification," violent ceremonies performed with the purpose of keeping alive values that are breaking down and being forgotten. But like Eric the Red, Williams was made modernity's servant in spite of himself: his nostalgic politics of local government were not opposed, but inevitably, helplessly, apposed to modernity.

When Kenneth Burke complained in his 1926 review of *In the American Grain* that "Ideology, while it is here, is totally secondary; it is never organized, [it] is low in the evolutionary scale," Williams conceded to Burke that the book's politics were "not complicated . . . not worked out . . . I have never been sufficiently devoted to that lore." However, Williams insisted that the book had an ideology, but "more over the writing than in it—which induces an imagistic style that can never be satisfactory to you I know. . . ."[36]

Burke was justified in questioning the place and subtlety of Williams's politics, as Williams acknowledged, but Burke missed a crucial point: the imagistic style is itself the ideology hovering over the writing of *In the American Grain*. For Williams had a scheme besides local government to argue, the antischeme of the book's poetics. His style, he felt, would annihilate time and death and make Aaron Burr and Daniel Boone fully present again. To read *In the American Grain* concretely would be to overcome one's fear of the imagination, to liberate one's self with senses waking and have contact with the past. Just as Williams hoped one would touch the past so intimately, so he aimed for one to encounter through poetry the present—even as it was evaporating in modernity. These were the politics of "contact."

11

Immediate Demands:
The Politics of "Contact"

In December 1920, Williams and Robert McAlmon published the first issue of *Contact* and made a set of last-ditch affirmations more post-Armory than postwar in spirit. Faced with a stalled literary scene now dominated by intellectuals and critics, they continued the avant-garde quest for new form and insisted that the artist knew best. Against the despair over American culture that wrote the steamship passages of expatriates, they stubbornly insisted that a distinctly American art the equal of any from Europe could be begin here and now.

McAlmon and Williams were also looking to recover the benevolent hegemony that art once supposedly possessed, the social power that Williams had thought it was on the verge of attaining before Sarajevo and Versailles. Although they dismissed the current New York scene for being full of "ideas of social revolution" as cold as the tea they were talked over and artists "weaken[ing] their work with humanitarianism," *Contact*'s publishers insisted that they were not "aesthetes" infatuated with "technique." McAlmon and Williams felt that their rejection of social commitment, moral duty, and political potential was itself socially purposeful. In fact, by rejecting such claims, they performed the one thing needful in American culture: "It is our object," wrote Williams, "to discover, if possible, the terms in which good taste can be stated here." From such terms would follow all else the culture lacked.[1]

McAlmon made clear the scope of their aspirations when he defended Williams's *Kora in Hell* from a hostile review in *Poetry* in 1921. Because the war had shattered European values, the American cultural context was utterly barren, he said; Americans had lost their bearings, and more and more of them refused to try to recover the old ones. Williams was only being modern and honest in *Kora* by recording the quest that "thousands" were now making for "a faith in the mere value of living out their lives rather than a religious explanation of existence." His coeditor's literary experiment was an effort to be "conscious of the new form in relation to the dubiety of the day." New form, and the new consciousness created by writing and reading it, would eventually dispel doubt, or provide a way of thinking that would.[2]

But if America was suffering a crisis of values, it was also emerging as a new social order—the order of modernity—which had its own prophets and disciplinarians of the mind. As McAlmon acknowledged in *Contact*, "Civilization . . . has now given up all pretense at aristocratic organization, or any organization, and is an economically accumulated society in which various sophistications of ideas compete for supremacy." Inadequate as those sophistications were (in his defense of *Kora,* McAlmon dismissed current interpretations of evolution, American pragmatism, and "the intelligible, rational, deducible" mind of science and traditional humanism), as the ideology of modernity and the mass-market culture, they were now supreme. And so, Williams said, America was more than ever "a bastard country which knows nothing of its debt to the artist."[3]

But that debt was incalculable, far more than the one owed to the businessmen, the scientists, and the intellectuals; only the artist could save modern America, not only from its despair but also its misleading success. For in a world of increasingly thin and abstract experience, only the artist could preserve individual sensibility and the immediacy of experience that enabled the discovery of values appropriate to the actual world—and the artist was the only thinker out to prove the priority of both.

Williams and McAlmon's manifesto against modernity was wrapped around their magazine's title on the covers of the first two issues. The first, published in December 1920, said

. . . . art may be the supreme hypocrisy of an
information-cultured people . . . . without

CONTACT

. . justifiable perhaps if it becomes at last actually
the way sensitive people live. . . . .

It was the same criticism of modernity that Williams would soon make in *The Great American Novel* and deepen in *In the American Grain.* In *Contact,* McAlmon did most of the explaining: Americans based their culture on experience at least once removed from their environment, he said; such detached "information" caused them to suffer unawares from "information provincialism, which so dulls the sensitivities, while informing the mind, of the average 'cultured' American."[4] Art was now a "supreme hypocrisy" because it had "degenerated" from its original religious impulse and function as the supreme mode of experience and expression into a "profession" in which one marketed some "sophistication" of an idea. Furthermore, as Williams emphasized in his essays, American art was based entirely on past or foreign forms, not on one's own experience, and therefore only pretended to clarify an American's world.

The cover of the second issue announced how the artist would resolve the problem laid out in the first issue. Although the artist was "adrift," he was

> . . . . . . finding a place in abstraction sensually
> realized through
>
> C O N T A C T
>
> with his loose world. . . . a vast discharge of energy
> forced by the impact of experience into form.

That, in one modernist sentence, was Williams's poetics of "contact."

What was this mode of perception and expression, and how would it enable Americans to arrive at sound values and transform their lives? At the foundation of contact was the hero of Williams's myth of the *Nuevo Mundo,* the lone individual, and it is from the hero's relation with that world that we shall start. From Williams's epistemology, we shall arrive at the poems of *Spring and All*—and at the same nostalgia as that he expressed with his politics of the local, and the same ambivalent relation between the poet and modern American society as Red Eric and Aaron Burr had with theirs.

Noting that in his poems Williams was "engaged in discovering the shortest route between subject and object," Kenneth Burke defined contact in 1922 as "man with nothing but the thing and the feeling of the thing."[5] As Williams himself put it in 1921, contact meant recovering the ability to perceive "an immediate objective world of actual experience" (SE, 33–34). To Williams, the "flesh every day that ever was is right at hand" (*Rome,* 18) and thus "knowledge is presence—nothing is ended—nothing is begun" (52). Knowledge was not some abstract dogma that one applied to concrete situations, but the senses' standing in "that now, instantly, always" (18) of the present. And poetry was the mode of such knowledge of immediacy: "[Poetry] is, I am, be—here," for the "clarity" achieved in writing was the counterpart of true knowledge: "It is a logos completely satisfying" (33).

Just as there was a *logos* at the heart of words, there was its counterpart in the perceiver, an autonomous self. For Williams and McAlmon, the self was constituted neither by socioeconomic relations, as a Marxist would say, nor by oedipal relations, as a Freudian would say, but by its "own" experience of the world. McAlmon especially emphasized this; discussing literary influence, he said, "Before a writer 'arrives,' he establishes his own particular apprehension of life which, utterly apart from his manner of writing, is strictly personal, temperamental and rooted within him as an individual so that no literary influence can obliterate it."[6]

For Williams, too, the natural order was comprised of things- and selves-in-themselves. As he explained to Marianne Moore in 1934, he had had "a sort of nameless religious experience" some time in late 1905 or 1906, "a sudden resignation to existence" which "made everything a unit and at the same time a part of myself." This experience—born of despair, he told her—produced the "inner security" she had noticed in his work (SL, 147).

Yet despite this sense of his autonomy and his concomitant sympathy with things, Williams found that in art as well as in life, "there is a constant barrier between the reader and his consciousness of immediate contact with the world. . . . all things [are] removed and impossible." Consequently, the reader "never knows and never dares to know . . . what he is at the exact moment that he is" (I, 89). What was this barrier and why, if the "eternal moment" of the present was readily available and expressible, did it exist?

It was a wall of imported or outdated modes of perception and values—all the clichés of false "culture." Thus in their *Contact* essays, McAlmon and Williams called for the clearing away of mediating values from the individual's experience of the world. "Our only insistances [*sic*]," they wrote in the first issue, "are upon standards which reality as the artist senses it creates, in contradistinction to standards of social, moral or scholastic value—hangovers from past generations no better equipped to ascertain value than we are." To their list of a priori, insulating "standards," Williams added religious faith, which, he said, was "no more than knowledge of the earth"; "the conventional, Tolstoian, mystical concept of faith has never been more than a superficial decoration permissible in ages of great knowledge of the earth and its uses."[7]

For it had been "by paying naked attention first to the THING itself," said Williams, that American "engineers and cobblers" had made shoes, bridges, "indexing systems, locomotives, printing presses, city buildings, farm implements" and the like world-famous, and so would its artists (SE, 35). Any a priori notion skewed the attention. Even trying to look consciously for figures of speech, or even merely deciding to record a day's experiences, he said, "fastens [the writer] down, makes him a—It destroys, makes nature an accessory to the particular theory he is following, it blinds him to his world" (I, 120). Neither man meant to exclude the use of the mind—rather, each meant to use it all. McAlmon best expressed their sense of proportion when he said, "Art I suspect is the intelligent effort to express energy in some form, rather than an intellectual effort to be imaginative or 'esthetic.'"[8]

To Williams, the intellect had to be subordinated to that energy, which was the body's. Throughout the 1920s, Williams located the source of knowledge, meaning, and power in the physical, and he consistently tried to reduce abstractions to their basis in the concrete.[9] Religion was "knowledge of the earth"; intelligence was "only the superficial appearance of [the] passage through the brain of force" (*Rome*, 56); the imagination was "an actual force, comparable to electricity or steam" (I, 120); those who marveled at works of art simply knew "nothing of the physiology of the nervous system" (123).

For "KNOWLEDGE," Williams wrote in *Rome*, "IS ABSOLUTELY NO-THING * BUT PLEASURE[,] an ENDLESS pursuit" that "leads to NOTHING but the instant of its pleasure" (56). The pleasure of the lover, the writer, even the logician, derived from their activities' "purposelessness—aside from motion the feeling of the force : pleasure : SOMETHING out of nothing" (57). This pleasure was the very basis of morality, and yet this force had been "fenced away by priests who have lost touch." Among these priests were prime ministers, real estate agents, boards of education, and lawyers—anyone he saw submitting to Puritanism, which inverted morality and called itself a "work ethic," or to higher education, "a low scheme to trick pleasure out of work" (32).

Thus in his poems he sought to break down those fences and give the reader the actual sensation of this motion and force. As he told John Riordan in 1926, "a work of art is not integrated by thought but by performance with sensual components"; thus he praised Riordan for reading poems "with your whole body."[10] The abstractions of criticism had to start from the "clear use of sensation . . . building upon the basis of what is observed," as Williams praised Kenneth Burke for doing in an essay on Jules Laforgue (SE, 36).

Recovering the use of one's sensations meant that he could know the actualities of the things around him—for an American, his locality in America. The concern Williams expressed in *The Great American Novel* about creating a genuinely American art and culture led him to define contact as both individualistic and nationalistic. McAlmon, who left for Europe in February 1921, soon disagreed publicly with Williams about the importance of place; such an emphasis, he argued, would only produce the sort of debilitating "humanitarianism" they distrusted: "One writes to clarify one's intelligent understanding of the universe rather than to express a social or religious hope, etc. In fact the contact is first with topnotch comprehension rather than with locality or race or mere environment."[11]

Williams, however, insisted that clear sensation produced such comprehension, and "the artist is limited to the range of his contact with the objective world":

> Contact always implies a local definition of effort with a consequent taking on of certain colors from the locality by the experience, and these colors or sensual values of whatever sort, are the only realities in writing, or as may be said, the essential quality in literature. (SE, 32)

Criticism as well "must originate in the environment it is intended for," he told Kenneth Burke in January 1921; he disliked reading European criticism on European writers because "the environment gets in the writing every time and it is inimical to me. I resent the feel I get from the composition."

Williams could have defined the spectrum of colors that the locality gave his work—did it include shadings from the region's economy, for instance?—but he dwelt more on what of the environment he was trying to keep out of his work than on what went in. Having made a considerable investment in being an identifiably American artist, Williams had to believe that art could be created out of his place. But he saw little in the present culture of the place that he could use; most of it had to be resisted. Thus, while he insisted that "there is a source in AMERICA for everything we do" (AG, 109), he also had to insist that the individual was not bound by the past or the present. Art, he replied to Harold Stearns, was a "self-related activity" shaped by the will of artists, not the age (RI, 63).

Williams's position on the artist and his environment remained, finally, the paradox he first wrote out in his 1915 essay, "Vortex": "I will express my emotions in the appearances . . . of the place in which I happen to be . . . [but] I will not make an effort to leave that place for I deny that I am dependent on any place" (RI, 58). Although Williams was morally committed to America, his paradoxical relation to one's place is deeply individualistic. The relationships he defined between his poetry and reality, and his poetry and society, had the same ambiguity. Eager to feel that his work was engaged with society, but equally eager to preserve his individualism, he constructed a conceptual seesaw of engagement and detachment, of opposition and apposition to the world and his "time."

His refusal of the usual terms of art's engagement implied to those still using them that he was socially irresponsible. So he was read by Van Wyck Brooks, John Gould Fletcher, and the woman who corners "Jimmy Doyle" at the Village party. But Williams felt as strongly as ever that he was performing an important social function: he was saving selves from the depredations committed on their senses and desires by society. In "Glorious Weather" and the prose sections of *Spring and All*, he replied to the critics of *The Freeman*, the seeker of the usual rhymed uplift, and the radical demanding allegiance to one of those causes he would not follow, explaining how his devotion to "naked attention" and formal experimentation served Coolidge Americans.

In *Spring and All* he set out to refute the Platonic argument, reinforced by centuries of Western representational art, that art is only a "'beautiful illusion,'" a realm separated from and subordinated to reality (I, 89). The hostility borne by socially concerned critics toward "technique" was based on this premise. Such men were accusing Williams of having "no faith whatever," of aiming at the "annihilation of life" by writing poetry that does not "go hand in hand with life" (88). Yet it was their own art and aesthetics that perpetuated divorce and despair: "There is not life in the stuff," Williams replied, "because it tries to be 'like' life" (129); their poetics, not his, were "especially designed to keep up the barrier between sense and the vaporous fringe which distracts the attention from its agonized approaches to the moment" (89).

His own poetics assumed that "composition is in no essential an escape from life" (101). The modern artist does not imitate an already existing thing, like the "traditionalists of plagiarism" (94); he uses one of the processes of nature, the imagination, that "actual force" (120). Williams did acknowledge that there was some qualititative difference between works of nature and art: "[Nature] is opposed to art but [also] apposed to it" (121). But although his work may resemble nothing in nature, it is "transfused with the same forces that transfuse the earth" (121).

Just as he equated his poems and poetics with natural objects and processes in *Spring and All,* so he identified them with history and society in an essay he wrote a few months before *Spring and All*'s publication. In "Glorious Weather," published in *Contact* in April 1923, he argued that

> The object of writing is to celebrate the triumph of sense.
>
> Note: in a poem such as Poe's ANNABEL LEE there is a record of the best sense of the time. We insist on this practical attitude toward writing as against the front of "pure aesthetics."

However, as his choice of "Annabel Lee" suggests, Williams's practical attitude, and his practices, were quite different from those who read the poem's content as that record. For Williams, that "sense is in the form"; it is "not carried as an extraneous 'meaning,' but is constituted by the work itself." The distinction in aesthetic theory between form and content (or abstraction and subject matter, as he also called them) was merely pragmatic, "a division between two types of material." A poet used both "materials" to make a form, which Williams defined as "everything in a work which relates to structural unity rather than to 'meanings' dragged over from former associations." Thus a poem was neither "a symptom" nor "a synthesis of its time," but was a self-reflexive protest and victory, written "to celebrate its own emergence as against everything (its time) to which it stands opposed." It was "a construction that proves itself able to exist even in spite of and over against everything in its time that is deadly."[12]

But to what in 1923 did the poem stand opposed? In "Glorious Weather," Williams included any value, state of mind, or connotation that hazed over the *logos* of a word or the "presence" of the thing to which it referred. In *Spring and All,* Williams named the same enemies of contact that he and McAlmon had named in their magazine essays—the "profitless engagements of the arithmetical" (I, 123), the habits and language of the scientific or the "acquisitive understanding," and "religious dogmatism" (115)—and described their pernicious effects on words:

> So long as the sky is recognized as an association
> is recognized in its function of vague accessory to vague words whose meaning it is impossible to rediscover
> its value can be nothing but mathematical[,] certain limits of gravity and density of air. . . .
> The man of imagination who turns to art for release and fulfilment [*sic*] of his baby promises contends with the sky through layers of demoded words and shapes. Demoded, not because the essential vitality which begot them is laid waste—this cannot be so, a young man feels, since he feels it in himself—but because meanings have been lost through laziness or changes in the form of existence which have let words empty. (100)

The poet had to give demoded words an "acid cleansing" (317) to enable the reader to sense that essential vitality of the word. He deployed the resources of syntax, semantic continuity, rhythm, and enjambment against "meaning." As Williams explained in a poem about *Spring and All* he sent to Monroe Wheeler, he had tried "to cut . . . off" every piece in the book

> from writing
> for the transference
> of ideas—
> to make it
> definitely
> an object
> of whatever shape
> lying upon the paper—[13]

By diverting the reader's attention from the "ideas" behind the words, the poet shifted it to their "sensual values" and so to the "logos immediately satisfying."

As with single words, so with texts. Since "the form of poetry is related to the MOVEMENTS of the imagination revealed in words" (133), one's movement through words had to give that purposeless pleasure underlying knowledge. In Rome, pondering the organization of a book, Williams described the structures of *Kora in Hell, Spring and All,* and *Rome* itself as an attempt to achieve such movement:

> *Not* a mere arrangement—laid side by side—but as if things strove with each other in the work*—*No* significance of the things as things (lost in a work of art *always*) but as they are *left* by the motion to show the force : are the force)
> So the making of the book *is* "things" striving together
>
> Nothing else—it doesn't matter what *is* encountered.
>
> But not a "composition"—it is a disruption
> BROKKEN [*sic*]   (*Rome,* 57)

But Williams is nowhere near as linguistically radical as some of his critical prose implies. He had heard the accusations of decadence leveled at Walter Arensberg's extreme experiments, and had no intention of exposing his work to them (even if he imitated Arensberg's word games in a poem on the verb "To Have Done Nothing"). Unlike "certain of the modern Russians whose work I have seen," who used "unoriented sounds in place of conventional words" and so "completely liberated" the poem, Williams felt that words could not be "dissociated from natural objects and specified meanings"—only from "the usual quality of that meaning."[14] For "facts" and words existed in mutual interindependence—provided those demoded meanings could be stripped away:

> The word is not liberated, therefore able to communicate release from the fixities which destroy it until it is accurately tuned to the fact which[,] giving [the word] reality, by [the fact's] own reality establishes its own freedom from the necessity of a word, thus freeing [the word] and dynamizing it at the same time. (I, 150)

Properly tuned words, then, are both engaged and detached from reality, as the poem as a whole is part of and apart from both nature and its time, engaging itself with them by disengaging its words from their worn-out meanings and revealing the *logos* at their core and the "dynamizing" movement of the imagination. And just as the words self-reflexively communicate their own release from such fixities and celebrate their "emergence," so the experience of reading them, Williams claimed, "liberate[s] the man to act in whatever direction his disposition leads" (150). By placing his work "in a world of new values" (116), the poet enables the reader "to enter a new world, there to have freedom of movement and newness" (134).

Besides providing a moral example of "the importance of personality . . . showing the individual, depressed before it, that his life is valuable—when completed by the imagination" (107), the work of art taught him how to arrive at new values for himself. The reader of a broken composition not only made sensual contact with the "words themselves," but drew out the latent syntactical and semantic relations among them. Williams learned this from reading the angular, astonishing poems of Marianne Moore: "one may seek long in those exciting mazes sure of coming out at the right door in the end. There is nothing missing but the connectives" (I, 311). He even noted that previews of films were "much more vivid + sensual" than the full narrative, because "the banality of sequence has been removed," and he judged "the force" of a piece of writing by reading it from end to beginning ("I find my own sensual pleasure really increased by so doing").[15]

Thus one learned to use the "practical corrective" of the self-reliant farmer and fisherman who, looking at the sky, pierced through the demoded meanings and "read their own lives there" (I, 100). Like the farmer, one faced the over-whelming presence of the world "bare-handed" and became its "composing / —antagonist" (99–100), naming it out of pure contact with it, giving it form and value with faculties that were now properly one's own. With his senses tuned to the things-in-themselves of his locality, he became autonomous and interindependent once more. As a man "intact, with all his senses waking" (AG, 206), he would govern his local environment and build an authentic local culture.

Such were the potential social and political effects of the poetics of contact. That these perceptual means were Williams's political ends is clear from his most explicit summary of the political function of his poetry, the 1926 draft of "What Is the Use of Poetry?" Attacking yet again the scientific and philosophical minds for being unable to "attain to any sense of reality," he asserted that poetry restored not only the individual's autonomy but also his power. It did so by restoring the very basis of his power, his senses and his imagination:

> . . . poetry, cutting through science and philosophy and a sterile life, is of use to the individual in that it rehabilitates a tangible personal periphery, the lack of which is the chief characteristic of modernity—where all men are known as unenviable fools— . . . This loss is largely the work of that essential inanity of science and philosophy well summarized in its effect by such a candid modern work as T.S. Eliot's *The Waste Land*.
>
> This force, poetry[,] rescues self-conception and self-respect wasted by an arid presumption accepting, in our dilemma as we do, any authority which is blatant enough to hold our attention away from despair. Poetry does this somewhat by giving a sight through philosophy + science which make their practitioners, apart from their professional agility, sentimental with a logical despair and rob them as individuals of certitude + potency . . . .
>
> But poetry pierces this also with a sense of life. Poetry restores authority to man by grace of the imagination.

As far as poems go to fulfill their author's aesthetic intentions, the poems of *Spring and All* fulfill Williams's. The success of his formal experiments, especially in playing syntactical ambiguities against line breaks and sentence shapes, and his "dynamizing" even small words such as the definite article "a" by forcing one to attend to their phonological and synactical energies—their own "immediate" qualities—has been celebrated by Hugh Kenner, J. Hillis Miller, Stephen Cushman, Henry Sayre, and others.[16]

It is when one begins to read Williams's poems for more than the thrill of their motion, when one with roused attention begins to supply his own connectives, that questions arise—not so much about the poetics as about the politics implied by them. If this suggests that Williams failed "to cut [the poem] off / from writing / for the transference / of ideas," I hope I have made it clear that Williams did not deny content and meaning a place in his poetics. But one's questions about what the poems "say" lead back to questions about how the poet says it: the politics circle around to the poetics, and from there spiral back to the epistemology and ideas about language underlying them.

Williams's universe of autonomous things and selves and words led him to the same impossibly individualist politics he expressed through his myth of the *Nuevo Mundo* in his 1920s social and political criticism. However successful he might have been in "restoring authority to man" through the imagination, the individuals he awakened could only feel defeated by modernity. Even the victories Williams could claim over modernity's materialism, mediation, intrusions, and erasures are marked by despair at winning the war, and by a longing to escape society altogether for the security of the "old mode" of art's autonomy.

Like "The Wanderer," *Spring and All* is another ambivalent dialogue between the urban world of New York and more pastoral territory. Nine years later, Williams is more confident and articulate in his own beliefs and more certain of what the city represents, and he uses the pastoral mode as both a protesting withdrawal from the city and an engagement with it, apposing the pastoral to the city, sometimes point-by-point, to oppose it more specifically. By more explicitly identifying the pastoral as the realm of the imagination, Williams sharpens the confrontation between poetry and the mentalities of modernity.

Above all, the politics of *Spring and All* lie in its confrontation between poetry and politics themselves—which is the more accurate mode of organizing the world?—and in poetry's celebration of its own emergence in spite of the stultifications of modernity. But as in "The Wanderer," so in *Spring and All:* despite Williams's assertions that his poems are engaged with their time, he gives us cause to wonder if they do not after all act more as a temporary refuge from an overwhelming history for the battered self than as a transformation of the city and the individual. When he uses his poetics of immediacy to challenge politics as a mode of acting in and organizing the world—and in some of Williams's grander assertions he does make the challenge—the poems cannot do much more than Aaron Burr did against the Federalists; they act at most as permanent troublers of an equally permanent peace.

After an exuberant destruction and re-creation of the world by the imagination in the opening prose sections, the "stark dignity of entrance" of Spring in the title poem affirms the persistence of contact, Eros, and poetry even in the "broad waste of muddy fields" of the American present. Williams then embarks on a quest that takes him through the city and out again, ending in the "savage" and erotic center of "The Wildflower." Before retreating from the city, Williams challenges the way it constricts the imagination and the self by constricting one's senses and erotic energy, offering one false substitutes for immediate experience, and destroying local ways of life.

In "At the Faucet of June" (I, 109–10), the "machine" of modernity intrudes into the backyard garden of sensual contact. After four stanzas in which "familiar things" are united syntactically to give the sense of their being "full of a song / inflated to / fifty pounds pressure / at the faucet of / June," the syntactic sequence is broken off—and out leaps "J.P.M." from behind "steel rocks," apparently to enjoy more of his "extraordinary privileges among virginity."

J.P. Morgan was reputed to be quite a satyr; Williams, however, makes him the inverse of a Pan, one who uses his privilege not to procreate but to sublimate: to buy European art treasures, and to "solve the core of whirling flywheels." The result is that his Morgan "cars are about / the finest on / the market today." "It"—that is, the erotic-imaginative "song of June"—"has come to motor cars," declining from the force of satyrical assault. As Williams puns by "leaving off the g," the "song" has been diminished to the "son," who was notorious in the early 1920s for using his parents' motor car to play the petting Pan.[17]

But Williams rescues the sexual "song" by asserting that although it "is impossible to say" now, it is also "impossible to underestimate." He closes the poem with a second syntactically governed sequence:

                         wind, earthquakes in

                         Manchuria, a
                         partridge
                         from dry leaves

The lower presssure of commas joins these objects, as if the song's pressure is now
diminished. Nevertheless, the juxtaposition of their names may startle us into
awakening to their phonological unity, and we may hear the song again at full
pressure in the "words themselves"—and acknowledge that we may have under-
estimated the power of the imagination.

    J.P. Morgan was an obvious target for a poet trying to use the pressure of
poetry against the pressure of modernity. But the city in which Morgan housed his
art and his power was still more of a threat than a challenge to Williams. In the fall
of 1923, he and Floss moved to a friend's apartment for a sabbatical before leaving
for Europe, and in "Flight to the City" (99–100), Williams wondered if he would
be able to "Burst it asunder / break through to the fifty words / necessary" and bring
his wife gifts "from the great end of a cornucopia / of glass." His second residence
in New York apparently stirred recollections of an earlier failure to overcome
modernity's constraints.

    In "Young Love" (113–15), Williams remembers an encounter of "fifteen
years" ago, during his internship at Child's Hospital, with a nurse he calls "Miss
Margaret Jarvis." She was his version of the "hyacinth girl," and, like Eliot's
narrator, Williams fails at a moment "when anything might have happened"
between them. Exactly what did happen is not clear, but instead of meeting the
power of her emotions with his own—her "sobs soaked through the walls /
breaking the hospital to pieces"—he wilted. "All I said was: there, you see, it is
broken." He "wrapped" himself around her—in fact, he says, "I was your
nightgown"—but all, finally, that he did for her passion was watch, and "merely
caress [her] curiously."

    Now he is disgusted with himself for not having been "clean" and gone
"straight to the mark." His passion shattered no hospital walls. Instead, like J.P.
Morgan, he has diverted his sexual energy into his profession and into his
middle-class world, and that life now overwhelms him: "in my life the furniture
eats me." As an artist, he should be destroying and recomposing the world with the
force of his passion:

                         Clean is he alone
                         after whom stream
                         the broken pieces of the city—
                         flying apart at his approaches

He should fragment and recompose like the cubist painter of the "great forces at
work" in the city, John Marin, whom Williams first met in March 1922 and who is

mentioned in the poem,[18] or Walt Whitman, whose democracy, Williams says in the prose immediately preceding the poem, "represents the vigor of his imaginative life" (112–13).

Here Williams elaborates upon the analogy between democracy and inclusiveness that he drew in the 1910s so that he can claim that the poetics of contact are democratic. The poet reaches beyond social values, attitudes, norms, and customs to identify imaginatively with everything-in-itself. Thus he shatters the hospital walls of the urban order preventing contact and recomposes it according to the "imaginative understanding" (113). It is a question of the imagination's power to compete with modernity's ways of perceiving, which exclude reality and yield only "fragmentary" understanding (112) and inadequate values.

But is the poetry of contact powerful enough? Williams had only a fragmentary understanding of himself and his world when he met Miss Jarvis ("What to want?" he asks at one point). Although he could empathize to the point that he became her "nightgown," he did not break through to the "fifty words necessary" for genuine contact. The poem is an admission, and an exorcism, of his fear of suffering the same defeat before the city as he suffered before Margaret Jarvis—and as she, too, has suffered; 15 years later, she still goes "about the city, they say / patching up sick school children" (114).

The delightful "Horned Purple" (135–36) implies that he was still more comfortable with the smaller-scale erotics and "inclusiveness" of Rutherford. Williams himself was still patching up sick schoolchildren in 1923, and on his rounds that spring he noticed that some of his fellow citizens threatened to make the town fly apart. He wonders at young men "of a certain sort—/ drivers for grocers or taxidrivers / white and colored" who wear "horned" lilac blossoms in their caps or over their ears. "What is it that does this?" he asks.

Knowing full well, he parodies the shocked tone of some of Rutherford's "leading citizens" and celebrates the young toughs' expression of lust: "Dirty satyrs, it is / vulgarity raised to the last power." He takes his characteristic moral stance here, straddling the Rutherford's class lines and holding up the "directness of 'common people'" (AG, 206) for the aesthetic and moral benefit of their social betters. This kind of democratic inclusiveness he could easily perform, perhaps too easily. As he said of poetry in "The Black Winds" (I, 103), "How easy to slip / into the old mode, how hard to / cling firmly to the advance."

Whatever doubts Williams felt about achieving freedom of the senses, they could only have been intensified by his attempts to oppose modernity's distortion of his own role as a democratic artist. In three poems in *Spring and All,* Williams attacked mass means of imaginative expression—ostensibly democratic forms—to assert that they were destroying the average person's potential for contact and preventing him or her from hearing the poet. He also responded obliquely to those calling for a "proletarian art" by celebrating the American masses' desire for beauty and art and condemning the false satisfactions of modern culture.

Yet if these poems are Williams at his most radically democratic in political implication, their force is undercut by the limitation of his politics to those most consistent with his poetics. For as "To Elsie" suggests, placing one's faith in immediate experience, individual imaginations and local government against modernity could only lead one to see damage that not even the poet of contact could repair.

His ambivalence—revolutionary democracy for all, or contact and poetry for each and every one?—lies at the heart of "At the Ball Game" (147–49), in which he celebrates baseball for being "all to no end / save beauty" and the brute force of the crowd: "It is alive, venomous / it smiles grimly / its words cut." This wild energy is the motive force of religious fanaticism and political apocalypse—"It is the Inquisition, the / Revolution"—for it is the power of the imagination:

> It is beauty itself
> that lives
>
> day by day in them
> idly—
>
> This is
> the power of their faces

But Williams (a lifelong New York Giants fan) did not notice how this power was being sublimated and dissipated as, at the turn of the decade, sports were transformed from local and participatory activities into mass spectacle, with the figures of Babe Ruth, Jack Dempsey, and other athletes amplified into celebrity by newspapers. Instead, just as in "The Wanderer" he insisted that the "one thing" that could unite the Paterson strikers was beauty, and not their common interest as an exploited class, so here he displaces political terms with those of poetry.

Ironically enough, in "Light Becomes Darkness" (127–28) he indicts motion pictures for doing just that. As his comments in "What Is the Use of Poetry?" show, he detested the passive habits of perception that film fostered. In "Light" he gives his hatred an extra edge: the movies not only stultify the senses, but by doing so displace what he feels is their potentially revolutionary force.

Williams's premise is that the movies are displacing religion—and also taking over its function as mass opiate. Church ritual, he begins, has been translated into a profane "passion play" "without sacrifice / of even the smallest / detail," right down to the organ.[19] He then takes what is for him an unexpected turn into abstract language and the philosophy of history and social change. The translatability of cathedral into movie house, like the organ music's ability to change the audience's emotion swiftly from woe to joy, demonstrates that "creation and destruction are simultaneous." Within religion, this means that the unity of church doctrine always turns into schism. This cycle, however, can be broken:

> But schism which seems
> adamant is diverted
> from the perpendicular
> by simply rotating the object
>
> cleaving away the root of
> disaster which it
> seemed to foster.

The passage is obscure—Williams may have been imitating Marianne Moore's diction—but I think Williams means that, just as religion leads one to think not of the present but of another life, so the movies divert one's attention from the root causes of social schism simply by "rotating" the "object" with which one is dissatisfied and preventing one's recognition that it is connected to those root causes.

And "thus / the movies are a moral force"—not, however, because they stir up passion with near-lewdness, as guardians of public chastity were currently charging. The movies in fact enforce "morality," a perverse Puritanism, by diverting sexuality and imagination from their true object, the pure present of the moment of contact. Those "priests" who fence in desire now preside in the projection booth, as the movie audience is "intoned / over by the supple jointed / imagination of inoffensiveness / backed by biblical rigidity."

It is a dispiriting diversion of the ferocious energy of the ball game's crowd, which in other times and places fostered the schism of the Inquisition, and the Bolshevik Revolution. But now the movie crowd has no true unity or force—only "the closeness and / universality of sand." The particles of this aggregation are nothing like their "female relative" in Russia, and so Williams cannot envision them as Leo Tolstoy could imagine her—being "injected / into the Russian nobility."

In "Light Becomes Darkness" he himself is guilty of "rotating the object"—his image of the Russian peasant woman—and cleaving away its "root"—the collective ideology of communism—which spelled disaster for his individualism. In his 1928 "A Democratic Party Poem," he called America a group of "decayed Soviets" which needed to recover their local rights rather than the means of production—radical politics in 1922, perhaps, but radically nostalgic.[20] Williams's most extended poem on the Bolshevik Revolution, "A Morning Imagination of Russia" of 1927 (CP, 303–6), also emphasizes regaining "touch"; if people regained ownership of the means of perception, they would rule themselves in local governments. And, more to the point for Williams, they could once again build their own local culture.

For the movies are modernity's false substitute for a people's "peasant traditions," as one of Williams's best-known poems makes clear. "To Elsie" (131–33) is his most poignant diagnosis of the failure of American culture, not least because in it Williams despairingly acknowledges his failure as the poet of contact to restore it.

"To Elsie" begins so resonantly that one may not hear what Williams means when he says, "The pure products of America / go crazy." The primary reference of the phrase is to the purest products of immediate contact with an American environment that Williams can find, isolated rural people in northern New Jersey or "mountain folk from Kentucky" such as those who for lack of a more appropriate image he idealized as local culture in *The Great American Novel*. Here in "To Elsie" he idealizes them again, but as the Gothic obverse of Ma Duncan. The local culture that once produced a woman who could talk to the earth and preach the "gospel of beauty" now yields "deaf-mutes, thieves / old names / and promiscuity between devil-may-care men . . . and young slatterns, bathed / in filth," who act out tawdry erotic rites that barely express their severely limited emotions.

They have gone crazy, Williams argues, from having "imaginations which have no / peasant traditions to give them / character." America's peasants are mere shells of the Italians Williams would praise in *Rome*, who, even if "their life is stupid and happy and horrible," are "free because they tie the grape and rich because the law is made to rob them and religion to enslave them and science to break them from their homes and possessions" (13)—that is, because they live in the immediate sensual relation with the land to which modern culture's law and religion and science are utterly hostile. The difference between the Italian "peasant" and the "vulgar" American, Williams wrote in 1927, was that the peasant is "placed" in his or her environment, and thus had a "clear sense" that the vulgar and "the learned" lacked (EK, 37).

But the chance of saving rural American folk is next to nil, for with no traditions to inherit, there is no past connection with the land to recover. At best, the "spirit" of the Indians, that "ghost of the land" that in *In the American Grain* Williams asserts still "moves in the blood, moves the blood" will be passed on through the genes, and a girl like Elsie will be born of a "marriage / perhaps / with a dash of Indian blood" (I, 132). Then, "hemmed round by murder and disease" in her degraded rural environment, she will be put in such extremities that she is "rescued by an / agent— / reared by the state and / sent out at fifteen to work in / some hard pressed / house in the suburbs" like the Williams's.[21]

Elsie thus "express[es] with broken / brain the truth about us," the pure products of the American tradition of the imagination that Williams tries to exorcise with *The Great American Novel* and *In the American Grain*: all Americans, whether they live in hills, suburbs, or cities, have inherited the inverse of "peasant traditions," the Puritanism that teaches us to fear contact and act

> as if the earth under our feet
> were
> an excrement of some sky

and we degraded prisoners
destined
to hunger until we eat filth

while the imagination strains
after deer
going by fields of goldenrod in

the stifling heat of September

Unable to believe that this pastoral landscape can be entered simply by making contact with the earth under our feet, we have lost our moral bearings. Without contact, no one develops "character" and values. As the poem concludes, there is "no one / to witness / and adjust, no one to drive the car."

Not even the poet? In "To Elsie," Williams's fear that it may simply be "too late to be Eric" seems to overwhelm him. It may well be too late for the poet of contact, the person whom Williams argued was most qualified to "witness," "adjust," and enable Americans to recover their senses. There will be no audience the size of the ball-game crowd for the poet, no community with the closeness and universality created by a lust for immediacy and beauty. At best the poet can hope to catch "isolate flecks" in which "something / is given off."

In portraying this culture of self-flagellation, Williams lashes himself as hard as he does Puritanism, perhaps because he realized that his poetics could not defeat the forces of modernity generated by that self-denying imagination. For Elsie represents not only the American imagination: she also embodies the history of its defeat by those forces. She was one of a series of state wards, perhaps in the county children's home for which Williams was the physician in 1921 and 1922, that the Williams family took in to help around the house. According to Williams's reminiscences, she was mentally and emotionally disturbed.[22] As a symbol of what modernity has done to the American imagination, she is the beaten ghost of Williams's heroine Elia Brobitza—raised in the kind of institutional setting that Brobitza refused to enter, dependent on a middle-class suburban family of the kind that Brobitza defied. Elsie can use her imagination only to wear "cheap jewelry" for the boys; Brobitza could dream so passionately of her old lover that he appeared to her.

Yet Elsie was in a certain sense rescued from a wretched rural existence by the state's child welfare institutions. That is, her savior was modernity's mentality about social affairs, one of the very things that destroyed the kind of imagination and culture which she embodies in Williams's poem. Williams would have acknowledged the irony, but perhaps not its full force, for the gap between Elsie the person and Elsie the figure of local culture resonates; it is also the ironic gap between Williams's politics and his poetics.

As the poet mourning the passing of her culture, Williams was caught in the same double bind as when he was a dutiful civil servant in the 1910s. Back then he took practically every post in the borough and the county having to do with public health while writing against the forces that created those jobs. Williams was entirely sincere in acting as police surgeon while writing "Portrait of a Woman in Bed." He knew he had to participate in modernity to mitigate illness and pain, and his townspeople were indeed better off with a town nurse, as Elsie was better off in his household than in the Ramapos hills. But his awareness of the gap between social reality and the terms in which he criticized it, I think, gave the cry of anguish that closes "To Elsie" a particular blue note. Not "they" but "we," he among them, will keep Elsie the person alive only by continuing to make Elsies—and ourselves—"crazy."

I readily grant that Williams's point was that, while modernity can mitigate the actual Elsie's lot, it cannot save that spirit of the Indian she figuratively carried in her blood. I am trying to understand why he felt that not even he could save her. Having defined the problem "aestheticocentrically," in moral and aesthetic terms that limited his politics to the politics of individual liberty and local government, Williams was forced by his own best intentions to sentimentalize what local culture he could find and not confront more forcefully the modernity erasing such a world. As long as he framed his challenge in terms of the individual imagination and local culture, he could not win. The "dash of Indian blood" in Elsie, then, finally represents little more than his own nostalgia for a golden age of contact.

If "To Elsie" raised the question to Williams of just how effectively his nostalgic politics and poetics could oppose their enemy, two poems in *Spring and All* show us what kind of victory he could win. Both "Rapid Transit" and "The Right of Way" are self-reflexive poems which celebrate their own triumphs over "deadly" elements of modernity, the particular "pieces of the broken city" which each makes "stream" along within its force field. But in their very joy they make one wonder if such temporary victories are the best that the poet who celebrates the imagination's ability to destroy and recreate the world can hope to do.

Williams told John Thirlwall in the 1950s that in "Rapid Transit" (146–47) he "was studying a presentation of the language as it is actually used," a statement that plays down the use to which he put such formal means. Of all the poems in *Spring and All*, perhaps "Rapid Transit" most successfully opposes itself and the imagination to modernity, for it does so by playing off the language "as it is actually used" and the values it bears against the poem's and the poet's.[23]

Williams begins by reciting one of those "mathematical" modern values, a statistic which "demodes" the terror of its very meaning: "Somebody dies every four minutes / in New York State—." He apparently means to invest the statement with some human significance, but he is cut off by a voice—a representative of the culture, who does not grant the imagination such power—telling him, "To hell with you and your poetry. / . . . What the hell do you know about it?" The poet, too, "will rot," the voice says; why should he have anything more valuable to say about death than anyone else—especially a poet whose work does not seem to be poetry at all? Williams does not respond just yet; instead, we hear some of modernity's poetry, "AXIOMS" on the problem of death:

> Do not get killed
>
> Careful Crossing Campaign
> Cross Crossings Cautiously

The poet may know nothing about death, but modern life's only counsel is, avoid it—by avoiding life. These axioms—propounded by Rutherford's borough government in a 1922 campaign to paint pedestrian crosswalks at dangerous intersections—are perfect examples of what Williams called the Puritan-bred "asininities of ignorant fear that forbid us to protect a doubtful freedom by employing it" (AG, 109). (His 1928 sequence, "Della Primavera Trasportata al Morale," has a profusion of such asininities—stoplights, parking signs, real estate notices, and directions to hospital wards.)

Then Williams responds with a few positive axioms of his own. By juxtaposing them on the page, he "dynamizes" them, trying to give the words themselves the life that their meanings denote:

> THE HORSES   black
>   &
> PRANCED   white

But then he apparently gives up: "What's the use of sweating over / this sort of thing, Carl, here / it is all set up[.]"

What is set up, we learn, is a complete substitute for poetry: "Outings in New York City" at Pelham Bay Park in the Bronx. "Ho for the open country," Williams half-ruefully, half-mockingly rhymes. For the rest of the poem Williams sings the praises of the park in clichés that could have come from a city brochure ("It's on Long Island Sound / with bathing, boating / tennis, baseball, golf, etc."). He then actually gives "Carl" specific (and accurate) instructions on which subway to take there, courtesy, as the last line advertises, of the "Interborough Rapid Transit Co."

However nice it was in the early 1920s, though, Pelham Bay Park is a far cry from the "new world" of "freedom of movement and newness" that a reader could enter in Williams's poems. Modernity's version of the pastoral is a thoroughly administered landscape, controlled by a city commission, brought to one's attention through the "demoded" language of advertising, and reached by a subway, all constraining one from using the freedom that such a landscape promises. Williams himself seems to be constrained, speaking in modernity's own voice as if he were resigned to modernity's having the freedom of the pastoral space "all set up" under its control.

But he is working judo on it, using its own force to throw it. This poem, like Marianne Moore's "Marriage," is an "anthology of transit" (I, 311), suppressing its connectives to heighten the pleasure of the ride and engage the reader in meaning-making.[24] By abruptly stopping on the I.R.T.'s name, depriving us of the usual sense of closure and any obvious indication of its meaning, the poem startles us awake to the fact that its poetry lies in the physical energies of "the language as it is actually used," which Williams releases, for example, by breaking the line at "here / it is all set up," and by stopping the poem short on the pun about poetry in the subway line's name. The poem's own rapid transit celebrates its emergence out of poetry's apparent defeat by "everything in its time that is deadly": modernity's lack of values that could reconcile one to death, its fear of making contact with life, and its hatred of the poetry and poet who could save one from both. By revitalizing the plainest talk from the "fixities" of modern language, poetry recovers its own turf: the false rest to be had in Pelham Bay Park is displaced by the energetic pastoral of the imagination.

It is unfair but necessary to ask: could Williams's version of true pastoral permanently supplant Pelham Bay Park, the dead language in which it is praised, and the values of modernity as a whole? Perhaps so—within the individual, if not out in the world. Perhaps the reader will reconceive poetry, thinking of it as a counterlandscape available for him to enter while he rides the I.R.T. Perhaps he will ask why he has to take a subway out of the city to enjoy the park's lesser pleasures, or even go so far as to try to make that urban world into poetry's pastoral of contact. But Williams was not so sanguine about the prospects of his revolution. Like the geography of "The Wanderer," that of "Rapid Transit" implies that even though poetry can appose itself line-by-line to the landscape, language, and values of modernity, it remains a realm of experience segregated from the urban world, set out on the city limits like Pelham Bay Park.

Such is also the situation of poetry and the poet implied in Williams's closest skirmish with modernity, "The Right of Way" (119–20). "The Right of Way" celebrates contact by reenacting it as an aimless automobile ride. The drive, like the mind making contact, is purposeless and directionless, the pleasurable sensation of the pure motion of the imagination. "Why bother where I went?" Williams asks, dismissing our need for direction and offering instead the pleasure of an "unrelated" sequence of immediate perceptions of the people he sees. He passed by them, he says, "with my mind / on nothing in the world / but the right of way / I enjoy on the road by / virtue of the law"—that is, the law of the imagination that grants one the pure freedom to drive one's senses around. By its virtue his perceptions are free of the fixities of business, "social or religious hope," moral judgment, or A-to-B thinking—everything that "blinds him to his world." He is even freed from having to mean something: this "spectacle" is "nameless," and its "supreme importance"—the sheer pleasure of such pure perception—speeds him by the people on the roadside "without a word" to them (or even to the notebook in which he often jotted things when driving).

Like "Rapid Transit," "The Right of Way" appropriates part of modernity—here an essential part, the automobile—and deftly strips it of its conventional meaning to displace it with the higher order of the imagination's way of seeing. But contact neither completely displaces modernity, nor breaks completely free from it. As Cecelia Tichi notes, the pleasures of pure perception celebrated here have been made possible by the stepped-up tempo of modern life.[25] If it is the imagination "upon which reality rides" (139), the imagination is riding here on the reality of rubber tires powered by the force of internal combustion. Although Williams opposes with a higher value each "deadly" connotation of his ride, his higher values still depend on those connotations to which they are apposed, and thus the degree of freedom from the modern world which the poem celebrates is qualified.

This ambiguous independence is the logical extension of the deepest assumptions of Williams's poetics and his politics. He may have known full well its limitations as the foundation of a social order, but in the prose following "The Right of Way" in *Spring and All,* he revealed how powerful his attraction to such dreaming was:

> The writer of imagination would find himself released from observing things for the purpose of writing them down later. He would be there to enjoy, to taste, to engage the free world, not a world which he carries like a bag of food, always fearful lest he drop something or someone get more than he, [*sic*]
>
> A world detached from the necessity of recording it, sufficient to itself, removed from him (as it most certainly is) with which he has bitter and delicious relations and from which he is independent—moving at will from one thing to another—as he pleases, unbound—complete. . . . (120–21)

This writer would have the same relation to his world as cleansed, tuned words have to facts, that interindependence of two completely self-sufficient things. Such autonomy would not be a divorce from the world, but a marvelous marriage with it in which he would somehow retain freedom of movement. Indeed, it would be an individualist's paradise, detached altogether from the necessities imposed by social life. With no sort of business to conduct, he could dispense even with the fundamental social instrument of language and not speak to others such as the roadside folk, or even to one's self.

But as Williams's optative mood in his commentary suggests, the fact that only outside social relations can such pure contact occur led him not to press his demand for it as far as a less sensible idealist might. He expected, as he said in *Rome,* "not revolution—but to clean it out of me" (44), and in poems such as

"Rapid Transit" and "The Right of Way" he offered his reader a way to see through and get clear of the "deadliness" of modernity. It was a momentary "relief" from the world which denied him the "fulfilment [*sic*] of his baby promises," though not a complete transformation of that world.

Williams defiantly proclaimed in the opening of *Spring and All* that "the imagination, intoxicated by prohibitions," will rise "to drunken heights to destroy the world" and reveal the true "meaning of 'art'" (90–91). He asserted even more defiantly throughout the volume that such an act would restore authority to the individual and enable him to make power his own once again. Yet the degree of his exuberance is finally a measure of his desperation. Although he succeeded in showing that an intimate concern with art's form was an intimate concern with the state of the mind and the world, and that this concern should win back art's hegemony from the vapid "information culture" of modernity and "sterile" science and philosophy, beneath all of his gestures he did not believe he could win.

Williams felt 1920s America trapped him in the same way that 1830s and 1840s America had trapped Edgar Allan Poe: the artist must be in complete opposition to his culture's values, even though he is not powerful enough to overcome them. "The driving force of a crudely repressive environment" had "forced into being" Poe's imagination and led him to create poems that gave one a "sense of completeness" by including "reality"; they did so, however, by giving one a "sense of escape from it." Just as this paradoxical relation set Poe "accurately, even inevitably . . . in his time" (111), so Williams's engagement-through-withdrawal, his opposition through apposition rather than transformation set him in his modern decade.

Given the extreme individualism and the purity of the immediate relations with the world that Williams both presumed and demanded, he could not help but feel that he was fighting a losing cause. The most he could demand of his poetics of contact is that they keep themselves and the self alive, holding open a "vantage" within modernity's framework of "sophistications" and "information" so the individual could sustain himself with moments of immediate experience.

Despite Williams's intention to break down the barrier between art and life, then, the *Nuevo Mundo* of "mass movement like a sea" (I, 175) continued to hold art at arm's length and view it as an autonomous social institution. Although Williams, more than any other American modernist poet, insisted that the "special 'place' which poems, as all works of art, must occupy" is "quite definitely the same as that where bricks and colored threads are handled" (312), the forces of modernity threatening to diffuse both experience and art into mere information forced him to fall back on the idea that art was a refuge, a transcendental Pelham Bay Park.

But if Williams devoted his poetic revolution in the early 1920s to ends that prevented him from making them prevail, he did not give up his premises; instead he withdrew to husband art's energies and bide his time. As he wrote to Kenneth Burke in the fall of 1924,

> Let me make myself clear as to my present attitude toward the enemy. It is indifferentism. You are perfectly right in saying that. . . . Within that indifferentism, however, I live at the white hot center. That is my theory. Indifferentism as far as present attack is concerned but no indifference inside. Inside I want it hotter than ever before. We must weed and sharpen our weapons with malice. (SL, 65)

Continuing to place the freedom of art and the individual at the center of his vision of the world, he also continued to volunteer blueprints for what he called in "L'Illégalité" "the restoration of democracy on another plan." As he explained "The Right of Way" to John Thirlwall in the early 1950s, the "unrelated event" which is the poem's subject is not his own freedom from the social world through which his imagination speeds, but the people he sees along the way—"the really important people to whom I can salute," the anonymous "woman in blue / who was laughing," the "boy of eight who was / looking at the middle of / the man's belly / at a watchchain" (I, 119).[26] By giving the reader a glimpse of their sheer presence, Williams meant to assert, however ironically it rings, their "supreme importance."

Conclusion: Seeds

"It is impossible to remake the country." Quite so, but it is not impossible to remake the country in the imagination, *but only, I will add, of known elements . . . [found] in the present on the only basis possible[,] as it is the only universal element we have[:] the local and universal element under our noses.*

William Carlos Williams

Here in Ronald Reagan's second term, it would be sheer hypocrisy to chide William Carlos Williams for despairing over the prospects for social and political change in the Coolidge era—which the Reagan era, with its ideological alliance of hypocritical nostalgia for small-town America and lust for big-city cash and power, all-too-dispiritingly resembles. But as this study demonstrates, the habits of mind about the individual, society, and art which Williams acquired in the first 40 years of his life impelled him to "remake" modern America into the *Nuevo Mundo* of "The Wanderer," *The Great American Novel,* and *Spring and All,* but at the same time ensured that "the land of his heart's desire" he envisioned could never become the actual country. The very principles by which he wrote his poems made him a socially concerned poet and weakened the politics implicit in what he wrote. His assumptions about the autonomy of the individual and of art, and the immediacy of experience which they should feel and express, set him up for a despair that perhaps he did not have to feel—and that socially concerned poets who can watch the Contragate hearing on postmodern television, and who can look back on Williams's dilemmas, surely do not have to know.

Williams's sense of himself as an autonomous individual ran extraordinarily deep. His early "nameless religious experience" led him to make himself the core of his life and work, with the result, as he explained to Marianne Moore in 1934, "I won't follow causes. I can't. The reason is that it seems so much more important to me that I *am*" (SL, 147). Even those ideas and values he opposed, much less those he shared with Rutherford, the medical profession, rebel New York, and Coolidge democracy, could only have reinforced his belief in the simple separateness of himself.

A note in his 1928 *Embodiment of Knowledge* sums up perfectly the ambiguous relation of the individual to society which he had embodied in the figures of Eric and Boone and Burr. At first he defined "the characteristic American *position* of intelligence" as "the pioneer turn of mind—the individual superior to authority," but then caught himself: "No, external to it, as connotated [*sic*] by our history, [our] temperament—the one [position] profitably to be observed" (EK, 9). As his early and busy civic life suggests, he resisted the temptations to acting out this "externality," even if he imagined talking to the stones. Having grown up among white-collar townsmen of the same "pioneer turn of mind" and learning to judge behavior on ethical rather than social or political grounds, he came to believe that other selves had, or should be capable of, his own combination of self-sufficiency and service, and he continued to think in terms of the local government of a community whose social relations, like those of the *Others* circle, could be the voluntary but "antagonistic / co-operation" (P, 177) of individuals assured of their equality and independence. Always resisting the dogma of a group unless that dogma protected the liberty of the individual, he would always have to insist that he was also "not against government, *not* against government" (SE, 194).

But modernizing America's threat to individual autonomy forced him to be more antagonistic than cooperative, as it made the power both of independent communities and of persons seem to evaporate, and Williams's hometown turned itself into a more city-minded place. Having defined the individual and society in terms of a fundamental separation, however, Williams found no new middle ground except resignation or consolatory thoughts of escape.

Saving the "I," of course, required saving the "am," the immediacy of individual experience by which the "elements" of all things were fully "known." His definition of things as having a little core of "essential vitality," like his conception of the individual, tended to exclude a middle in which thing-as-such and thing-as-mediation could somehow meet. Kenneth Burke correctly observed in 1921 that Williams had a habit of defining the "barrier" between the individual and the world as a twin conflict between the individual's "desires" and abstract principles, and between Nature and Culture (the "ideas man has erected above nature"). Culture and Nature, like the individual in his antagonistic cooperation with his community, were separate but joined, opposed and apposed to each other, and so Williams drew a gray line between them. The "coercions of nature" that he wanted to deal with, as Burke noted, included iron rails as well as iron ore. Contact would strip away Culture from those rails and let them be seen for themselves; by facing such coercions of Nature in this pure state, one could build a new, appropriate American culture.[1]

But modern American culture threatened too often to make such pure experience vapid, stifling Betty Putnam's singing, making Rutherfordians into "gulls" of religion when there were gulls in the air to be seen, showing the mere "information" of motion pictures and displacing one's own passion. Finding so much in the way of immediacy, Williams tended to view society itself as the enemy of his poetics. Not having begun from the premise that society is "always already" weaving one's self and one's world, he assumed that he could wrestle the world into the shape of his desire in some space apart from society. If Culture by definition tainted one's experience, then the artist had to break free from it altogether to have pure experience—which Williams so often represented as a move into nature, "a return of culture to the ground," a "descent to the ground of [one's] desire."

He made a similar shift toward nature in his thinking about language. He saw language, or "words," as being affected by a socially created network of meanings and values, but for him they had been created prior to history and had an inviolable core. Thus he valued the blunt "commonness" of Old Bach and the "perfections" he heard in lower-class speech—but for their vitality and freedom from artifical restraints on desire and the natural self. Although he knew that "meanings have been lost through changes—[in] the form of existence," he spoke of restoring words by taking them all the way out of their social contexts, away from the discourses of science, philosophy, and commerce, back to a "wordless / world / without personality" (I, 119) in which the Adamic personality of the poet could rename and recover the word's vitality.

But once the words had been stolen "back" from modernity and renewed in that wordless world, as they were so deftly in "Rapid Transit," would their purity survive back in Manhattan? If one can know the "elements" locally and immediately and become one's own self only by remaking it all outside of time and history "in the imagination," how does one get back? The poet in the bourgeois world has not been able to overcome his interindependence with the world from which he declares himself free and which in return declares him banished from power. Ironically, the conditions Williams placed on remaking "the country in the imagination" prevented him from crossing the crucial borderline between art's autonomy and its engagement.

Although his fundamental despair, the "resignation toward existence" (SL, 147) on which, he told Marianne Moore, his very self was founded, might have led him to plan "to live in this world with people as they are because you can't change anybody" (LRN, 20), as he wrote to himself in 1914, something equally strong drove him to write a large body of socially concerned verse and to insist that it was the most important "record" of "its time." The country he remade in the realm of the imagination pressed in apposition against America so closely that Williams had to remind his readers that he was, after all, writing poems. But having defined the individual and society in terms of such fundamental separation, and having identified all social mediation as the enemy of immediacy, Williams could find no middle ground except withdrawal. And so, even though he could claim the presence of "reality" and a "sense of completeness" more rightfully for his own work than Poe's, he also offered a "sense of escape" and "relief."

But he had been brought up to believe that "art is intrinsic it is not a plaything," and he did not give up trying to make it so. And it was indeed "not impossible" to remake modernity and the country "in the imagination." I have questioned the efficacy of Williams's imaginary America and suggested that the Constitution he wrote for the country would not have enabled its society to work, unless all of its citizens had an extraordinary willingness to cooperate voluntarily. That is, it would work only if it were a small town, a state, a nation of men like Williams.

But if he was condemned to despair about "remaking the country" through poetic revolution by his revolutionary aims, those aims were nonetheless honorable and decent. And if he brought reality over into Santiago Grove but could not bring it back, reality remains there, in the realm of the imagination, where it has formed "seeds" of possibility, demands to consider the problem again. The fate of Williams's "burning desire to be something to the common" should warn poets to beware the seductions of American individualism and autonomy and the modernist artist's ideology of immediacy. And yet Williams's poems, which, to use his favorite democratic term, "include" more of America more generously than those of any of other major modernist, do finally achieve an aesthetic and moral victory over their own political limitations—which were not Williams's alone, but those of modern America and modernist art.

Notes

Unpublished material in special collections is referred to as follows: *Buffalo*: Poetry Collection, Lockwood Memorial Library, State University of New York at Buffalo. References are made according to Neil Baldwin and Steven L. Meyers, *The Manuscripts and Letters of William Carlos Williams in the Poetry Collection of the Lockwood Memorial Library, State University of New York at Buffalo: A Descriptive Catalogue* (Boston: G.K. Hall & Co., 1978). *Yale*: Collection of American Literature, The Beinecke Rare Book and Manuscript Library, Yale University. A letter and name following refer to the library's cataloguing. *Chicago*: *Poetry* Papers, Joseph Regenstein Library, University of Chicago. *Delaware*: Special Collections, Hugh M. Morris Library, University of Delaware. *Penn*: Rare Books and Special Collections, Pattee Library, The Pennsylvania State University. *Maryland*: Special Collections, McKeldin Library, University of Maryland. *Virginia*: William Carlos Williams Collection, Barrett Library, University of Virginia. *Fairleigh-Dickinson*: Williams material at the Department of English, Fairleigh-Dickinson University, Rutherford Campus. *Private*: Material in private possession.

Williams family members are referred to with these abbreviations: Edgar I. Williams, EW; Florence Herman Williams, FH or FW; Helene Hoheb Williams, HHW. The typescript of *Selected Letters* at the Beinecke contains many letters not in the published version; I refer to it as (Yale SL). A previously unpublished letter found in Paul Mariani's *William Carlos Williams: A New World Naked* is cited as (Mariani).

Much of my local history comes from Rutherford's two major newspapers of the period: the *American,* founded in 1892, and the *Republican,* founded in 1905. The *Republican* absorbed the *American* in February 1915 and was renamed the *Republican and Rutherford American.* I refer to it simply as the *Republican.*

Introduction

1. "Enthusiasms": Dr. William Eric Williams to author, 7 Feb. 1983.

2. Dijkstra, RI, 11; Weaver, *William Carlos Williams: The American Background* (Cambridge: Cambridge University Press, 1971), 89–114 (quotation from 90); Mariani, 651.

3. Levertov, "Poetry and Revolution: Neruda Is Dead—Neruda Lives," *Light Up the Cave* (New York: New Directions, 1981), 130; Breslin, *William Carlos Williams: An American Artist* (New York: Oxford University Press, 1971), 22.

4. Townley, *The Early Poetry of William Carlos Williams* (Ithaca: Cornell University Press, 1975), 53–54. Breslin, 38, asserts that Williams's "critical ideas underwent little growth or modification" after the 1910s, an assertion that Cecelia Tichi uses to justify bringing material from Williams's whole career to bear on his thinking in the 1910s and 1920s ("Twentieth Century

Limited," *William Carlos Williams Review* 9.1–2 [Fall 1983], 70 n. 4). But even if Williams used the same ideas in the 1950s as in the 1910s, we have to ask what they mean as a response to a new historical context.

5. In *American Literature and Social Change* (Bloomington: Indiana University Press, 1983), 11–16, Michael Spindler details the shift in America from an "economy of production" to an "economy of consumption" between 1890 and 1920, with useful statistics on capital formation and growth.

6. Tilly, *An Urban World* (Boston: Little, Brown, 1974); Wiebe, *The Search for Order 1877–1920* (New York: Hill and Wang, 1967), 166.

7. Lasch, *The New Radicalism in America, 1884–1963* (New York: Vintage Books, 1967), xiv; Eagleton, *Literary Theory: An Introduction* (Minneapolis: University of Minnesota Press, 1983), 194; Levertov, "On the Edge of Darkness: What Is Political Poetry?" *Light Up the Cave*, 116.

8. De Tocqueville, *L'Ancien régime et la révolution,* cited in Yehoshua Arieli, *Individualism and Nationalism in American Ideology* (1964; rprt. Baltimore: Penguin, 1966), 192.

9. Johns, *Times of Our Lives* (New York: Stackpole and Sons, 1937), 128; Aaron, *Writers on the Left: Episodes in American Literary Communism* (New York: Harcourt, Brace & World, 1961), 6; Fishbein, *Rebels in Bohemia: The Radicals of* The Masses, *1911–1917* (Chapel Hill: University of North Carolina Press, 1982), 66 and passim.

10. Bürger, *Theory of the Avant-Garde* (Minneapolis: University of Minnesota Press, 1984). He is responding to more pessimistic arguments about art's autonomy and impotence in an increasingly rationalized social order made by the Frankfurt School, particularly Herbert Marcuse and T.W. Adorno. See Adorno's "Lyric Poetry and Society" (1957; *Telos*, no. 20 [Summer 1974], 56–71) on the illusory freedom from society of even the lyric. Berman, *All that Is Solid Melts into Air* (New York: Simon and Schuster, 1982), emphasizes the ambivalence caused artists by capitalism's Faustian drive for "development" and their combined alienation and complicity in the process: "All forms of modernist art and thought have a dual character: they are at once expressions of and protests against the process of modernization" (235). In *Children of the Mire* (Cambridge: Harvard University Press, 1974), Paz asserts that poets' "response to and awareness of the discord between society and poetry" is "the central, often secret, theme of poetry since the Romantic era" (v). I regret that Jerrold Seigel's brilliant study of *Bohemian Paris* (New York: Viking Penguin, 1986) appeared too late for me to use.

11. Burger, 24; Sonnenberg, "Left Literary Notes: Masses Old and New," *Radical America* 3 (Nov. 1969), 71, quoted in Fishbein, 184.

12. "Lazy Verse" in *Journalism vs. Art* (New York: Alfred A. Knopf, 1916), 90; *Enjoyment of Poetry* (1913; rprt. New York: Charles Scribner's Sons, 1951), 130.

13. "Letter to the Editor," *Gryphon,* no. 2 (Fall 1950), 32.

14. Paz, 43–44.

Chapter 1

1. On economic "incorporation"—and its effect on American culture—see Alan Trachtenberg, *The Incorporation of America: Culture and Society in the Gilded Age* (New York: Hill and Wang, 1982). For the transformation of American small towns in the 1890s and 1900s, see Richard Lingeman, *Small-Town America* (Boston: Houghton Mifflin, 1980), 258–363 and Wiebe, 44–75.

2. Lingeman, 409.

3. "Seventy Years Deep," *Holiday* 16.5 (Nov. 1954), 54; *Republican,* 3 Jan. 1916.

4. Quoted in Kenneth T. Jackson, *Crabgrass Frontier: The Suburbanization of the United States* (New York: Oxford University Press, 1985), 79.

5. Lingeman, 286; Jackson, 72.

6. James A. Hands, *A Brief History of Rutherford, New Jersey* (Rutherford, N.J., 1956), n.p. See also Reid Howell, "The History of Rutherford, New Jersey," in Frances A. Westervelt, *The History of Bergen County, 1620–1923* (New York: Historical Publishing Co., 1923), vol. 1, 311, referred to henceforth as "Howell." *News* editorial quoted in *Republican,* 20 March 1915.

7. See Hands for details of the incorporation dispute.

8. Kipp's name was also spelled "Kip." He was described in the 1920 *Year Book* of the Bergen County Historical Society: "He was reputed to be one of the wealthiest men in this part of New Jersey, although his mode of living was simple and luxuries had no attraction for Mr. Kip. . . . He was an extremely conservative man and disapproved of large public expenditures of money. The problem of taxation was with Mr. Kip at all times a mighty interesting proposition" (Howell, 309).

9. The crossing was not "improved" until 1914 or 1915 (Howell, 327), though the improvement was apparently without much success; the *Republican* was still editorializing on the crossing in the early 1920s.
    News editorial quoted in *Republican,* 20 March 1915.

10. Details of Rutherford's growth: Hands; Howell; Rosalind Meyers, *Rutherford, New Jersey and Its Schools* (Rutherford, N.J., 16 Dec. 1935); *The Evolution of the Borough of Rutherford* (Borough of Rutherford Municipal Planning Project, June 1939); *The Free Public Library of Rutherford* (Rutherford, N.J.: Free Public Library of Rutherford, 1944). Union Club: interview with Fred Bunker, former borough purchasing agent and assistant business administrator, 5 Aug. 1982. "Long-Time Resident": W.P. Elliot, *Things Old and New In Rutherford* (Rutherford, N.J., 1898), quoted in Alice Cooke Brown, *A Social History Of Rutherford, New Jersey,* Diss. New York University School of Education, 1948, 435.

11. Lloyd Haberty, *Newspapers and Newspaper Men of Rutherford* (Rutherford, N.J., n.d.), 4–5, 9–11.

12. "Hackensack Ring": *Bergen County Panorama* (Hackensack, N.J.: Bergen County Board of Chosen Freeholders, 1941), 37–38. Information on Democratic power in neighboring towns from election results in the *Republican* and *American.*

13. Shibboleth: Theodore Roosevelt, "Where We Cannot Work with Socialists," *The Outlook* 91 (20 May 1909), 619–23.

14. "The Art of Poetry," *Paris Review* 32 (Summer-Fall 1964), 1.

15. *Republican,* 29 Aug. 1914. See Richard Hofstadter, *The Age of Reform* (New York: Vintage, 1955), 182–85, on ethnic tensions underlying Progressives' condemnation of "machine" politics.

16. "1928: A Musty Old Democratic Party Poem of the Campaign before Last" (Buffalo A769b).

17. Mariani, 23. Kipp: Howell, 310.

18. *Industrial Directory for New Jersey, 1915.* William Eric Williams, "The Doctor," *WCW Review* 9.1–2 (Fall 1983), 36. Free blacks and ethnic groups: *Bergen County Panorama,* 169–81.

19. "Questions and Answers—From a Radio Program," undated typescript (Yale Za Williams Uncat).

20. Eckart quoted by Andrew Giarelli, "The Medical Nature of William Carlos Williams," *Journal of the Medical Society of New Jersey* 80:9 (Sept. 1983), 738.

21. Mariani, 9–14.

22. Floss Herman Williams recalled that Becton, Dickinson, and the Williams boys courted the local "belles" at a nearby lake (Edith Heal, "Floss," *William Carlos Williams Newsletter* 3.1 [Spring 1977], 5).

23. Townley, 53–54.

24. Date and proceeds from *Betty Putnam*: *American*, 8 July 1909, and *Republican*, 10 July 1909. The Kirmess dances (in which Floss performed): *Republican*, 24 Nov. 1910.

25. "As Sung in 'The Mikado,'" *Republican*, 20 May 1909.

26. David Fedo, *William Carlos Williams: A Poet in the American Theater*, Diss. Boston Univerity 1972, 12.

27. *Betty Putnam* (Yale Za Williams 28). All quotations in my text are from this typescript.

28. *Republican*, 10 July 1909.

29. *Sauerkraut to the Cultured: A Nieu Amsterdam Comedy* (Yale Za Williams 214a), 4. Page numbers in my text refer to this typescript. The play, less provocatively titled *Johan Bach's Daughter*, was advertised in the *Republican* and the *American* for three weeks before the performance. Except for a passing mention in the *Republican*'s 19 Nov. article on the Kirmess, that it was "well received," the play was not reviewed. According to the program in the *American*, 10 Nov. 1910, the play was directed by Williams's father, and Williams himself played Karl Minnewit.

30. WCW to H.H. Lewis, 30 Dec. 1938 (Yale Za Williams Uncat).

31. "Vote of confidence": Bergen *Herald-News*, 9 Nov. 1954. "All that remains": quoted by William A. Caldwell, "William Carlos Williams: The Doctor," *Journal of the Medical Society of New Jersey* 80.9 (Sept. 1983), 709–11. Caldwell attended the dinner and took notes of Williams's words.

32. F.B.I. file on Williams, archives of the Department of Justice. The F.B.I. investigated Williams as part of its work on the treason case against Ezra Pound. The policeman's description resembles one given by Dr. William Eric Williams of a "characteristic attitude" of his father's: "poet busy creating" ("The Physical," *WCW Review*, 8.1 [Spring 1982], 7).

Chapter 2

1. On small-community stress, see Wiebe, 44–75, and especially Hofstadter, who emphasizes immigration's creation of the difference between the Yankee middle-class conceptions of politics and the urban machine's.

2. Michael Kammens, *A Season of Youth: The American Revolution and the Historical Imagination* (New York: Knopf, 1978), 72; Wiebe, 57.

3. Information on the G.A.R.'s New Jersey activities from Bunker interview. On Burrows, see *Rutherford Illustrated* (Rutherford, N.J.: Rutherford Printing Co., 1892), 11. For hagiographical genealogy, see Howell and especially J.M. Von Valen, *History of Bergen County, N.J.* (New York: New Jersey Publishing & Engraving Co., 1900).

4.   "Rutherford's Prince of Poets Lays Writing to Frustration," Bergen *Herald-News*, n.d. [1949] (WCW microfilm, Rutherford Free Library).

For more on Williams's need to feel American, see his letter to Horace Gregory, 22 July 1939 (SL, 185), and his vision of the multiracial, multicultural society of Mayaguez, Puerto Rico, where "the light" of "tolerance" caused "the breakdown of old rigidities" (YMW, 35).

Williams's address book is now at Yale (Za Williams Uncat), dated by Williams, "French Hospital, December 25, 1906," on the first page.

5.   "Magna Carta": "My Years at Horace Mann" (Yale Za Williams 168). Grant: WCW to EW, 16 Nov. 1904 (Yale SL).

6.   "Indifferent": from Thirlwall typescript, "Conversation with William Carlos Williams," 25 June 1953 (Yale Za Williams Uncat). In *Ezra Pound's Pennsylvania* (Toledo: The Friends of the University of Toledo Libraries, 1976), 30, Noel Stock lists Pound's curriculum and reprints the poem, "Ezra On the Strike," from the Jenkinstown *Times-Chronicle*, 8 Nov. 1902 (34).

"Many sessions": Thirlwall, "Conversation." "Trusts": Pound to WCW, 6 Feb. 1907 (Buffalo).

7.   Duncan: WCW to EW, 22 Aug. 1908 (Buffalo). "The Real American," rev. of Nicholas Murray Butler, *The American as He Is, The Outlook* 91 (20 March 1909), 623–26. "Be sure": WCW to EW, 18 March 1909 (Yale SL).

8.   Columbus: Mariani, 88. "Infuse": WCW to FH, 15 May 1910 (Mariani, 88). The reading lists are reprinted in appendix B of Townley, 186–89.

9.   Williams wrote Edgar on 13 Feb. 1907 (Buffalo) promising to send him a manuscript, so he was writing plays by then. Which one is unknown. We do know of seven plays that had American themes. There are the three typescripts, *A September Afternoon, Betty Putnam*, and *Sauerkraut To the Cultured*. On 19 Nov. 1908 (Buffalo), Williams mentioned to Edgar a play with four characters set in Fort Carolina, Florida around 1600; in late November 1909, Williams wrote Floss from Leipzig that he was working on a play about Christopher Columbus (Mariani, 83). Among the notes and fragments of nine plays in his notes from 1908 to 1911 are file cards for *A Quaker Soak* (Townley, 49–50).

And there is *Plums*, described by Vivien Koch in *William Carlos Williams* (Norfolk, Conn.: New Directions, 1950), 148, but which has not been seen since. *Plums*, Koch says, concerned "a landowner whose intelligence and cultivation have brought prosperity and eminence to the Hudson Valley and who, by aristocratic allegiances as well as self-interest, is with the British [in the American Revolution]. The Yankees, represented by two plum-stealing soldiers, are shown as crass, marauding, and unperceptive of the true quality of the land they would 'free.'"

"So American": WCW to EW, 18 March 1909 (Yale SL).

10.   A copy of the Union Club fair program is on file at the New Jersey History Room of Messler Library, Fairleigh-Dickinson.

11.   "Single tax men": *American*, 8 Oct. 1896. Borough single-tax proposals: *American*, 26 Oct. 1893.

12.   Pound to WCW, 7 Jan. 1958 (Yale Za Pound).

13.   Bell, "The Background and Development of Marxian Socialism in the United States," in *Socialism and American Life*, ed. Donald Drew Egbert and Stow Persons (Princeton: Princeton University Press, 1952), vol. 1, 267.

On Williams and Social Credit, Mike Weaver, 103–11, is still best. Kitty Hoagland has testified to Williams' enthusiasm for both Social Credit and the cooperative (interview with author, 10 Aug. 1982); see also Don Cox, "Two Glimpses of Williams," *WCW Review* 8.2 (Fall

1982), 29–30. Williams owned a copy of coop organizer Paddy the Cope's *My Story* (London: Jonathan Cape, 1939), which is now at Fairleigh-Dickinson. See also Williams's draft of a speech on becoming a member of the board of directors of the Co-Operative Consumers' Society of Bergen County filed with an October 1938 brochure of the organization's (Buffalo G73).

14. Webb: Norman and Jeanne MacKenzie, *The Fabians* (New York: Simon and Schuster, 1977), 61.

15. Hillquit quoted in Bell, 284; Bell, 269. I rely here on Bell's mordant anatomy, hostile as it is, of what he calls "the Golden Age of American Socialism."

16. John Spargo, *The Spiritual Significance of Socialism* (New York: W.B. Huebsch, 1908), 48.

17. Gannet, "Things Most Commonly Believed by Us" (1887), cited by George Willis Cooke, *Unitarianism in America: A History of Its Origin and Development* (Boston: American Unitarian Association, 1902), 227. Cooke, 275, notes that 40,000 copies of "Our Faith" had been sold by 1902, so Williams's classroom undoubtedly had one. Williams recalled the slogan in his *Autobiography*, 22, and parodied it in *The Great American Novel* (I, 164).

18. *American*, 12 Jan. 1893.

19. "Abundantly": *American*, 22 Dec. 1892.

20. "Not exclusive": *American*, 22 Dec. 1892. The Unitarian Society's 1920 profession is quoted by Weaver, 2.

21. Cooke, 343, 349, 442.

22. Copies of Leonard Levi Paine's *The Ethnic Trinities and Their Relations to the Christian* (New York: Houghton Mifflin, 1901) and *Noble Lives and Deeds*, ed. Edward A. Horton (Boston: Unitarian Sunday-School Society, 1895) are among Williams's books at Fairleigh-Dickinson.

23. WCW to EW, 18 March 1906 (Buffalo).

24. Hofstadter, 5, notes that the number of members of the "new" middle class octupled between 1897 and 1910, whereas the "old" middle class only doubled.

25. Hofstadter, 5-11.

26. Contemporaries recognized that Roosevelt was involving the federal government in new activity. See Mark Sullivan, *Our Times: The United States, 1900–1925* (New York: Charles Scribner's Son's, 1926–33), vol. II, 420–46. Wilson: *American*, 3 Nov. 1910.

27. "Decent": WCW to EW, 7 Nov. 1905 (Buffalo). *The Outlook*: WCW to EW, 18 March 1909 (Yale SL); Roosevelt's essay, 619–23, immediately preceded "The Real Americans," 623–26.

28. All quotations from *A September Afternoon* are from the typescript (Yale Za Williams 221a), 5–7.

29. Steffens, "Philadelphia: Corrupt and Contented," *McClure's Magazine* (July 1903), incorporated into *The Shame of the Cities* in 1904.

30. On the defeat of reform in 1909 and Lippman's challenge, see Justin Kaplan, *Lincoln Steffens* (New York: Simon and Schuster, 1974), 166–78; on the transformation of Progressive discourse, see also Lasch, 141–83, and Wiebe, 164–95.

Chapter 3

1. "Pioneering": Cooke, 438–39. "Rules": WCW to EW, 18 March 1906 (Buffalo).

2. Nietzsche: see Henry May, *The End of American Innocence* (1959; rprt. Chicago: Quadrangle Books, 1964), 206–10. Williams wrote Viola Baxter Jordan on 24 Dec. 1914 to tell her husband Virgil that "[Thus Spake] Zarathustra has been sold out at Brentano's long since," but whether Williams was buying a copy for Jordan or himself is impossible to say (Yale Za Jordan). "Creeds": WCW to FH, 28 Nov. 1909 (Mariani, 83).

3. Quotations about the dramatists are from notecards Williams made during the course (Private).

4. Notebook, Yale Za Williams 174.

5. WCW to EW, 22 June 1908 (Buffalo). Williams's account of his internships (A, 76–105) is much enriched by Mariani, 52–75.

6. *New Republic* cited by Aaron, 14. "Interest": Hilda Doolittle to WCW, 12 Feb. 1908 (Buffalo F159).

7. Mariani, 8–9.

8. WCW to HHW, 27 May 1906 (Yale SL).

9. Bledstein, *The Culture of Professionalism* (New York: W.W. Norton, 1976), 96–98.

10. A.M.A.: Wiebe, 113–16. Osler, "The Student Life" in *The Student Life and Other Essays* (Boston and New York: Houghton Mifflin, 1931), 14. Tichi (*WCW Review,* 68–69) explores Osler's impact on Williams.

11. See "Health for the People" (Yale Za Williams 113), a draft of an essay from the 1940s, in which he blasted the A.M.A. for suing a group of doctors who formed a cooperative practice and lauded a current bill in Congress to establish a national health plan. He bent his scruples on local government here because he felt that "the only alternative is Federal regulation" of a "business gang." But see his 1938 short story, "To Fall Asleep," for his assertion that medicine under socialism depended on individual excellence (FD, 177–84).

12. WCW to EW, 18 March 1906 and 22 March 1906 (Buffalo); Osler, 5.

13. WCW to Monroe, [1915] (Chicago).

14. Bledstein, 90, 87–88.

15. Paul Starr, *The Social Transformation of American Medicine* (New York: Basic Books, 1982), 217 and 220–32.

16. See Bledstein, 54–55, on the professional's conception of "human nature"; on treating "universal facts of human nature" ahistorically, see Roland Barthes, "The Great Family of Man," in *Mythologies,* trans. Annette Lavers (New York: Hill and Wang, 1972), 100–102.

17. "Three Professional Studies," *Little Review* 5.10–11 (Feb.-March 1919), 36–39. See Dr. William Eric Williams, "The Doctor," *WCW Review,* 9.1–2 (Fall 1983), xx.

18. Gompers, *Seventy Years of Life and Labor* (1925; rprt. in 1 vol. New York: E.P. Dutton, 1943), 251.

19. Phillip A. Taft, *The A.F.L. in the Time of Gompers* (New York: Harpers, 1957), 42. Socialist-trade unionist fight: Bell, 252–56. "Sentimental": "P'eas," an unpublished improvisation on Herman (Buffalo 123c).

20. Williams paraphrased Roosevelt (IM, 174) from a newspaper account of the contract scandal (Buffalo B51).

21. Among the typescripts of *In the Money* at Buffalo are six 1903 newspaper articles about the scandal (Buffalo B51), which Williams followed closely in the novel—and which Joe Stecher, using details most likely given to Williams by Herman, painstakingly corrects (WM, 183–97).

22. "P'eas."

23. Heal, "Flossie," *WCW Review*, 9.

24. Osler, 15; Tichi, *WCW Review*, 68; WCW to EW, [1908] (Yale SL).

25. WCW to EW, 6 April 1909 (Yale SL). "A Street Market, N.Y., 1908," Mariani, 71.

26. "A Local Beauty Spot," *American*, 11 Aug. 1910. The letter is attributed to "a Rutherford boy, writing from the American Academy in Rome to a friend here."

27. "Antidote": WCW to EW, 8 July 1908 (Buffalo).
    Williams may also have read Spargo's *The Spiritual Significance of Socialism*, the abbreviated title of which is scribbled in the pocket notebook he carried around in the fall and winter of 1910–11. Spargo, a leader of the American Socialist party, asserted that socialism would create "the equality of opportunity out of which will develop a diversity of genius and attainment undreamed of yet" (60–61).

28. Wilde, *The Soul of Man* (London: Arthur L. Humphreys, 1907), 5.

29. Wilde, 14, 41.

30. Wilde, 55, 48, 47.

31. WCW to EW, 18 March 1908 (Yale SL).

32. Williams, "A Symposium on 'The Politics of the Unpolitical,'" *View*, 4.2 (Summer 1944), 61. Read, *The Politics of the Unpolitical* (London: George Routledge and Sons, 1943), 153 and 160.

Chapter 4

1. Aisen, "The Latest Evolution in Art and Picabia," *Camera Work*, Special Number (June 1913), 14.

2. "Notes on '291': Watercolors by John Marin," *Camera Work*, nos. 42–43 (Apr.-July 1913), 18.

3. Milton W. Brown, *American Painting from the Armory Show to the Depression* (Princeton: Princeton University Press, 1955), 54. This study and Brown's *The Story of the Armory Show* (Joseph Hirshorn Foundation, 1968) survey press reaction to the Armory Show.

4. See Davies's chart of modern art's lineage in *Arts and Decoration* (March 1913), 150, and Brown, *The Story*, 90–91. Pine tree: William I. Homer, *Alfred Stieglitz and the American Avant-Garde* (Boston: New York Graphics Society, 1977), pl. 81, 166.

5. I rely here on Joseph R. Conlin, *Big Bill Haywood and the Radical Union Movement* (Syracuse: Syracuse University Press, 1969), 137–40, and Joyce Kornbluh, ed., *Rebel Voices: An I.W.W. Anthology* (Ann Arbor: University of Michigan Press, 1964).

6. Pageant: See Robert Rosenstone, *Romantic Revolutionary: A Biography of John Reed* (New York: Vintage Books, 1981), 124–30, and Kornbluh's richer account, including a reprint of the pageant program. Haywood's poetry: Hutchins Hapgood, *A Victorian in the Modern World* (1939; reprt. Seattle: University of Washington Press, 1972), 293.

7. Rosenstone, 127. Sanger: Mari Jo Buhle, *Feminism and Socialism in the United States, 1820–1920*, Diss. University of Wisconsin, 1974, 321–22, and 341–42n.75.

8. "The Day in Bohemia": Rosenstone, 94–96. "Self-conscious": Rosenstone, 104. The history of the Village from 1910 to 1917 is told by Rosenstone; Albert Parry, *Garrets and Pretenders: A History of Bohemianism in America* (New York: Covici-Friede, 1933), 267–304; and many participants' accounts or autobiographies. "Imagiste": Kreymborg, *Troubadour* (New York: Boni and Liveright, 1925), 205–6.

9. Reed in Paterson: Rosenstone, 117–32. *The Masses*: see Fishbein passim; Aaron, 18–25; and the autobiographies of Floyd Dell, Max Eastman, Louis Untermeyer, and Art Young. Illustrators at the Armory Show: see the show catalogue in Brown, *The Story*, 220–301.

10. Hapgood quoted in Rosenstone, 129. Bourne: "Pageantry and Social Art," unpublished ms., cited in Arthur Frank Wertheim, *The New York Little Renaissance: Iconoclasm, Modernism, and Nationalism in American Culture, 1908–1917* (New York: New York University Press, 1976), 56.

11. Rutherford newspapers said nothing about the Paterson strike. Peter Kipp, however, had banking interests in Paterson and went there almost every day (Howell, 310).

12. WCW to HHW, 27 April 1916 (quoted in William Eric Williams, M.D., "William Carlos Williams: My Father the Doctor," *Journal of the Medical Society of New Jersey* 80.9 (Sept. 1983), 674.

13. "Imagisme" and "A Few Don'ts by an Imagiste," *Poetry* 1.6 (March 1913), 198–206.

14. Rereading Whitman: Breslin, 19. Traubel: Aaron, 7, and Emma Goldman, *Living My Life* (1931; rprt. New York: Dover Press, 1970), vol. 1, 567.

15. Hueffer, "Post-Impressionism—Some Speculations," Pt. I, *Poetry* 2.5 (Aug. 1913), 179. Rodman: Wertheim, 64–65.

16. Pound and Aldington: Pound to WCW, [Summer-early Fall] 1913 (Buffalo). Pound and Kemp: Noel Stock, *The Life of Ezra Pound* (New York: Avon, 1970), 198. Pound, Kreymborg, and Williams: Pound to Kreymborg [*Troubadour*, 204–5], and Pound to WCW, [Summer-early Fall] 1913 (Buffalo). Pound and Reed: Pound used four lines from Reed's "Sangar" (*Poetry* 1.3 [Oct. 1912], 71–74) with meaning-changing ellipses, to head "Pax Saturni" (*Poetry* 2.1 [April, 1913], 8). Reed sent "A Word to Mr. Pound" in *Poetry* 2.3 (June 1913), 112–13. Mabel Dodge Luhan: quoted by Reed to Eddy Hunt, 16 Dec. 1913 (Rosenstone, 151).

17. "Speech Rhythm" (Yale Za Jordan) reprinted in Weaver, 82–83.

18. Documentation of Williams's activities in 1913, as for all of the early 1910s, is scanty. Several important sources have not turned up or been made available. Some of Pound's letters to Williams are extant, but Williams's to Pound have vanished. Only a few letters between Williams and Charles Demuth have turned up, as is the case for letters between Williams and Alfred Kreymborg. Only three of the letters at Yale from Williams to Viola Baxter Jordan are from 1913, none of them between 26 January and 9 October, when he would have been most likely to discuss the Armory Show, the Paterson strike and the pageant. Williams's seven letters to Harriet Monroe (Chicago) in 1913 do not refer to these events. No correspondence between Williams and New York artists and radicals of 1913 is catalogued in library collections.

The Armory Show: the only positive evidence about Williams's attendance is his wife's statement that he did not (Heal, "Flossie," 11). Mariani (106) suggests that Williams may have gone without Floss's knowledge—but Williams undermines his own claim to have gone (A, 134) by recalling details of the 1917 exhibition of the Society of Independents. William Marling,

William Carlos Williams and the Painters, 1909–1923 (Athens, Ohio: Ohio University Press, 1982), 1–2, makes the most sensible case for Williams's not attending.

Paterson pageant: Williams does not refer to it in "The Wanderer," his 1913–14 poem on Paterson, and mentions it only once, at secondhand, in *Paterson*. He recalled going to hear Billy Sunday preach in Paterson (A, 391), but that was in 1915; he does not mention going out in 1913 to nearby Haledon to hear the I.W.W. speakers at the mass meetings held during the strike.

19. Marling, 1–2. Williams and O'Neill: Louis Shaeffer, *O'Neill: Son and Playwright* (Boston: Little, Brown, 1968), 376.

20. Williams, Notebook (Yale Za Williams 174).

21. Pound in New York: Stock, *Life of EP*, 135. "Out of touch": Pound to WCW, 21 May 1909 (*The Letters of Ezra Pound 1907–1941*, ed. D.D. Paige [New York: Harcourt, Brace & World, 1950], 7–8).

22. Pound to WCW, 11 Sept. 1920 (*Letters of EP*, 159). Stock mentions no visit to Mouquin's. One poet who did dine there was Kreymborg (*Troubadour*, 127).

23. *Selected Prose 1909–1965*, ed. William Cookson (New York: New Directions, 1973), 113. See *Poetry* 12.6 (Sept. 1918), 310–12, and *Literary Digest* (9 Aug. 1924), for poems and a few biographical details on Welsh. He was published through the 1910s in conventional magazines—*Scribner's, Harper's,* and *The Forum.*

24. Marling, 26.

25. Marling, 25–26, misdates Demuth's return to America as in 1913, places *The Azure Adder* in *Rogue* rather than in *The Glebe*, 1.3 (Dec. 1913), and says that Demuth had known Stieglitz and exhibited at 291 before his 1912 trip to Paris. However, Homer, 295–98, lists no Demuth show at 291 and dates his return to America in the spring of 1914 (302). Marling's errors lead him to think that Demuth was more available to help Williams than he actually was.

26. Hartley, Demuth, and Steiglitz: Homer, 286 n.92. Kreymborg and Demuth: *Troubadour*, 167, 134, and 210. Kreymborg met Demuth at 291, but gives no date; according to Homer, it was spring 1914 at the earliest. *Azure Adder: Troubadour*, 132–33. Kreymborg may have had the manuscript as early as 1909; he had to have asked Cournos before 1911, when Cournos moved to London.

27. *Letters of EP*, 27. *Rogue* circle: *Troubadour*, 218–20, and Wertheim, 100–103.

28. Pound to WCW, [1912] (Buffalo). Magazines at the Bonis': *Troubadour*, 209.

29. Havel: Rosenstone, 143. Only Man Ray (*Self-Portrait* [Boston: Little, Brown, 1963], 40) says he met Williams in 1913, when Williams was one of "two new faces" at Grantwood one day—but the other new face, Eastman, (*Love and Revolution: My Journey through an Epoch* [New York: Random House, 1964], 139), says he did not meet Williams at all, and Kreymborg, who Ray says was there, did not meet Williams until 1914.

30. *Troubadour*, 202.

31. Meetings: *Troubadour*, 113 (Hartley); 163–65 (Stieglitz; Kreymborg recalled Rodin drawings on exhibit at 291, which, according to Homer, dates his first visit between 2 and 21 Jan. 1908); 127 (Mouquin's); 126 (Kilmer); 208 (the Bonis).

32. Roth's caricature is reproduced in Parry, 271.

33. WCW to Orrick Johns, 30 Oct. 1916 (Delaware).

34. *Troubadour*, 309. Kreymborg wrote Williams on 9 Nov. 1916 (Buffalo F280) full of praise for Reed.

35. Bryant: Kreymborg to WCW, 9 Nov. 1916. Reed's whereabouts: Rosenstone, 260.

36. Williams's account of meeting Reed at Ridge's: A, 142.

    They may have discussed Billy Sunday's preaching in Paterson in 1915; Reed wrote a scathing story for *The Metropolitan* about the evangelist's financial backing, details of which Williams, who may have gone to hear Sunday then, used years later in *Paterson* (Weaver, 213).

    As with *Insurgent Mexico,* there is no sign that Williams read Reed's *Ten Days that Shook the World.*

37. Gold: see Aaron, 213. This was "A New Program for Writers" in the literary branch of the John Reed Club (itself formed in late 1929) which Gold announced in the January 1930 issue of *The New Masses.*

Chapter 5

1. On Village individualism, see Aaron, 6, and especially Fishbein, who pays careful attention to the incoherences in the Village rebels' politics, and to whom I am much indebted. She concludes that they "failed to articulate a social dynamic that would explain the relationship between institutional changes and the transformation of consciousness" (39). Similarly, they failed to define the relationship between their radical politics and their art. As Max Eastman told Daniel Aaron in 1957, "No, there just wasn't any blending of poetry with revolution [in *The Masses*]. Nobody wrote any revolutionary poetry that was any good" (Aaron, 25).

2. Bourne, "Paul Elmer More," *The New Republic* VI (April 1916), in *War and the Intellectuals: Collected Essays, 1915–1919,* ed. Carl Resek (New York: Harpers, 1964), 168.

3. "Free": "America: Chances and Remedies," I, *The New Age* 12.1 (1 May 1913), 10.

4. "Henry James," *Little Review* 5.4 (Aug. 1918), 26 (*Literary Essays of Ezra Pound* [New York: New Directions, 1968], 296).

5. "Humanity": "Provincialism the Enemy," IV, *The New Age* 21.14 (2 Aug. 1917), 308 (*Selected Prose,* 200). "Those things": "Patria Mia," IX, *The New Age* 11.27 (31 Oct. 1912), 635. I cite from the originally published version of this essay since the one published in *Selected Prose* has significant excisions. "Personality": "Provincialism the Enemy," II, *The New Age* 21.12 (19 July 1917), 268, 269 (*Selected Prose,* 193, 194).

6. "Patria Mia," VII, *The New Age* 11.25 (17 Oct. 1912), 588. Chace, *The Political Identities of Ezra Pound and T.S. Eliot* (Stanford: Stanford University Press, 1973), 36, 16. I am much indebted to Chace's analysis here.

7. "The New Sculpture," *The Egoist* 1.4 (16 Feb. 1914), 68.

8. "Patria Mia," V, *The New Age* 11.23 (3 Oct. 1912), 539, and X, *The New Age* 12.1 (7 Nov. 1912), 12.

9. "America: Chances and Remedies," II, *The New Age* 13.2 (8 May 1913), 34, and I, 10.

10. "The Serious Artist," I-II, *The New Freewoman* 1.9 (15 Nov. 1913), 162 (*Literary Essays,* 44).

11. "The New Sculpture," 68.

12. "Implies one": "America: Chances and Remedies," I, 10. "Exempt": "Henry James," *Little Review* 26 (*Essays,* 296).

13. "Provincialism the Enemy," IV, 308 (*Selected Prose*, 199).

14. *Troubadour*, 162. My biographical information here is taken from *Troubadour*.

15. "Group standards": Benjamin de Casseres, "Decadence and Mediocrity," *Camera Work*, no. 32 (Oct. 1910), 39. "Coercions": John Weischel, "Cosmism or Amorphism?" *Camera Work*, nos. 42–43 (April-July 1913), 74. Williams's books at Fairleigh-Dickinson include a 1915 issue of *Camera Work*, but no earlier ones. Kreymborg: *Troubadour*, 117.

16. *Mushrooms* (New York: John Marshall, 1916).

17. *Troubadour*, 259–62. Poet Orrick Johns had passed the job with Konta to Kreymborg, who passed it on to another *Others* poet, Skipwith Cannell.

18. "Friend": *Troubadour*, 238.

19. Ray and Woolf: Ray, *Self-Portrait*, 33–34. Johns, *Time of Our Lives*, 224. The later visitors and residents of Grantwood are from an interview with Grantwood artist William Tisch (David S. Heeren, "Ridgefield Art Colony Recalled in Octogenarian's Reminiscence," Bergen *Record*, n.d., n.p.) and a memoir by another resident, William E. Monaghan ("Those Were the Days, My Friend, Those Were the Days"). Both are on file at the Ridgefield Public Library, Ridgefield, N.J.

20. Joseph M. Flora, "Bob Brown," *Dictionary of Literary Biography*, vol. 4: *American Writers in Paris, 1920–1939*, ed. Karen Lane Rood (Detroit: Gale Research Co., 1980), 60–64. Komroff murals: Tisch, "Ridgefield Art Colony." Komroff left for the Soviet Union some time in 1917.

21. *Rogue* 1.8 (15 July 1915), 3.

22. "Paradox": *Troubadour*, 218. "A Bas Patriotism, or To Hell with Arithmetic," *Rogue* 1.7 (15 June 1915), 4.

23. Grantwood weekends: Williams, A, 135–36; Johns, 223–27, *Troubadour*, 238–43. Homer, 184.

24. Woolf, "The Liberty I Loathe" and "On Seeing the Garment Workers Strike," *The Glebe* 1.1 (Sept. 1913), 11, 14. Johns, 220. Sanborn: Edmund Brown to WCW, 11 Feb. 1919 (Buffalo F63).

25. Moore, "To Statecraft Embalmed," *Others* 1.6 (Dec. 1915), 104, and "Radical," *Others*, 5.4 (March 1919), 15. Hoyt, "Retort," *Others* 3.3 (Sept. 1916), 54.

26. Lasch, 286.

27. "America, Whitman, and the Art of Poetry," *The Poetry Journal* 8.1 (Nov. 1917), 29.

28. WCW to Edmund Brown, [1916] (Virginia 7456a).

Chapter 6

1. WCW to Viola Baxter, 30 Oct. 1911 (Yale Za Jordan).

2. "Dead forms": WCW to FH, 16 Jan. 1910 (Mariani, 83). WCW to Baxter, 15 Oct. 1911 (Yale Za Jordan).

3. WCW to EW, 6 April 1909 (Yale SL).

4. Monroe, "The New Beauty," *Poetry* 2.1 (April 1913), 22–23. Ficke, "Poetry," *Poetry* 1.1 (Oct. 1912), 1–2.

5. "Note by the Editor," *The Lyric Year* (New York: Mitchell Kennerly, 1912), viii. "Second Avenue" is on 132–37.

6. Johns, *Times of Our Lives*, 203–4.

7. Williams and Earle: Mariani, 100–101.

8. *Poetry* 2.1 (April 1913), 22.

9. *Poetry* 2.5 (Aug. 1913), 180, 185, 183, 179.

10. WCW to Monroe, 30 Aug. 1913 (Chicago). Article title: WCW to Monroe, 29 Sept. 1913 (Chicago); Weaver thinks the text he reprints (82–83), which he found in the Jordan papers at Yale, is a later version of Williams's submission. I quote from Weaver's text. "It's good": WCW to Viola Baxter Jordan, 11 June 1914 (Yale Za Jordan).

11. "A Few Don'ts by an Imagiste," 201, 202. "Letter to an Australian Editor," *Briarcliff Quarterly* 3.2 (Oct. 1946), 205–8.

12. "Patria Mia," VI, *The New Age* 11.24 (10 Oct. 1912), 564; Barzun: "Paris," *Poetry* 3.1 (Oct. 1913), 29.

13. Pound, "A Peal of Iron," *Poetry* 3.2 (Dec. 1913), 112; Bynner, "One of the Crowd," *Poetry* 1.5 (Feb. 1913), 53–55.

14. Pound to WCW, 19 Dec. 1913 (*Letters of EP*, 28).
    I cite the text of "The Wanderer" as originally published in *The Egoist* 1.6 (16 March 1914), 109–11. The numerous changes Williams made before reprinting it in *Al Que Quiere!* in 1917 are, with one exception noted below, stylistic, all aimed at bringing the poem's "rococo" style closer to "the simple order of natural speech."

15. Monroe, "The New Beauty," 23. Pound, "Commission," *Poetry* 2.1 (April 1913), 10–11 (*Personae* [New York: New Directions, 1926], 88–89).

16. "Tenzone," in *Lustra* (London, 1916) (*Personae*, 81).

17. Mabel Dodge Luhan, *Movers and Shakers* (New York: Harcourt, Brace & Co., 1936), 96–122, and Emma Goldman, *Living My Life*, vol. 2, 523.

18. Between 1914 and 1917, Williams added six lines here:

> "Never while the air's clear coolness
> Is seized to be a coat for pettiness;
> Never while richness of greenery
> Stands a shield for prurient minds;
> Never, permitting these things unchallenged
> Shall my voice of leaves and varicolored bark
>   come free through!"

The relation of this attack on American morality to the criticism in the "Broadway" and "Paterson—the Strike" sections is not clear. Is the "brutality" of the Paterson community petty? Is the fear of the eroticism displayed by his muse and her young pursuers on Broadway prurient?

Williams probably added "prurience" because by 1917 he had taken a lot of flak for openly expressing eroticism. Kreymborg said that Williams's work in *Others* drew more hostile mail than anyone else's: "Shy though Bill was in person, blank paper let loose anything he felt about everything, and he frankly and fearlessly undressed himself to the ground. Not since the days of old Walt had an American gone quite so far, and readers were shocked all over again" (*Troubadour*, 242). In 1917, during wartime, Williams feared that the censor would deny *Al Que Quiere!* mailing privileges. He told publisher Edmund Brown, "I have not tried to force forward things that I was morally certain would bring trouble. I have really tried to be unobjectionable—mais quoi!" (WCW to Brown, 5 Feb. 1917; Yale Za Williams Uncat).

19. Williams had sent Zukofsky his 1928 "Democratic Party Poem," in which he argued that recovering "the sense of local responsibility" and autonomy was "the only hope for continued freedom in a democracy" (Buffalo A76). Zukofsky, a serious student of Marxism, advised him that such politics were Jeffersonian, not Bolshevik, and that industrialization had rendered them anachronistic (Zukofsky to WCW, 10 July 1931; Buffalo F711).

20. I reproduce the draft of the poem (Buffalo A295) as best I can—it is heavily marked for revisions. I date it by its presence the same typescript of "Breakfast," which first appeared in *Complete Collected Poems* in 1938. Details of the history of Santiago Grove are from Howell, 328–29, and from conversations with Rutherford residents Professor John Dollar and Ed Brouillard.

Chapter 7

1. Weaver, 23–29.

2. Weaver assumes with no evidence that Williams read *The New Freewoman* before Pound urged him to do so in a letter of 29 Dec. 1913 (*Letters of EP*, 27). But Williams's letter of 1 Jan. 1914 to Viola Baxter Jordan (SL, 27) indicates that he did not. Marling, 68, notes Hartley's interest in egoism.

3. "Views and Comments," *The Egoist* 1.5 (2 March 1914), 95; "Views and Comments" 1.7 (1 April 1914), 125; "Skyscapes and Goodwill" 1.2 (15 Jan. 1914), 26.

4. "Liberty, Law, and Democracy" 1.1 (1 Jan. 1914), 2; "Views and Comments" 1.7 (1 April 1914), 125; "Views and Comments" 1.1 (1 Jan. 1914), 4.

5. Carter, "The Public Ownership of the Artist" 1.2 (15 Jan. 1914), 32. Pound, "Wyndham Lewis" 1.12 (15 June 1914), 233.

6. "The Art of the Future," *The New Freewoman* 1.10 (1 Nov. 1913), 183. See H.D.'s "Cities," *The Egoist* 3.7 (1 July 1916), 102, or Aldington's "Notes on the Present Situation" 1.17 (1 Sept. 1914), 326.

7. "Correspondence: The Great Sex Spiral: A Criticism of Miss Marsden's 'Lingual Psychology'" 4.3 (April 1917), 46, and 4.7 (Aug. 1917), 110–11.

8. Williams to John Thirlwall in Thirlwall, "Comments on *Collected Earlier Poems*" (Yale Za Williams Uncat).
   The play was published in *Others* 5.5 (April-May 1919), 1–16, and I quote it from there; "Portrait of a Woman in Bed," *Others* 3.4 (Dec. 1916) (CP, 87–88). Brobitza's words are the same in play and poem; in the play she is interrupted several times by the Poor Master, and lines of her poem become her response to him. Whether Williams conceived the poem or the play first is not known.

9. In "Sample Prose Piece: The Three Letters," *Contact*, no. 4 [Summer 1921], 10, Williams groups Robitza, his grandmother, and the Baroness Elsa Freytag von Loringhoven as fierce social outcasts of a kind that kindled his imagination.
   "Face of the town": "Comments on CEP." In Williams' conversation with Thirlwall, he makes it clear that Robitza's "house" was not the Ivison "castle." There was nothing in the Rutherford newspapers about Robitza's eviction.

10. "Views and Comments," *The Egoist* 1.9 (1 May 1914), 163.

11. WCW to Monroe, 13 Jan. 1921 (Chicago).

12. "Notes From a Talk on Poetry," *Poetry* 14.4 (July 1919), 213, 215. Professor Doolittle is Williams's example.

13. "Notes," 211, 213.

14. "Notes," 213, 212.

15. "America, Whitman, and the Art of Poetry," 29.

16. "Belly Music," *Others* 5.6 (July 1919), 31.

17. "America, Whitman, and the Art of Poetry," 35.

Chapter 8

1. Growth figures from the 1930 federal census (in Myers, 20). *Directory,* 467–68.

2. Howell, 325, 328.

3. *Republican,* 3 Jan. 1916.

4. "A Local Beauty Spot," *American,* 11 Aug. 1910. Williams's presence at the playground was noted in the *Republican,* 11 July 1914; "A Playground Appeal," *Republican,* 25 July 1914.

5. "The Town Nurse," *Republican,* 23 Jan. 1915. Mayor Black: *Republican,* 3 Jan. 1916.

6. WCW to Monroe, 10 Feb. 1919 (Chicago).

7. Details on the schools from Myers. Mayor: *Republican,* 14 May 1921. The West Side Improvement Association—the new residents' answer to the Town Improvement Association, testimony in itself to the strains imposed on Rutherford's social structure by growth—was a major force in the school fight.

8. Police surgeon: *Republican,* 6 Jan. 1917. Mosquito commission: Jessie Leslie to WCW, 17 Jan. 1916 (Buffalo F332) confirms the date. The circumstances are unknown. Williams's letter of resignation from the county children's home (15 Dec. 1922) was read into the minutes of the Board of Chosen Freeholders of Bergen County for that year. Thanks to Ray Ralph of the Bergen County Historical Society for pointing it out.

9. The monthly social club that Williams helped found in 1916, the Polytopic Club, spent little time on politics. According to the minutes of the club meetings (now in the possession of Professor John Dollar of Fairleigh-Dickinson), the only evening with a political agenda was the first meeting in October 1916, on the Wilson-Hughes presidential campaign. Only a few meetings in the 1910s were on social or civic topics—discussions of "the high cost of living" and "government ownership" and Williams's talk on the work of the mosquito commission. The minutes make no reference to Williams's opinions.

10. WCW to HHW, 27 April 1916 (Mariani, 131).

11. "Woman Walking" (CP, 66), first published in *The Egoist* 1.2 (1 Dec. 1914), 444. In *Al Que Quiere!,* Williams cut this line, thus playing down his restlessness in Rutherford.

12. See Mariani, 133–34 and 144–45, on the volume's titling.

13. Williams's search for an image "large enough to embody the whole knowable world about me" (A, 391), which eventually resulted in *Paterson,* began early on with his "American" plays. Sometimes he sought it in Rutherford, as here and in the 1929 "Genesis" (Buffalo B40). *The Build-Up,* however, is his only completed work whose subject was the Rutherford community itself.

14. Hoagland interview, 11 Aug. 1982.

15. Eastman, *Enjoyment of Poetry,* 115.

16. By the "townspeople" poems, I mean those that Williams addressed, usually by that term, to Rutherford as a community. One could assemble another group of "townspeople" poems in which Williams portrays or addresses a single person from Rutherford, such as "Canthara" (CP, 78) or "Portrait of a Young Man with a Bad Heart" (90), or "Divertimento" (100). I confine myself here to the former group, in which Williams presents himself as the "poet of democracy" on a local scale.

17. WCW to Viola Baxter Jordan, 24 June 1914 (Yale Za Jordan).

18. "Comments on CEP."

Chapter 9

1. "Further Announcement," *Contact*, no. 1 (Dec. 1920), 10.

2. "Futile arguments": WCW to HHW, 26 Aug. 1915 (Yale Za Williams 221); WCW to Brown, 30 April 1917 (Yale Za Williams Uncat). The present location of the preceding "blasting letter" is unknown.

3. "From Dr. Williams," *Republican*, 12 May 1917.

4. Paul Williams, "A Letter to My Father on His 100th Birthday," *WCW Review* 10.1 (Spring 1984), 4; Williams's appointments: *Republican*, 19 Jan. 1918 (board of health), 3 Aug. 1918 (food administrator). There were seven Food Administration notices in the paper between August and December either written or signed by him. Memorial Day: *Republican*, 29 May 1920.

5. "Editorial Notes," *Republican*, 23 Oct. 1920, and 6 Nov. 1920; Williams, "Reader-Critic," *The Little Review* 5.9 (Jan. 1919), 64. See also "Yours, O Youth" of 1921: at first Pound succeeded in London, Williams said, "But in the end they played Wilson with him" (SE, 35).

6. "Salaried": *Republican*, 7 April 1917; Gompers: "The Man about Town," *Republican*, 1 May 1920; "Profiteers": *Republican*, 24 April 1920; T.I.A.: "T.I.A. Tips," *Republican*, 10 March 1917. Williams, "The Supply of Sugar," *Republican*, 2 Aug. 1919.

7. See Robert K. Murray, *Red Scare: A Study in National Hysteria* (New York: McGraw-Hill, 1955). Murray emphasizes psychological forces rather than political or economic motives, but, given the ugliness of events, his bias is understandable. Sandburg's role: Eastman, *Love and Revolution*, 138.

8. WCW to Monroe, 13 Jan. 1921 (Chicago).

9. *Being Geniuses Together, 1920–1930*, rev. and with supplementary chapters by Kay Boyle (Garden City: Doubleday, 1968), 87, 1.

10. Williams's despair at losing his "springtime" was compounded by his father's death on Christmas Day, 1918; in fact, it forced him to justify his writing much more than the war did. See "Three Professional Studies," written the week after, for the anxiety about writing it caused him.

11. Turner, *Shall It Be Again?* (New York: W.B. Huebsch, 1922), 418; Williams's copy at Fairleigh-Dickinson is unmarked. Pound, "Credit Power and Democracy," *Contact*, no. 4 [Summer 1921], 1. Williams's copy of Douglas at Fairleigh-Dickinson is the 1931 American edition.

12. "Four Foreigners," *The Little Review* 5.5 (Sept. 1919), 36.

13. "Glorious Weather," *Contact*, no. 5 (June 1923), [4].

14. WCW to Monroe, 28 April 1919 (Chicago).

15. According to Homer, Demuth divided his time between Lancaster and New York; he also spent time at Dr. Frederick M. Allen's Morristown Physiatric Institute, which opened in June 1920 (Arthur Krosnick, "William Carlos Williams and Charles Demuth," *Journal of the Medical Society of New Jersey* 80.9 [Sept. 1983], 704).

16. Paz, *Marcel Duchamp: Appearance Stripped Bare* (New York: Seaver Books, 1981), 11–12. On Williams's long struggle with Duchamp's poetics, see Henry M. Sayre, "Ready-Mades and Other Gestures: The Poetics of Marcel Duchamp and WCW," *Journal of Modern Literature* 8.1 (1980), 3–22, and Marling, 55–67.

17. "Glorious Weather," [3].

18. Hartley, "The Importance of Being Dada" in *Adventures in the Arts* (New York: Boni and Liveright, 1921), 252. Marling, 67–80, is quite good on the homoerotic tensions that ultimately separated them.

19. Anderson, "The Essential Thing," *The Little Review* 3.1 (March 1916), 23, and "What the Public Doesn't Want" 4.4 (Aug. 1917), 20–21; Goldman, *Living My Life,* vol. 2, 530–31; Anderson, "The Labor Farce," *Little Review* 3.6 (Sept. 1916), 16.

20. "Belly Music," 31, 27; "Sample Prose Piece: The Three Letters," 11.

21. "Reader-Critic," *The Little Review* 5.9 (Jan. 1919), 64; "Reader-Critic," *Little Review* 9.3 (Autumn 1922), 60.

22. See Williams's remarks against Dell in WCW to Burke, 24 March 1921 and 12 May 1921 (Penn), and Freud in WCW to Burke, 27 April 1921 (Penn). On *The New Masses,* see WCW to Pound, [March 1926] (SL, 69). See also WCW to H.H. Lewis, 28 April 1937 (Yale Za Williams Uncat), where he recounts meeting "a person named [Joseph] Freeman [one of the founders of *The New Masses*]. . . . To me, of course, the name meant nothing."

23. WCW to Burke, "Monday" [1921] (Penn).

24. "Belly Music," 32; "The High Cost of Waste," *The Dial* 67 (6 Sept. 1919), 179–80.

25. "A Man versus The Law," *The Freeman* 1.15 (23 June 1920), 348–49. In *A History of* The Freeman: *Literary Landmark of the Early Twenties* (New York: Columbia University Press, 1963), Susan J. Turner accurately characterizes the nostalgic so-called "radicalism" of the magazine.

26. *Crazy Man* (New York: Harcourt, Brace, 1924), 134, 196; see also Carley's manifesto, 133–36. Coffey's letters to WCW (Buffalo F1118–1121) help confirm Bodenheim's characterization of Coffey's beliefs.

27. Details of Coffey's career from: *Crazy Man*; "A Man versus the Law," and Coffey to WCW (Buffalo F1118–1121). See also Conrad Aiken's novel *Conversation,* which features a character based on Coffey.

28. "A Man versus the Law," 348; "To a Friend of Mine" is quoted here as published in *Poetry* 13.6 (March 1919), 302. Williams later made the last two lines more assertive (see CP, 158). Not long after Williams was ticketed, one J.C. Chapman wrote an open letter to the Rutherford paper complaining about having to buy a ticket for a police pension fund-raiser under similar duress (*Republican,* 23 July, 1920).

29. "A Man versus the Law," 348.

30. "A Man versus the Law," 349.

31. Goldman, vol. 1, 468, vol. 2, 706; Carnevali, *The Autobiography of Emanuel Carnevali*, compiled and ed. by Kay Boyle (New York: Horizon Press, n.d.), 117–18.

32. Boyle, letter to author, 15 Oct. 1983.

33. Reed to Max Eastman, quoted in Rosenstone, 347; Frost's limerick in Untermeyer, *Bygones* (New York: Harcourt, Brace, & World, 1962), 45.

34. Cowley, *Exile's Return: The Works and Days of the Lost Generation* (New York: Penguin, 1956), 53.

    The National Archives, which holds some of the files compiled on radicals by the Bureau of Investigation during the war and the Red Scare, has no files on Williams or the artists with whom he associated most. References to Lola Ridge are scattered through files of the General Intelligence Division index, which was a reference index of publicly available information on radicals. However, the archives has none of the Bureau of Investigation files that were kept open after 1924 by the F.B.I. So whether the government's surveillance of artists extended beyond the Office of the Postmaster—charged only with censoring magazines—remains an open question. My thanks to Susan Rosenfeld Falb of the Civil Archives Division, who helped research this question.

35. Dell, "A Psycho-Analytic Confession," *The Liberator* 3 (April 1920), 15–19. On Rolland, Barbusse, and *The Liberator*, see Aaron, 50–55.

36. Cowley, 71, 72–73. By 1923, however, Cowley was exhorting Kenneth Burke to write "political manifestoes" for a special issue of *Broom* (162).

37. *Post-Adolescence*, in *McAlmon and the Lost Generation*, ed. Robert E. Knoll (Lincoln: University of Nebraska Press, 1962), 127, 129.

38. WCW to Edmund Brown, [1916] (Virginia 7456); WCW to Burke, 31 March 1921 (Penn); WCW to Wheeler, 20 Aug. 1923 (Maryland).

39. WCW to Turner, [1921] (Yale Za Williams Uncat).

40. *Post-Adolescence* (Knoll, 116).

41. *Autobiography of Emanuel Carnevali*, 146. Williams, "Gloria!" *Others*, 5.6 (July 1919), 3.

42. *Autobiography of Emanuel Carnevali*, 85.

43. *Autobiography of Emanuel Carnevali*, 86, 78, 73, 160, and 84. Carnevali's struggle as an immigrant undoubtedly stirred both Williams's sympathy and his deep-seated anxiety about being American.

44. "Arthur Rimbaud," *Others* 5.4 (March 1919), 22–23; *Autobiography of Emanual Carnevali*, 160, 173.

45. *Autobiography of Emanuel Carnevali*, 143–44. Carnevali made "My Night at Lola's," 141–48, out of the speech he gave at Ridge's.

46. "Notes from a Talk on Poetry," 213.

47. "Gloria!," 3; "Belly Music," 26.

48. "Gloria!," 3; "Belly Music," 27; "Gloria!," 3.

49. *Autobiography of Emanuel Carnevali*, 80, 142. "Against the Middle-Aged Mind," *Poetry* 24.1 (April 1924), 45–50.

50. "The Italics Are God's," *Contact*, no. 4 [Summer 1921], 15; "Glorious Weather," *Contact*, no. 5 (June 1923), 2; "Belly Music," 32.

51. Stearns, "Illusions of the Sophisticated," *The Freeman* 1 (15 Dec. 1920), 321.

52. "What Is the Use of Poetry?" (Buffalo C150).

Chapter 10

1. Hamilton, "Economics," in *Civilization in the United States: Essays by Thirty Americans,* ed. Harold Stearns (New York: Harcourt, Brace & Co., 1922), 266.

2. "L'Illégalité aux Etats-Unis," *Bifur,* no. 2 (25 July 1929), 96, 97. I have translated the essay back into English from the French translation ("from the American") by Georgette Camille.

3. "The Ghost of Peter Kipp," *Republican,* 22 Jan. 1921.

4. Chemistry laboratories: Meyers, 21.

5. William E. Leuchtenberg, *The Perils of Prosperity, 1914–32* (Chicago: University of Chicago Press, 1958), 95.

6. Williams, "A New High School," *Republican,* 8 Jan. 1921; "Greatest Mass Meeting" and "Unanimous Petition of the Physicians of Rutherford," 14 May 1921; "From the Physicians," 28 May 1921, a reply to an editorial published the week before which attacked the physicians; "A Statement on the School Question," 7 May 1921; WCW to Kenneth Burke, 10 June 1921 (Penn). Williams told Burke he could not help feeling, "'Ah if this energy were only going into art!'"
   Williams was not a member of the school board, as Mariani, 183, has it; his brother Edgar was elected in February 1922.

7. *Republican,* 21 May 1921.

8. "The Return of Peter Kipp," *Republican,* 25 March 1922; "The Return of Peter Kipp," *Republican,* 8 April 1922.

9. *Bergen County Panorama,* 45–47.

10. I have estimated growth from conflicting figures in Meyers, *The Free Public Library of Rutherford,* and a story on tax rates in the *Republican,* 6 May 1921.

11. *Republican,* 22 Oct. and 17 Dec. 1921.

12. Taxes: *Republican,* 6 May 1921; Kennedy: "PAL Notes," 23 Sept. 1922; Mayor: annual message, 7 Jan. 1928.

13. *Republican,* 29 May 1922.

14. Leuchtenberg, 185–86, is best on the automobile's role in modernization. Automobile licenses: *Republican,* 16 Dec. 1922; trolley fares: 28 May 1921; bus lines: 11 Sept. 1920.

15. *Republican,* 18 Nov. 1922; Metzgar, "We're Thankful," 2 Dec. 1922.

16. *Republican,* 25 June and 2 July 1921, and Tichi, *WCW Review,* 62–65. For Williams and automobiles, see William Eric Williams, "Cars," *WCW Newsletter* 3.2 (Fall 1977), 1–5.

17. Appliance advertisements: *Republican,* 15 and 22 May 1920; Robert S. Lynd and Helen Merrell Lynd, *Middletown: A Study in Modern American Culture* (1929; rprt. New York: Harcourt, Brace & World, 1956), 45–47.

18. Backyard theater: WCW to Edmund Brown, 11 July 1919 (Virginia 7456a).

19. *The Dial* 68 (June 1920), 684.

20. *Republican,* 22 April 1922.

21. Leuchtenberg, 158–77, is best on the role of new economic roles of women in the "sexual revolution." For lively detail, see Allen, 73–101; for the contribution of Greenwich Village—largely to style and rhetoric—see Cowley, 63–65.

22. *Republican,* 24 April 1920.

23. *Republican,* 29 July 1922. The speaker was citing British historian James Bryce.

24. *Republican,* 10 Dec. 1921; Williams, AG, foreword.

25. *Republican,* 24 April 1920.

26. "With a Light Heart" (Buffalo B38).

27. WCW to Brown, 26 Dec. [1921 or 1922] (Yale Za Williams Uncat).

28. Dewey, 687.

29. "Information culture": *Contact,* no. 1 (Dec. 1920), cover.

30. Berman, *All that Is Solid Melts into Air,* 37–86 and 96.

31. Williams's defense of Burr has brought similar charges down on him. Walter Sutton has argued that, unlike Pound's Jefferson-Adams Cantos, *In the American Grain* lacks any sense of civic responsibility. But Williams would have classed Sutton with the "schemers" or Protestant-bound Federalists who despised, feared, and were secretly jealous of Burr—by his own lights, Williams was telling them what they most desperately needed. Whether it was realistic or not is another question, as Williams unwillingly acknowledged (Sutton, *"In the American Grain* as Proto-Epic," *WCW Review* 11:1 (Spring 1985), 1–5.

32. On the psychology and culture of abundance, see Bourne, "Paul Elmer More" (*War and the Intellectuals,* 168) and Warren I. Sussman, *Culture as History* (New York: Pantheon, 1984), xix-xxx.

33. Williams overlooks elementary sociology here: immigration from southern Europe explains the "growth" of Catholicism in the 1920s better than poetics.

34. Williams, "L'Illégalité aux Etats-Unis," 99. Prohibition, as Leuchtenberg argues (213–17), was not so much prorural virtue as antiurban.

35. "L'Illégalité aux Etats-Unis," 95–103.

36. Burke, "Subjective History," New York *Herald Tribune Books,* 14 March 1926; rprt. in *William Carlos Williams: A Critical Anthology,* ed. Charles Tomlinson (Baltimore: Penguin, 1972), 88; WCW to Burke, 15 March 1926 (Penn).

Chapter 11

1. "Revolution": McAlmon, "Insistences," *Contact,* no. 3 [Spring 1921], 12; "humanitarianism": joint editorial, no. 1 (Dec. 1920), 1; Williams, "Further Announcement," no. 1 (Dec. 1920), 10.

2. McAlmon, "Concerning 'Kora in Hell,'" *Poetry* 18.1 (April 1921), 54–59.

3. McAlmon, "Modern Artiques," *Contact,* no. 2 (Jan. 1921), 9–10; Williams, "Sample Prose Piece: The Three Letters," 10–11.

4. "Modern Artiques," 9–10.

5. Burke, "Heaven's First Law," *The Dial* 72 (Feb. 1922), 198, 199. Burke assumed that "Form in literature must always have its beginnings in idea"—the very concept that Williams was trying to overthrow with contact.

6. McAlmon, "Contact and Genius," *Contact*, no. 4 [Summer 1921], 16.

7. Joint editorial, *Contact*, no. 1 (Dec. 1920), 1; Williams, "Further Announcement," 10.

8. "Insistences," 17.

9. See especially his introduction to two poems by Marianne Moore (*Contact*, no. 2 [Jan. 1921], 1). In a 1927 review of a physiology book, he said hopefully, "There is a lust in us all today to get back to the body as a basis of power" ("Water, Salts, Fat, Etc.," *New York Evening Post*, 31 Dec. 1927, 7. The text in I, 357–63, is revised.)

10. WCW to Riordan, [July] 1926, and 26 Jan. 1926 (Virginia 7456g).

11. "Contact and Genius," 16.

12. *Contact*, no. 5 (June 1923), 1, 2.

13. "Puppy Sitting on His Tail," enclosed in a letter to Monroe Wheeler, 27 Sept. 1923 (Maryland).

14. Which "Russian poets" Williams had in mind is not known.

15. "What Is the Use of Poetry?"

16. Kenner's "Syntax in Rutherford" in *The Pound Era* (Berkeley: University of California Press, 1971), 397–406, and his discussion of Williams in *A Homemade World: The American Modernist Writers* (New York: Knopf, 1975) remain the best descriptions of how Williams's words actually work. They are joined by Miller's *Poets of Reality: Six Twentieth-Century Writers* (rev. ed., New York: Atheneum, 1969) and by Cushman's *William Carlos Williams and the Meanings of Measure* (New Haven: Yale University Press, 1985), which excels on Williams's use of enjambment. Sayre's *The Visual Text of William Carlos Williams* (Urbana: University of Illinois Press, 1983) overstates the domination of visual over aural patterns in Williams's poems but makes an important point.

17. Leo Marx, *The Machine in the Garden: Technology and the Pastoral Ideal in America* (1964; rprt. Oxford: Oxford University Press, 1978), 11–24, argues that such an interruption of idyllic revery by machinery as Williams presents here is an archetype of the American imagination's uneasy relation with American society.

18. A letter from Marin to Williams of 6 March 1922 (Buffalo F391) sets up a meeting between them, which, judging from Marin's tone, was their first.

19. The Rivoli Theater in Rutherford, opened in 1921, had an organ rather than a piano for the accompaniment of silent films. The Rivoli is now the William Carlos Williams Center for the Performing Arts.

20. Buffalo A769b.

21. I join James Guimond in wishing we knew Williams's views of the theories of rural poverty current in the early 1920s, such as the "nature versus nurture" debate and the eugenics movement. I suspect that Williams would have dismissed them, wanting to believe that the "lack of peasant traditions" failed to give the rural poor "character"; the rural poverty he wants to ameliorate is a poverty of the spirit.

    It must be said that in "To Elsie" Williams misguidedly assumes that some cultural traits are somehow contained in the genes and can be inherited along with a "dash of Indian blood." But compared to what others made of this assumption—consider novelist Gertrude Atherton's claim, based on the "fact" that "human nature is largely a matter of the cephalic index," that American fiction was declining because "long-headed" Nordic peoples were "being rapidly bred out by the refuse of Europe"—Williams's use of it is more easily forgiven. Guimond, "William Carlos Williams: His Art," *Journal of the Medical Society of New Jersey,* 80:9 (Sept. 1983), 733; Atherton quoted approvingly in "Inferior Races in American Fiction," *The Literary Digest* (29 April 1922), 27–29.

22. Williams told Thirlwall that Elsie was "slightly demented" and something of a "pyromaniac" ("Comments on CEP").

23. "Comments on CEP."

24. Williams praises Moore's work in the prose immediately preceding "Rapid Transit" (I, 145–46).

25. Tichi, *WCW Review,* 62–65. She does not emphasize that Williams intended his poetics of "speed" to oppose the very spirit-killing aspects of modern life that the automobile embodied in its production and marketing; its transforming the American landscape, family, and neighborhood; and its symbolizing "freedom" and "power" and "class."

26. "Comments on CEP."

Conclusion

1. Burke, "Heaven's First Law," 199–200.

Selected Bibliography

Collected Writings by William Carlos Williams

The Autobiography of William Carlos Williams. New York: Random House, 1951. Rprt. New York: New Directions, 1967.

A Book of Poems: Al Que Quiere! Boston: The Four Seas Company, 1917.

The Build-Up. New York: Random House, 1952. Rprt. New York: New Directions, 1968.

The Collected Earlier Poems. Norfolk, Conn.: New Directions, 1951.

The Collected Later Poems. Norfolk, Conn.: New Directions, 1950; with "The Lost Poems, 1944–1950," 1963.

The Collected Poems of William Carlos Williams. Vol. 1: 1909–1939. Edited by A. Walton Litz and Christopher MacGowan. New York: New Directions, 1986.

The Embodiment of Knowledge. Edited with an introduction by Ron Loewinsohn. New York: New Directions, 1974.

The Farmers' Daughters: The Collected Stories of William Carlos Williams. Norfolk, Conn.: New Directions, 1961.

I Wanted to Write a Poem. Reported and edited by Edith Heal. Boston: Beacon Press, 1958; rev. 1967. Rprt. New York: New Directions, 1978.

Imaginations. Containing *Kora in Hell,* 1920; *Spring and All,* 1923; *The Great American Novel,* 1923; *The Descent of Winter,* 1928; *A Novelette [January] and Other Prose,* 1932. Edited with introductions by Webster Schott. New York: New Directions, 1970.

In the American Grain. New York: Albert and Charles Boni, 1915. Rprt. New York: New Directions, 1956.

In the Money. Norfolk, Conn.: New Directions, 1940.

Interviews with William Carlos Williams. Edited with an introduction by Linda Welsheimer Wagner. New York: New Directions, 1976.

Many Loves and Other Plays: The Collected Plays of William Carlos Williams. Norfolk, Conn.: New Directions, 1961.

Paterson. Norfolk, Conn.: New Directions, 1963.

Pictures from Breughel and Other Poems. Norfolk, Conn.: New Directions, 1962.

Poems by William C. Williams. Rutherford, N.J., 1909.

A Recognizable Image: William Carlos Williams on Art and Artists. Edited with an introduction and notes by Bram Dijkstra. New York: New Directions, 1978.

Rome. Edited with an introduction by Steven Ross Loevy. *Iowa Review,* 9:3 (Summer 1978), 1–65.

Selected Essays of William Carlos Williams. New York: Random House, 1954. Rprt. New York: New Directions, 1969.

The Selected Letters of William Carlos Williams. Edited with an introduction by John C. Thirlwall. New York: McDowell, Obolensky, 1957.

Voyage to Pagany. New York: The Macauley Company, 1928. Rprt. with an introduction by Harry Levin. New York: New Directions, 1970.
White Mule. Norfolk, Conn.: New Directions, 1937.
Yes, Mrs. Williams: A Personal Record of My Mother. New York: McDowell, Obolensky, 1959. Rprt. with a foreword by William Eric Williams. New York: New Directions, 1982.

Uncollected Writings by William Carlos Williams

"The Advance Guard Magazine." *Contact* 1.1 (Feb. 1932), 86–90.
"America, Whitman, and the Art of Poetry." *The Poetry Journal* 8.1 (Nov. 1917), 27–36.
"Belly Music." *Others* 5.6 (July 1919), 25–32.
The Comic Life of Elia Brobitza. *Others* 5.5 (April-May 1919), 1–16.
"Correspondence: The Great Sex Spiral: A Criticism of Miss Marsden's 'Lingual Psychology.'" *The Egoist* 4.3 (April 1917), 46, and 4.7 (Aug. 1917), 110–11.
"Four Foreigners." *The Little Review* 6.5 (Sept. 1919), 36–39.
"From Dr. Williams." *Rutherford Republican and Rutherford American* 28.9 (12 May 1917), 1.
"From the Physicians." *Rutherford Republican and Rutherford American* 36.13 (28 May 1921), 7.
"Gloria!" *Others* 5.6 (July 1919), 3–4.
"Glorious Weather." *Contact*, no. 5 (June 1923), [1–4].
"Hospital Funds." *Rutherford Republican* 21.6 (2 May 1914), 1.
"L'Illégalité aux Etats-Unis." Translated from the American by Georgette Camille. *Bifur*, no. 2 (25 July 1929), 95–103.
Introduction to two poems by Marianne Moore. *Contact*, no. 2 (Jan. 1921), 1.
"Letter to an Australian Editor." *Briarcliff Quarterly* 3.2 (Oct. 1946), 205–8.
Letter to the Editor. *Gryphon*, no. 2 (Fall 1950), 32.
"The Little Red Notebook." Edited by Dr. William Eric Williams. *William Carlos Williams Review*, Centennial Issue 9.1–2 (Fall 1983), 1–34.
"A Man versus the Law." *The Freeman* 1.15 (23 June 1920), 348–49.
"A New High School." *Rutherford Republican and Rutherford American* 36.18 (8 Jan. 1921), 1.
"Notes from a Talk on Poetry." *Poetry* 14.4 (July 1919), 211–16.
"Reader-Critic." *The Little Review* 5.9 (Jan. 1919), 64.
"Reader-Critic." *The Little Review* 9.3 (Autumn 1922), 60.
"Sample Prose Piece: The Three Letters." *Contact*, no. 4 [Summer 1921], 10–13.
"Seventy Years Deep." *Holiday* 16.5 (Nov. 1954).
"The Situation in American Writing: Seven Questions." *Partisan Review* 6.4 (Summer 1939), 41–44.
"Speech Rhythm." Rprt. in Mike Weaver, *William Carlos Williams: The American Background* (Cambridge: Cambridge University Press, 1971), 82–83.
"A Statement on the School Question." *Rutherford Republican and Rutherford American* 37.9 (7 May 1921), 1.
"The Supply of Sugar." *Rutherford Republican and Rutherford American* 32.21 (2 Aug. 1919), 1.
"A Symposium on 'The Politics of the Unpolitical.'" *View* 4.2 (Summer 1944), 61–62.
"Three Professional Studies." *The Little Review* 5.10–11 (Feb.-March 1919), 36–44.
"The Town Nurse." *Rutherford Republican* 22.18 (23 Jan. 1915), 1, 4.
"Water, Salts, Fat, Etc." Review of Logan Clendening, M.D., *The Human Body*, New York *Evening Post*, 31 Dec. 1927, 7.

Related Works

Aaron, Daniel. *Writers on the Left: Episodes in American Literary Communism*. New York: Harcourt, Brace & World, 1961.
Allen, Frederic Lewis. *Only Yesterday: An Informal History of the 1920s*. New York: Harper & Row, 1931.

Arieli, Yehoshua. *Individualism and Nationalism in American Ideology*. 1964; rprt. Baltimore: Penguin, 1966.

Baldwin, Neil, and Meyers, Steven L. *The Manuscripts and Letters of William Carlos Williams in the Poetry Collection of the Lockwood Memorial Library, State University of New York at Buffalo: A Descriptive Catalogue*. Foreword by Robert Creeley. Boston: G.K. Hall and Co., 1978.

Bergen County Panorama. Hackensack, N.J.: Bergen County Board of Chosen Freeholders, 1941.

Berman, Marshall. *All that Is Solid Melts into Air: The Experience of Modernity*. New York: Simon and Schuster, 1982.

Bledstein, Burton J. *The Culture of Professionalism: The Middle Class and the Development of Higher Education in America*. New York: W.W. Norton, 1976.

Bodenheim, Maxwell. *Crazy Man*. New York: Harcourt, Brace, 1924.

Bourne, Randolph. *War and the Intellectuals: Collected Essays, 1915–1919*. Ed. with an introduction by Carl Resek. New York: Harpers, 1964.

Breslin, James. *William Carlos Williams: An American Artist*. New York: Oxford University Press, 1971.

Brooks, Van Wyck. *America's Coming-of-Age*. New York: W.B. Huebsch, 1915.

Brown, Alice Cooke. *A Social History of Rutherford, New Jersey*. Diss. New York University School of Education, 1948.

Brown, Milton W. *American Painting from the Armory Show to the Depression*. Princeton: Princeton University Press, 1955.

———. *The Story of the Armory Show*. Joseph Hirshhorn Foundation, 1968.

Buhle, Mari Jo. *Feminism and Socialism in the United States, 1820–1920*. Diss. University of Wisconsin, 1974.

Bürger, Peter. *Theory of the Avant-Garde*. Trans. Michael Shaw with a foreword by Gunther Schulte-Strasse. Vol. 4, Theory and History of Literature. Minneapolis: University of Minnesota Press, 1984.

Burke, Kenneth. "Heaven's First Law." Rev. William Carlos Williams, *Sour Grapes. The Dial* 72 (Feb. 1922), 197–200.

———. "Subjective History." Rev. William Carlos Williams, *In the American Grain. New York Herald Tribune Books*, 14 March 1926; rprt. in *William Carlos Williams: A Critical Anthology*. Ed. Charles Tomlinson. Baltimore: Penguin, 1972, 86–89.

Carnevali, Emanuel. *The Autobiography of Emanuel Carnevali*. Compiled and ed. by Kay Boyle. New York: Horizon Press, n.d.

Carter, Paul. *The Twenties in America*. Rev. ed. New York: Thomas Y. Crowell Company, 1975.

Chace, Richard. *The Political Identities of Ezra Pound and T.S. Eliot*. Stanford: Stanford University Press, 1973.

Civilization in the United States: An Inquiry by Thirty Americans. Ed. Harold Stearns. New York: Harcourt, Brace & Co., 1922.

Conlin, Joseph R. *Big Bill Haywood and the Radical Union Movement*. Syracuse: Syracuse University Press, 1969.

Cowley, Malcolm. *Exile's Return: The Works and Days of the Lost Generation*. New York: Penguin, 1956.

Cushman, Stephen. *William Carlos Williams and the Meanings of Measure*. Yale Studies in English 193. New Haven: Yale University Press, 1985.

Dell, Floyd. *Homecoming*. New York: Farrar and Rinehart, 1933.

———. *Intellectual Vagabondage: An Apology for the Intelligentsia*. New York: George H. Doran and Co., 1926.

———. "A Psycho-Analytic Confession." *The Liberator* 3 (April 1920), 15–19.

Dewey, John. "Americanism and Localism." *The Dial* 68 (June 1920), 684–88.

Duffey, Bernard. *The Chicago Renaissance in American Letters: A Critical History*. East Lansing: Michigan State College Press, 1954.

Eastman, Max. *Enjoyment of Poetry*. 1913; rprt. New York: Charles Scribner's Sons, 1951.

———— . *Journalism vs. Art.* New York: Alfred A. Knopf, 1916.

———— . *Love and Revolution: My Journey through an Epoch.* New York: Random House, 1964.

Egbert, Donald Drew, and Persons, Stow, eds. *Socialism and American Life.* 2 vols. Princeton: Princeton University Press, 1952.

The Evolution of the Borough of Rutherford. Borough of Rutherford Municipal Planning Project, June 1939.

Fedo, David. *William Carlos Williams: A Poet in the American Theater.* Diss. Boston Univerity, 1972.

Fishbein, Leslie. *Rebels in Bohemia: The Radicals of* The Masses, *1911–1917.* Chapel Hill: University of North Carolina Press, 1982.

The Free Public Library of Rutherford. Rutherford, N.J.: Free Public Library of Rutherford, 1944.

Goldman, Emma. *Living My Life.* 1931; rprt. in 2 vols. New York: Dover Press, 1970.

Gompers, Samuel. *Seventy Years of Life and Labor: An Autobiography.* New York: E.P. Dutton, 1925; rprt. in 1 vol., 1943.

Haberty, Lloyd. *Newspapers and Newspaper Men of Rutherford.* Rutherford, N.J., n.d.

Hands, James A. *A Brief History of Rutherford, New Jersey.* Rutherford, N.J., 1956.

Hapgood, Hutchins. *A Victorian in the Modern World.* 1939; rprt. Seattle: University of Washington Press, 1972.

Hartley, Marsden. *Adventures in the Arts.* New York: Boni and Liveright, 1921.

Hofstadter, Richard. *The Age of Reform.* New York: Vintage Books, 1955.

Homer, William I. *Alfred Stieglitz and the American Avant-Garde.* Boston: New York Graphics Society, 1977.

Jackson, Kenneth T. *Crabgrass Frontier: The Suburbanization of the United States.* New York: Oxford University Press, 1985.

Johns, Orrick. *Times of Our Lives: The Story of My Father and Myself.* New York: Stackpole Sons, 1937.

Kammens, Michael. *A Season of Youth: The American Revolution and the Historical Imagination.* New York: Knopf, 1978.

Kaplan, Justin. *Lincoln Steffens: A Biography.* New York: Simon and Schuster, 1974.

Kenner, Hugh. *A Homemade World: The American Modernist Writers.* New York: Alfred A. Knopf, 1975.

———— . *The Pound Era.* Berkeley: University of California Press, 1971.

Koch, Vivien. *William Carlos Williams.* Norfolk, Conn.: New Directions, 1950.

Kornbluh, Joyce, ed. *Rebel Voices: An I.W.W. Anthology.* Ann Arbor: University of Michigan Press, 1964.

Kreymborg, Alfred. *Mushrooms.* New York: John Marshall, 1916.

———— . *Troubadour: An Autobiography.* New York: Boni and Liveright, 1925.

Lasch, Christopher. *The New Radicalism in America, 1884–1963: The Intellectual as a Social Type.* New York: Vintage Books, 1967.

Leuchtenberg, William E. *The Perils of Prosperity, 1914–32.* Chicago: University of Chicago Press, 1958.

Lingeman, Richard. *Small-Town America: A Narrative History, 1620–the Present.* Boston: Houghton Mifflin, 1980.

Link, Arthur S. *Woodrow Wilson and the Progressive Era.* New York: Harper & Row, 1954.

Lippman, Walter. *Drift and Mastery: An Attempt to Diagnose the Current Unrest.* 1914; rprt. with introduction and notes by William E. Leuchtenberg. Englewood Cliffs: Prentice-Hall, 1961.

Luhan, Mabel Dodge. *Movers and Shakers.* New York: Harcourt, Brace & Co., 1936.

Lynd, Robert S., and Lynd, Helen Merrell. *Middletown: A Study in Modern American Culture.* 1929; rprt. New York: Harcourt, Brace & World, 1956.

The Lyric Year. Ed. Ferdinand Earle. New York: Mitchell Kennerly, 1912.

McAlmon, Robert. *Being Geniuses Together, 1920–1930.* Rev. and with supplementary chapters by Kay Boyle. Garden City: Doubleday, 1968.

_____ . *McAlmon and the Lost Generation: A Self-Portrait*. Ed. with a commentary by Robert E. Knoll. Lincoln: University of Nebraska Press, 1962.

Mariani, Paul. *William Carlos Williams: A New World Naked*. New York: McGraw-Hill, 1981.

Marling, William. *William Carlos Williams and the Painters, 1909–1923*. Athens, Ohio: Ohio University Press, 1982.

Marx, Leo. *The Machine in the Garden: Technology and the Pastoral Ideal in America*. 1964; rprt. Oxford: Oxford University Press, 1978.

May, Henry. *The End of American Innocence: A Study of the First Years of Our Own Time*. 1959; rprt. Chicago: Quadrangle Books, 1964.

Meyers, Rosalind. *Rutherford, New Jersey and Its Schools*. Rutherford, N.J., Dec. 16, 1935.

Miller, J. Hillis. *Poets of Reality: Six Twentieth-Century Writers*. Rev. ed. New York: Atheneum, 1969.

Monroe, Harriet. *A Poet's Life: Seventy Years in a Changing World*. New York: Macmillan, 1938.

Murray, Robert K. *Red Scare: A Study in National Hysteria*. New York: McGraw-Hill, 1955.

Noble Lives and Deeds. Forty Lessons, By Various Writers, Illustrating Christian Character. Ed. Edward A. Horton. Boston: Unitarian Sunday-School Society, 1895.

Others: An Anthology for 1917. Ed. Alfred Kreymborg. New York: Alfred A. Knopf, 1917.

Paine, Leonard Levi. *The Ethnic Trinities and Their Relations to the Christian*. New York: Houghton Mifflin, 1901.

Parry, Albert. *Garrets and Pretenders: A History of Bohemianism in America*. New York: Covici-Friede, 1933.

Paz, Octavio. *Children of the Mire: Modern Poetry from Romanticism to the Avant-Garde*. Trans. Rachel Phillips. Cambridge: Harvard University Press, 1974.

_____ . *Marcel Duchamp: Appearance Stripped Bare*. Trans. Rachel Phillips and Donald Gardner. New York: Seaver Books, 1981.

Pound, Ezra. "America: Chances and Remedies," I. *The New Age* 13.1 (1 May 1913), 9–10.

_____ . "America: Chances and Remedies," II. *The New Age,* 13.2 (8 May 1913), 34.

_____ . "America: Chances and Remedies," III. *The New Age,* 13.3 (15 May 1913), 57–58.

_____ . "America: Chances and Remedies," IV. *The New Age,* 13.4 (22 May 1913), 83.

_____ . "America: Chances and Remedies," V. *The New Age,* 13.5 (29 May 1913), 115–16.

_____ . "America: Chances and Remedies," VI. *The New Age,* 13.6 (5 June 1913), 143.

_____ . *The Collected Early Poems of Ezra Pound*. Ed. Michael King with an introduction by Louis L. Martz. New York: New Directions, 1976.

_____ . "Credit Power and Democracy." *Contact,* no. 4 [Summer 1921], 1.

_____ . "A Few Don'ts by an Imagiste." *Poetry* 1.6 (March 1913), 200–206.

_____ . "Imagisme." *Poetry* 1.6 (March 1913), 198–200.

_____ . *The Letters of Ezra Pound 1907–1941*. Ed. D.D. Paige. New York: Harcourt, Brace & World, 1950.

_____ . *Literary Essays of Ezra Pound*. Ed. with an introduction by T.S. Eliot. New York: New Directions, 1968.

_____ . "The New Sculpture." *The Egoist,* 1.4 (16 Feb. 1914), 67–68.

_____ . "Paris." *Poetry* 3.1 (Oct. 1913), 29.

_____ . "Patria Mia," I. *The New Age* 11.19 (5 Sept. 1912), 445.

_____ . "Patria Mia," II. *The New Age* 11.20 (12 Sept. 1912), 466.

_____ . "Patria Mia," III. *The New Age* 11.21 (19 Sept. 1912), 491–92.

_____ . "Patria Mia," IV. *The New Age* 11.22 (26 Sept. 1912), 515–16.

_____ . "Patria Mia," V. *The New Age* 11.23 (3 Oct. 1912), 539–40.

_____ . "Patria Mia," VI. *The New Age* 11.24 (10 Oct. 1912), 564.

_____ . "Patria Mia," VII. *The New Age* 11.25 (17 Oct. 1912), 587–88.

_____ . "Patria Mia," VIII. *The New Age* 11.26 (24 Oct. 1912), 611–12.

————— . "Patria Mia," IX. *The New Age* 11.27 (31 Oct. 1912), 635–36.

————— . "Patria Mia," X. *The New Age* 12.1 (7 Nov. 1912), 12.

————— . "Patria Mia," XI. *The New Age* 12.2 (14 Nov. 1912), 33–34.

————— . "A Peal of Iron." *Poetry* 3.2 (Dec. 1913), 112.

————— . "Provincialism the Enemy," I. *The New Age* 21.11 (12 July 1917), 244–45.

————— . "Provincialism the Enemy," II. *The New Age* 21.12 (19 July 1917), 268–69.

————— . "Provincialism the Enemy," III. *The New Age* 21.13 (26 July 1917), 288–89.

————— . "Provincialism the Enemy," IV. *The New Age* 21.14 (2 Aug. 1917), 308–9.

————— . *Selected Prose 1909–1965.* Ed. William Cookson. New York: New Directions, 1973.

————— . "Wyndham Lewis." *The Egoist* 1.12 (15 June 1914), 233.

Ray, Man. *Self-Portrait.* Boston: Little, Brown, 1963.

Read, Herbert. *The Politics of the Unpolitical.* London: George Routledge and Sons, 1943.

Rosenstone, Robert. *Romantic Revolutionary: A Biography of John Reed.* New York: Vintage Books, 1981.

Rutherford Illustrated. Rutherford, N.J.: Rutherford Printing Co., 1892.

Sayre, Henry M. *The Visual Text of William Carlos Williams.* Urbana: University of Illinois Press, 1983.

Schapiro, Meyer. "Rebellion in Art." *America in Crisis: Fourteen Crucial Episodes in American History.* Ed. Daniel Aaron. New York: Alfred A. Knopf, 1952, 192–225.

Seigel, Jerrold. *Bohemian Paris: Culture, Politics, and the Boundaries of Bourgeois Life, 1830–1930.* New York: Viking Penguin, 1986.

Shaeffer, Louis. *O'Neill: Son and Playwright.* Boston: Little, Brown, 1968.

Spargo, John. *The Spiritual Significance of Socialism.* New York: W.B. Huebsch, 1908.

Spindler, Michael. *American Literature and Social Change: William Dean Howells to Arthur Miller.* Bloomington: Indiana University Press, 1983.

Starr, Paul. *The Social Transformation of American Medicine.* New York: Basic Books, 1982.

Stock, Noel. *Ezra Pound's Pennsylvania.* Toledo: The Friends of the University of Toledo Libraries, 1976.

————— . *The Life of Ezra Pound.* New York: Avon, 1970.

Sullivan, Mark. *Our Times: The United States 1900–1925.* 5 vols. New York: Charles Scribner's Sons, 1926–1933.

Sussman, Warren I. *Culture as History: The Transformation of American Society in the Twentieth Century.* New York: Pantheon Books, 1984.

Taft, Phillip A. *The A.F.L. in the Time of Gompers.* New York: Harpers, 1957.

Tashjian, Dickran. *Skyscraper Primitives: Dada and the American Avant-Garde.* Middletown: Wesleyan University Press, 1975.

Tichi, Cecelia. "Twentieth Century Limited." *William Carlos Williams Review,* Centennial Issue 9.1–2 (Fall 1983), 49–72.

Tilly, Charles. *An Urban World.* Boston: Little, Brown, 1974.

Townley, Rod. *The Early Poetry of William Carlos Williams.* Ithaca: Cornell University Press, 1975.

Trachtenberg, Alan. *The Incorporation of America: Culture and Society in the Gilded Age.* New York: Hill and Wang, 1982.

Turner, John Kenneth. *Shall It Be Again?* New York: W.B. Huebsch, 1922.

Turner, Susan J. *A History of* The Freeman: *Literary Landmark of the Early Twenties.* New York: Columbia University Press, 1963.

Untermeyer, Louis. *Bygones.* New York: Harcourt, Brace & World, 1962.

————— . *From Another World.* New York: Harcourt, Brace, 1933.

————— . "'Others' and Others." *The New Republic* 13 (16 March 1918), 211–13.

Von Valen, J.M. *History of Bergen County, N.J.* New York: New Jersey Publishing & Engraving Co., 1900.

Wallace, Emily Mitchell. *A Bibliography of William Carlos Williams.* Middletown: Wesleyan University Press, 1968.

Weaver, Mike. *William Carlos Williams: The American Background.* Cambridge: Cambridge University Press, 1971.

Wertheim, Arthur Frank. *The New York Little Renaissance: Iconoclasm, Modernism, and Nationalism in American Culture, 1908–1917.* New York: New York University Press, 1976.

Westervelt, Frances A. *The History of Bergen County, 1620–1923.* New York: Historical Publishing Co., 1923.

Wiebe, Robert H. *The Search for Order, 1877–1920.* New York: Hill and Wang, 1967.

Wilde, Oscar. *The Soul of Man.* London: Arthur L. Humphreys, 1907.

Williams, Edgar I. "How It Looks to a Man Returned from Overseas." *Rutherford Republican and Rutherford American* 32.5 (12 April 1919), 1.

[Williams, Edgar I.] "A Local Beauty Spot." *Rutherford American* 32.23 (11 Aug. 1910), 5.

Williams, Paul. "A Letter to My Father on His 100th Birthday." *William Carlos Williams Review* 10.1 (Spring 1984), 1–4.

Williams, William Eric, M.D. "Cars." *William Carlos Williams Newsletter* 3.2 (Fall 1977), 1–5.

———. "The Doctor." *William Carlos Williams Review*, Centennial Issue 9.1–2 (Fall 1983), 35–42.

———. "Money." *William Carlos Williams Review*, Centennial Issue 9.1–2 (Fall 1983), 42–43.

———. "The Physical." *William Carlos Williams Review* 8.1 (Spring 1982), 1–7.

———. "William Carlos Williams: My Father the Doctor." *Journal of the Medical Society of New Jersey* 80.9 (Sept. 1983), 673–76.

Index